Model-Based Software Analysis with C#

This book teaches model-based analysis and model-based testing, important new ways to write and analyze software specifications and designs, generate test cases, and check the results of test runs. These methods increase the automation in each of these steps, making them more timely, more thorough, and more effective.

Using a familiar programming language, testers and analysts will learn to write models that describe how a program is supposed to behave. The authors work through several realistic case studies in depth and detail, using a toolkit built on the C# language and the .NET framework. Readers can also apply the methods in analyzing and testing systems in many other languages and frameworks.

Intended for professional software developers, including testers, and for university students, this book is suitable for courses on software engineering, testing, specification, or applications of formal methods.

Jonathan Jacky is a Research Scientist at the University of Washington in Seattle. He is experienced in embedded control systems, safety-critical systems, signal processing, and scientific computing. He has taught at the Evergreen State College and has been a Visiting Researcher at Microsoft Research. He is the author of *The Way of Z: Practical Programming with Formal Methods*.

Margus Veanes is a Researcher in the Foundations of Software Engineering (FSE) group at Microsoft Research. His research interests include model-based software development, validation, and testing.

Colin Campbell has worked on model-based testing and analysis techniques for a number of years in industry, for companies including Microsoft Research. He is a Principal of the consulting firm Modeled Computation LLC in Seattle (www.modeled-computation.com). His current interests include design analysis, the modeling of reactive and distributed systems, and the integration of components in large systems.

Wolfram Schulte is a Research Area Manager at Microsoft Research, managing the FSE group, the Programming Languages and Methods (PLM) group, and the Software Design and Implementation (SDI) group.

Model-Based Software
Testing and Analysis
with C#

Jonathan Jacky
University of Washington, Seattle

Margus Veanes
Microsoft Research, Redmond, Washington

Colin Campbell
Modeled Computation LLC, Seattle, Washington

Wolfram Schulte
Microsoft Research, Redmond, Washington

CAMBRIDGE
UNIVERSITY PRESS

CAMBRIDGE UNIVERSITY PRESS
Cambridge, New York, Melbourne, Madrid, Cape Town, Singapore, São Paulo, Delhi

Cambridge University Press
32 Avenue of the Americas, New York, NY 10013-2473, USA

www.cambridge.org
Information on this title: www.cambridge.org/9780521886550

First published 2008

Printed in the United States of America

A catalog record for this publication is available from the British Library.

Library of Congress Cataloging in Publication Data

Model-based software testing and analysis with C# / Jonathan Jacky . . . [et al.].
   p. cm.
Includes bibliographical references and index.
ISBN-13: 978-0-521-88655-0 (hardback)
ISBN-13: 978-0-521-68761-4 (pbk.)
ISBN-10: 0-521-68761-6 (pbk.)
1. Computer software – Testing.   2. Computer software – Quality control.
3. C# (Computer program language)   I. Jacky, Jonathan. II. Title.
QA76.76.T48M59   2008
005.13′3–dc22   2007027740

ISBN   978-0-521-88655-0 hardback
ISBN   978-0-521-68761-4 paperback

Contents

Preface

This book teaches new methods for specifying, analyzing, and testing software. They are examples of *model-based analysis* and *model-based testing*, which use a model that describes how the program is supposed to behave. The methods provide novel solutions to the problems of expressing and analyzing specifications and designs, generating test cases, and checking the results of test runs. The methods increase the automation in each of these activities, so they can be more timely, more thorough, and (we expect) more effective. The methods integrate concepts that have been investigated in academic and industrial research laboratories for many years and apply them on an industrial scale to commercial software development. Particular attention has been devoted to making these methods acceptable to working software developers. They are based on a familiar programming language, are supported by a well-engineered technology, and have a gentle learning curve.

These methods provide more test automation than do most currently popular testing tools, which only automate test execution and reporting, but still require the tester to code every test case and also to code an oracle to check the results of every test case. Moreover, our methods can sometimes achieve better coverage in less testing time than do hand-coded tests.

Testing (i.e., executing code) is not the only assurance method. Some software failures are caused by deep errors that originate in specifications or designs. Model programs can represent specifications and designs, and our methods can expose problems in them. They can help you visualize aspects of system behavior. They can perform a *safety analysis* that checks whether the system can reach forbidden states, and a *liveness analysis* that identifies dead states from which goals cannot be reached, including deadlocks (where the program seems to stop) and livelocks (where the program cycles endlessly without making progress). Analysis uses the same model programs and much of the same technology as testing.

This book is intended for professional software developers, including testers, and for university students in computer science. It can serve as a textbook or supplementary reading in undergraduate courses on software engineering, testing, specification, or applications of formal methods. The style is accessible and the emphasis is practical, yet there is enough information here to make this book a useful introduction to the underlying theory. The methods and technology were developed at Microsoft Research and are used by Microsoft product groups, but this book emphasizes principles that are independent of the particular technology and vendor.

The methods are based on executable specifications that we call *model programs*. To use the methods taught here, you write a model program that represents the pertinent behaviors of the implementation you wish to specify, analyze, or test. You write the model program in C#, augmented by a library of data types and custom attributes. Executing the model program is a simulation of the implementation (sometimes called an animation). You can perform more thorough analyses by using a technique called *exploration*, which achieves the effect of many simulation runs. Exploration is similar to model checking and can check for safety, liveness, and other properties. You can visualize the results of exploration as state transition diagrams. You can use the model program to generate test cases automatically. When you run the tests, the model can serve as the oracle (standard of correctness) that automatically checks that the program under test behaved as intended. You can generate test cases in advance and then run tests later in the usual way. Alternatively, when you need long-running tests, or you must test a reactive program that responds to events in its environment, you may do *on-the-fly testing*, in which the test cases are generated in response to events as the test run executes. You can use *model composition* to build up complex model programs by combining simpler ones, or to focus exploration and testing on interesting scenarios.

In this book, we demonstrate the methods using a framework called NModel that is built on the C# language and .NET (the implementations that are modeled and tested do not have to be written in C# and do not need to run in .NET). The NModel framework includes a library for writing model programs in C#, a visualization and analysis tool mpv (Model Program Viewer), a test generation tool otg (Offline Test Generator), and a test runner tool ct (Conformance Tester). The library also exposes the functionality of mpv, otg, ct, and more, so you may write your own tools that are more closely adapted to your environment, or that provide other capabilities.

To use this technology, you must write your own model program in C# that references the NModel library. Then you can use the mpv tool to visualize and analyze the behavior of your model program, in order to confirm that it behaves as you intend, and to check it for design errors. To execute tests using the test runner ct, you must write a test harness in C# that couples your implementation to the tool. You can use the test generator otg to create tests from your model program in advance, or let ct generate the test on the fly from your model program as the test run executes. If you wish, you can write a custom *strategy* in C# that ct uses to maximize coverage according to criteria you define.

To use the NModel library and tools, the only additional software you need is the .NET Framework Redistributable Package (and any Windows operating system capable of running it). The NModel framework, as well as .NET, are available for download at no cost.

This book is not a comprehensive survey or comparison of the model-based testing and analysis tools developed at Microsoft Research (or elsewhere). Instead, we focus on selected concepts and techniques that we believe are the most important for beginners in this field to learn, and that make a persuasive (and reasonably short) introduction. We created the NModel library and tools to support this book (and further research). We believe that the simplicity, versatility, and transparency of this technology makes it a good platform for learning the methods and experimenting with their possibilities. However, this book is also for readers who use other tools, including Spec Explorer, which is also from Microsoft Research and is also in active development. Other tools support many of the same methods we describe here, and some that we do not discuss. This book complements the other tools' documentation by explaining the concepts and methods common to all, by providing case studies with thorough explanations, and by showing one way (of many possible ways) that a modeling and testing framework can support the techniques that we have selected to teach here.

This book is a self-contained introduction to modeling, specifications, analysis, and testing. Readers need not have any previous exposure to these topics. Readers should have some familiarity with an object-oriented programming language such as Java, C++, or C#, as could be gained in a year of introductory computer science courses. Student readers need not have taken courses on data structures and algorithms, computing theory, programming language semantics, or software engineering. This book touches on those topics, but provides self-contained explanations. It also explains the C# language features that it uses that are not found in other popular languages, such as attributes and events.

Although this book is accessible to students, it will also be informative to experienced professionals and researchers. It applies some familiar ideas in novel ways, and describes new techniques that are not yet widely used, such as on-the-fly testing and model composition.

When used with the NModel framework, C# can express the same kind of state-based models as many formal specification languages, including Alloy, ASMs, B, Promela, TLA, Unity, VDM, and Z, and also some diagramming notations, including Statecharts and the state diagrams of UML. Exploration is similar to the analysis performed by model checkers such as Spin and SMV. We have experience with several of these notations and tools, and we believe that modeling and analysis do not have to be esoteric topics. We find that expressing the models in a familiar programming language brings them within reach of most people involved in the technical aspects of software production. We also find that focusing on testing as one of the main purposes of modeling provides motivation, direction, and a practical emphasis that developers and testers appreciate.

This book is divided into four parts. The end of each part is an exit point; a reader who stops there will have understanding and tools for modeling, analysis, and testing up to that level of complexity. Presentation is sequential through Part III, each chapter and part is a prerequisite for all the following chapters and parts. Chapters in Part IV are independent; readers can read one, some, or all in any order.

This book provides numerous practical examples, case studies, and exercises and contains an extensive bibliography, including citations to relevant research papers and reports.

Acknowledgments

Parts of this book were written at Microsoft Research. The NModel framework was designed and implemented at Microsoft Research by Colin Campbell and Margus Veanes with graph viewing functionality by Lev Nachmanson.

The ideas in this book were developed and made practical at Microsoft Research from 1999 through 2007 in the Foundations of Software Engineering group. Contributors included Mike Barnett, Nikolaj Bjorner, Colin Campbell, Wolfgang Grieskamp, Yuri Gurevich, Lev Nachmanson, Wolfram Schulte, Nikolai Tillman, Margus Veanes, as well as many interns, in particular Juhan Ernits, visitors, university collaborators, and colleagues from the Microsoft product groups. Specific contributions are cited in the "Further readings" chapters at the end of each part.

Jonathan Jacky especially thanks Colin Campbell, who introduced him to the group; Yuri Gurevich, who invited him to be a visiting researcher at Microsoft; and Wolfram Schulte, who arranged for support and resources while writing this book. Jonathan also thanks John Sidles and Joseph Garbini at the University of Washington, who granted him permission to go on leave to Microsoft Research. Jonathan thanks his wife, Noreen, for her understanding and encouragement through this project. Jonathan's greatest thanks go to his coauthors Colin, Margus, and Wolfram, not only for these pages but also for the years of preparatory work and thought. Each made unique and absolutely essential individual contributions, without which this book would not exist.

Margus Veanes thanks the members of the Foundations of Software Engineering group, in particular Yuri Gurevich, for laying a mathematical foundation upon which much of his work has been based, and Colin Campbell, for being a great research partner. Finally, Margus thanks his wife, Katrine, and his sons, Margus and Jaan, for their love and support.

Colin Campbell would like to thank Jim Kajiya for his technical vision and steadfast support of this project over almost a decade. Colin also acknowledges a profound debt to Yuri Gurevich for teaching him how to understand discrete systems as evolving algebras and to Roberta Leibovitz, whose extraordinarily keen insight was welcome at all hours of the day and night.

Wolfram Schulte thanks Wolfgang Grieskamp and Nikolai Tillmann, who designed and implemented the Abstract State Machine Language and substantial parts of Spec Explorer 2004; both tools are predecessors of the work described here. He also wants to express his gratitude, to many testers, developers, and architects in Microsoft. Without their willingness to try new research ideas, their passion to push the limits of model-based testing and analysis, and their undaunted trust in his and his coauthors' capabilities, this book would not exist – thank you.

Part I

Overview

1 Describe, Analyze, Test

Creating software is a notoriously error-prone activity. If the errors might have serious consequences, we must check the product in some systematic way. Every project uses *testing*: check the code by executing it. Some projects also *inspect* code, or use *static analysis* tools to check code without executing it. Finding the best balance among these *assurance methods*, and the best techniques and tools for each, is an active area of research and controversy. Each approach has its own strengths and weaknesses.[1]

The unique strength of testing arises because it actually executes the code in an environment similar to where it will be used, so it checks all of the assumptions that the developers made about the operating environment and the development tools.

But testing is always incomplete, so we have to use other assurance methods also. And there are other important development products besides code. To be sure that the code solves the right problem, we must have a *specification* that describes what we want the program to do. To be sure that the units of code will work together, we need a *design* that describes how the program is built up from parts and how the parts communicate. If the specification or design turns out to be wrong, code may have to be reworked or discarded, so many projects conduct *reviews* or *inspections* where people examine specifications and designs. These are usually expressed in *informal* notations such as natural language and hand-drawn diagrams that cannot be analyzed automatically, so reviews and inspections are time-consuming, subjective, and fallible.

In this book we teach novel solutions to these problems: expressing and checking specifications and designs, generating test cases, and checking the results of test runs. The methods we describe increase the automation in each of these activities, so they can be more timely, more thorough, and (we expect) more effective.

---

[1] Definitions for terms that are printed in italics where they first appear are collected in the Glossary (Appendix C).

We also teach a technology that realizes these solutions: the NModel modeling and testing framework, a library and several tools (applications) built on the C# language and .NET. However, this technology is not just for .NET applications. We can use it to analyze and test programs that run outside .NET, on any computer, under any operating system. Moreover, the concepts and methods are independent of this particular technology, so this book should be useful even if you use different languages and tools.

In the following sections we briefly describe what the technology can do. Explanations of how it works come later in the book.

1.1   Model programs

We express what we want the program to do – the *specification* – by writing another much simpler program that we call a *model program*. We can also write a model program to describe a program *unit* or *component* – in that case, it expresses part of the *design*. The program, component, or system that the model program describes is called the *implementation*. A single model program can represent a *distributed system* with many computers, a *concurrent system* where many programs run at the same time, or a *reactive program* that responds to events in its environment.

A model program can act as executable documentation. Unlike typical documentation, it can be executed and analyzed automatically. It can serve as a prototype. With an analysis tool, it can check whether the specification and design actually produce the intended behaviors. With a testing tool, it can generate test cases, and can act as the *oracle* that checks whether the implemenation passes the tests.

In the NModel framework, model programs are written in C#, augmented by a library of attributes and data types. Methods in the model program represent the *actions* (units of behavior) of the implementation. Variables in the model program represent the *state* (stored information) of the implementation. Each distinct combination of values for the variables in the model program represents a particular state (situation or condition) of the implementation.

Within a model program, we can identify separate *features* (groups of related variables and methods). We can then perform analysis or testing limited to particular features or combinations of features.

We can write separate model programs and then combine them using *composition*. Composition is a program-transformation technique that is performed automatically by our analysis and testing tools, which can then analyze or test from the composed program. Composition is defined (and implemented by the tools) in a way that makes it convenient to specify interacting features, or to limit analysis and testing to particular scenarios, or to describe temporal properties to check during analysis.

To see how to write a model program, we can refer to traditional, informal specifications and design documents. Sometimes there is already an implementation we can inspect or experiment with. Sometimes a designer will write the model program first, going directly from ideas to code. There is no algorithm or automated method for deriving a model program – we have to use judgment and intuition. But there are systematic methods for *validating* a model program – checking that it behaves as we intended.

Writing a model program does not mean writing the implementation twice. A model program should be much smaller and simpler than the implementation. To achieve this, we usually select just a subset of the implementation's features to model. A large implementation can be covered by several small model programs that represent different subsets of features. Within each subset, we choose a *level of abstraction* where we identify the essential elements in the implementation that must also appear in the model. Other implementation details can be omitted or greatly simplified in the model. We can ignore efficiency, writing the simplest model program that produces the required behaviors, without regard for performance. Thanks to all this, the model program is much shorter and easier to write than the implementation, and we can analyze it more thoroughly. "The size of the specification and the effort required in its construction is not proportional to the size of the object being specified. Useful and significant results about large program can be obtained by analyzing a much smaller artifact: a specification that models an aspect of its behavior."[2]

We use the term *preliminary analysis* for this preparatory activity where we select the subset of features to include, identify the state and the actions that we will represent, and choose the level of abstraction.

Writing a model program can be a useful activity in its own right. When we (the authors) write a model program, we usually find that the source materials provided to us – the informal specifications and design documents – are ambiguous and incomplete. We can always come up with a list of questions for the architects and designers. In the course of resolving these, the source materials are revised. Clarifications are made; future misunderstandings with developers and customers are avoided. Potential problems and outright errors are often exposed and corrected.

1.2 Model-based analysis

Model-based analysis uses a model program to debug and improve specifications and designs, including architectural descriptions and protocols. Model-based analysis can also help to *validate* the model programs themselves: to show that they actually

---

[2] The quotation is from Jackson and Damon (1996).

do behave as intended. The model program is expressed in a *formal* notation (a programming language), so it can be analyzed automatically. Analysis uses the same model programs and much of the same technology as testing.

Runs of the model program are *simulations* (or *animations*) that can expose problems by revealing unintended or unexpected behaviors. To perform a simulation, simply code a main method or a unit test that calls the methods in the model program in the order that expresses the scenario you wish to see. Then execute it and observe the results.

We can analyze the model program more thoroughly by a technique called *exploration*, which achieves the effect of many simulation runs. It is our primary technique for analyzing model programs. Exploration automatically executes the methods of the model program, selecting methods in a systematic way to maximize coverage of the model program's behavior, executing as many different method calls (with different parameters) reaching as many different states as possible. Exploration records each method call it invokes and each state it visits, building a data structure of states linked by method calls that represents a *finite state machine* (FSM).[3]

The mpv (Model Program Viewer) tool performs exploration and displays the results as a *state-transition diagram*, where the states appear as bubbles, the *transitions* between them (the method calls) appear as arrows, and interesting states and transitions are highlighted (see, e.g., Chapter 3, Figures 3.8–3.11).

The input to mpv is one or more model programs to explore. If there is more than one, mpv forms their composition and explores the composed program. Composition can be used to limit exploration to particular scenarios of interest, or to formulate temporal properties to analyze.

It can be helpful to view the result of exploration even when you do not have a precise question formulated, because it might reveal that the model program does not behave as you intend. For example, you may see many more or many fewer states and transitions than you expected, or you may see dead ends or cycles you did not expect.

Exploration can also answer precisely formulated questions. It can perform a *safety analysis* that identifies *unsafe* (forbidden) states, or a *liveness analysis* that identifies *dead states* from which goals cannot be reached. To prepare for safety analysis, you must write a Boolean expression that is true only in the unsafe states. Exploration will search for these unsafe states. To prepare for liveness analysis, you must write a Boolean expression that is true only in *accepting states* where the program is allowed to stop (i.e., where the program's goals have been achieved). Exploration will search for dead states, from which the accepting states cannot be reached. Dead states indicate *deadlocks* (where the program seems to stop running

---

[3] Exploration is similar to another analysis technique called *model checking*.

and stops responding to events) or *livelocks* (where the program keeps running but can't make progress). The mpv tool can highlight unsafe states or dead states.

There is an important distinction between finite model programs where every state and transition can be explored, and the more usual *"infinite"* model programs that define too many states and transitions to explore them all. Recall that a state is a particular assignment of values to the program variables. Finite programs usually have a small number of variables with finite domains: Booleans, enumerations, or small integers. The variables of "infinite" model programs have "infinite" domains: numbers, strings, or richer data types.

To explore "infinite" model programs, we must resort to *finitization*: execute a finite subset of method calls (including parameters) that we judge to be representative for the purposes of a particular analysis. Exploration with finitization generates an FSM that is an *approximation* of the huge *true FSM* that represents all possible behaviors of the model program. Although an approximation is not complete, it can be far more thorough than is usually achieved without this level of automation. Along with abstraction and choosing feature subsets, approximation makes it feasible to analyze large, complex systems.

We provide many different techniques for achieving *finitization* by *pruning* or *sampling*, where the analyst can define rules for limiting exploration. Much of the analyst's skill involves choosing a finitization technique that achieves meaningful coverage or probes particular issues.

1.3   Model-based testing

Model-based testing is testing based on a model that describes how the program is supposed to behave. The model is used to automatically generate the test cases, and can also be used as the *oracle* that checks whether the *implementation under test* (IUT) passes the tests.

We distinguish between *offline* or *a priori testing*, where the test case is generated before it is executed, and *online* or *on-the-fly testing*, where the test case is generated as the test executes. A test case is a *run*, a sample of behavior consisting of a sequence of method calls. In both techniques, test cases are generated by exploring a model program. In offline testing using the otg tool (Offline Test Generator), exploration generates an FSM, the FSM is *traversed* to generate a scenario, the scenario is saved in a file, and later the ct tool (Conformance Tester) executes the test by running the scenario. In online testing, ct creates the scenario on-the-fly during the test run. The ct tool executes the model program and the IUT in *lockstep*; the IUT executes its methods as exploration executes the corresponding methods in the model program, and the model program acts as the oracle to check the IUT.

To use ct, you must provide one or more model programs and write a *test harness* that couples your IUT to the tool. If you provide more than one model program, ct composes them and explores their composition. In this context, composition is usually used to limit exploration to particular scenarios. If you wish, you can write a custom *strategy* in C# that ct uses to maximize test coverage according to criteria you define.

We distinguish between *controllable actions* of the IUT that can be executed on demand by the test tool and *observable actions* of the IUT that the test tool can only monitor. Method calls are controllable actions, while events (including message arrival and user's input such as keystrokes and mouse clicks) are observable actions. Observable actions are usually *nondeterministic*: it is not possible for the tester to predict which of several possible observable actions will happen next. We can classify systems by their controllability and determinism. *Closed systems* are fully controllable and deterministic. *Reactive systems* have both controllable and observable actions. Some systems are uncontrollable, with only observable actions; a log file is a simple example of such a system.

Some test tools can only handle closed systems. Such tools can be used to test reactive systems by creating a *sandbox* where normally observable actions are made controllable by the test harness (which can be made to generate messages or events on demand). But a sandbox is not realistic and is not always technically feasible. The ct tool can accommodate observable events, which means, for example, that it can test an IUT at one end of a network connection. On-the-fly testing works well for reactive systems because it can deal efficiently with nondeterminism.

1.4 Model programs in the software process

Model programs can change the way we develop software. We can begin checking and testing development products earlier in the project.

To see how this works, it is helpful to represent software project activities and schedule in a V-diagram (Figure 1.1). The horizontal axis represents time, beginning with the project concept at the left and ending with the product delivery on the right. The vertical axis represents the *level of integration*, with the entire product at the top, and the smallest meaningful units of software (classes and other types in C#) at the bottom. A traditional project begins at the upper left with a product concept, then works down the left side of the V, creating a specification that describes what the product should do, and a design that describes how the product should be built up from units. At the bottom of the V, developers code and test individual units. Then the project works up the right side, integrating and testing larger collections of units, until the complete product is delivered. (In projects with frequent releases, there can be a V-diagram for each release.)

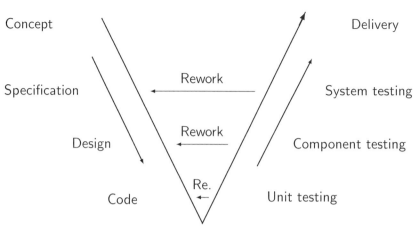

Figure 1.1. V-diagram showing traditional software project activities and schedule.

The V-diagram shows how each kind of testing activity (on the right side) is supposed to check one kind of development product (at the same level on the left side). This reveals the problem with traditional sequential development: the products that are produced first (the specification and high-level system design) are tested last (by tests on the integrated system, using scenarios suggested by customers or their representatives among the developers). Therefore, defects in these first products might not be discovered until much later, after code has been written from them. The diagram shows how the costs of rework escalate as defects are discovered later in the project.

It would be better if we could check each product as soon as it is produced. We would like to check and correct the specification and design as we work down the left side of the V, before we code the units. Then, soon after the unit tests pass, the integrated system should just work – with few unpleasant surprises.

Something like this is already being tried at the unit level (down at the point of the V). In *test-driven development*, developers write each unit test case before its code, and execute it as they code. When the code for each unit is completed, it has already passed its unit tests.

Now it is possible to apply the same principle of immediate feedback to other development products. Analysis with model programs can check specifications and designs, much like unit tests check code, so problems can be detected and fixed immediately (Figure 1.2).

Analyzing and testing models is common in many branches of engineering, where builders cannot depend on testing the end product in order to expose major defects. No one plans to crash an airplane or collapse a bridge! Instead, engineers create mathematical models – such as block diagrams for circuits and control systems, or

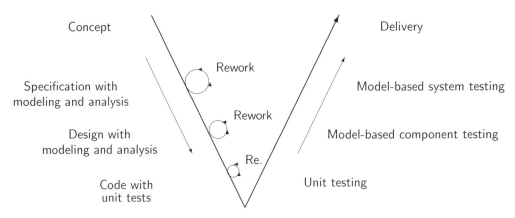

Figure 1.2. V-diagram showing opportunities for model-based testing and analysis.

finite element models for structures – and even build physical models (to test in wind tunnels, etc.). Our model programs are analogous to the models used in other branches of engineering.

Model-based analysis and testing are each useful in their own right. A project might use either or both. Figure 1.2 shows several opportunities for using them, but a particular project might take only one or two. We know of projects where architects used model programs just to debug protocols early in the project, and testing was performed in the usual way. We know of others where testers wrote model programs just for testing components that had been specified and designed in the usual way. Moreover, we can model specifications (by modeling the system behavior visible to users) or designs (by modeling the behavior of components only visible to developers) or both (as shown in Figure 1.2). It is not necessary to model everything; projects typically focus their modeling efforts on the system behaviors or components that are the most novel, critical, or intricate.

Although model programs can be helpful during specification and design, this book emphasizes model-based testing. Many of our examples assume that an implementation is already in hand or on the way, so the model is based on the implementation (not the other way around). We usually model subsets of features that are about the right size for a tester's work assignment (a typical test suite). We usually choose a level of abstraction where actions in the model correspond to actions in the implementation that are easy to observe and instrument (such as calls to methods in its API).

Moreover, we believe that the tester's point of view is especially helpful in keeping the models grounded in reality. In order to perform conformance testing, which involves lockstep execution of the model with the implementation, the tester must write a *test harness* that couples the implementation to the model through the test

tool. This test harness makes the correspondence between the model and the implementation completely explicit. Writing this harness, and the subsequent lockstep
execution itself, closes the loop from the model back to the implementation. It vali-
dates the model with a degree of thoroughness that is not easily achieved in projects
that do not use the models for testing.

1.5 Syllabus

This book teaches how to write and analyze model programs, and how to use them
to test implementations. Here is a brief summary of the topics to come.

   The book is divided into four parts. The end of each part is an exit point; a reader
who stops there will have coherent understanding and tools for modeling, analysis,
and testing up to that level of complexity. Presentation is sequential through Part III,
each chapter and part is a prerequisite for all following chapters and parts. Chapters
in Part IV are independent; readers can read one, some, or all in any order. Each
part concludes with a guide to futher reading, an annotated bibliography of pertinent
literature including research papers.

   Part I shows what model-based testing and analysis can do; the rest of the book
shows how to do it.

   Chapter 1 (this chapter) is a preview of the topics in the rest of the book.

   Chapter 2 demonstrates why we need model-based testing. We exhibit a software
defect that is not detected by typical unit tests, but is only exposed by executing
more realistic scenarios that resemble actual application program runs. We preview
our testing techniques and show how they can detect the defect that the unit tests
missed.

   Chapter 3 demonstrates why we need model-based analysis. We exhibit a program
with design errors that cause safety violations (where the program reaches forbidden
states), deadlocks (where the program seems to stop running and stops responding to
events), and livelocks (where the program keeps running but can't make progress).
We preview our analysis and visualization techniques and show how they can reveal
the design errors, before beginning any testing.

   Part II explains modeling, analysis, and testing with finite models that can be
analyzed exhaustively. (The systems that are modeled need not be finite.)

   Chapter 5 introduces the modeling library and explains how to write model programs.

   Chapter 6 introduces our primary model-based analysis technique, exploration.
We introduce the analysis and visualization tool, mpv (Model Program Viewer), and
explain how it can reveal errors like those discussed in Chapter 3.

   Chapter 7 introduces features and model composition, which are used to build
up complex model programs by combining simpler ones, to focus exploration and

testing on interesting scenarios, and to express temporal properties to check during analysis.

Chapter 8 introduces model-based testing for closed systems (fully controllable systems with no nondeterminism). We show how to generate test suites using the tool `otg` (Offline Test Generator). We show how to write a test harness for the implementation, and how to execute the generated test suites using our test runner tool `ct` (Conformance Tester). We discuss test coverage.

Part III extends our methods to "infinite" models that cannot be analyzed exhaustively.

Chapter 10 describes modeling with data types that have "infinite" domains, such as numbers and strings, and collection types, such as sets, bags, sequences, and maps, which provide rich data structures.

Chapter 11 is about analyzing systems with complex state. It discusses pruning techiques for sampling or finitizing "infinite" state spaces.

Chapter 12 introduces on-the-fly testing, where the test scenarios are created as the test executes, as a strategy for testing systems with "infinite" state space.

Part IV discusses several advanced topics. In contrast with previous parts, the presentation here is not sequential so you may read these chapters in any order.

Chapter 14 discusses composition as a technique for building up complex models from simple ones.

Chapter 15 discusses modeling with objects. We explain the complications that are introduced by objects and describe the solutions provided by the library and tools.

Chapter 16 discusses reactive systems that include observable actions that cannot be controlled by the tester. We discuss on-the-fly testing as a strategy for dealing with nondeterminism.

There are several appendices.

Appendix A describes the attributes and classes provided by the modeling library, which are used for writing model programs.

Appendix B describes the command-line options for `mpv` (Model Program Viewer), `otg` (Offline Test Generator), and `ct` (Conformance Tester).

Appendix C is a glossary that provides definitions for all of the terms that are printed in italics where they first appear.

This book also provides a bibliography and an index.

2 Why We Need Model-Based Testing

This chapter demonstrates why we need model-based testing, with a small but complete working example. We exhibit a software defect that is not detected by typical unit tests, but is only exposed by executing more realistic scenarios that resemble actual application program runs. We conclude that, in order to generate and check the realistic scenarios required for thorough testing, we will need more automation than is provided by the popular unit testing tools. We preview our testing techniques and show how they can detect the defect that the unit tests missed.

This chapter concerns testing methods. We also have analysis methods that can detect errors that arise during specification or design. We demonstrate an example that motivates our analysis methods in Chapter 3.

In this chapter, we also review some features of the technologies we use: the C# language, the .NET framework, and the NUnit testing tool.

2.1 Client and server

Suppose we are developing a laboratory instrument system comprising a temperature sensor connected to an embedded computer, a network, and another computer used for data storage and analysis (Figure 2.1). This is a client/server system. The server, a temperature-monitoring program, runs on the embedded computer. The client, a data-logging program, runs on the other computer. The programs communicate using the TCP/IP protocol, so the client could use the Internet to connect to a server in a remote factory or weather station.

First we start the server program `Monitor` by typing a command at the embedded computer:

```
Monitor 128.95.165.121 8023 1
```

The command-line arguments are the IP address and port number that the server should use, and the number of successive client connections to accept before exiting.

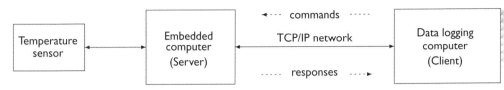

Figure 2.1. Remote instrument, a client/server system.

At the data storage computer, we invoke the client program `Logger`:

```
Logger 128.95.165.121 8023 3 10 F
```

Here the command line arguments are the server host IP address and port number, the number of temperature samples to acquire before exiting, the time interval between samples in seconds, and the units (Celsius or Fahrenheit) for expressing the samples. `Logger` then acquires the samples and writes them to the console, along with a time stamp and information about the server.

```
2006-10-26 13:12:42Z Temperature server at port 8023 reports   72.2 F
2006-10-26 13:12:52Z Temperature server at port 8023 reports   72.4 F
2006-10-26 13:13:02Z Temperature server at port 8023 reports   72.5 F
```

`Monitor` also writes messages about client connections to the console on the embedded computer.

```
2006-10-26 13:12:34Z Temperature server binds port 8023
2006-10-26 13:12:42Z Temperature server accepts connection
2006-10-26 13:13:12Z Temperature server connection closed
2006-10-26 13:13:12Z Temperature server exits
```

It might seem that not much could go wrong with such a simple system. But we have already experienced failures, and some have been intermittent and difficult to reproduce. Therefore, we have resolved to test and analyze the system thoroughly, to discover the different ways it can fail, in order to prepare for correcting defects or designing a more robust system.

Before we can describe our testing and analysis, we must explain a bit more about how our programs work.

2.2 Protocol

Our two programs implement a *protocol*, an agreement about how to work together. A protocol is defined by rules for forming messages and rules that constrain the ordering of the messages. In this example, the "messages" in the protocol are the method calls coded by developers, not the actual messages that travel over the network. In this protocol, the server starts first, and waits for a connection from a client. The client connects to the server and sends a command: the string T to request a temperature measurement. The server responds by sending back the temperature, expressed in a string such as 72.1. Then the client may send another command, or it may close the connection and exit. If the client closes, the server may wait for another client to connect, or it may also exit. The server can only accommodate one client connection at a time.

2.3 Sockets

We implement our protocol using *sockets*, an *application programming interface* (API) for communicating over TCP/IP networks. The socket API is one of the fundamental technologies of the Internet and is familiar to many developers. The .NET framework provides an implementation of this API in the Socket class in the System.Net.Sockets namespace.

Establishing a connection requires several steps, where each partner calls methods in the socket API in a particular sequence (Figure 2.2). In the Server, Socket creates a *listener socket*, Bind associates it with an IP address and a port number, and Listen prepares for a connection. Accept makes the connection and creates a *connection socket* to use for that connection. In the Client, Socket creates a socket and Connect makes the connection. Once the connection is made, both partners call Send and Receive to exchange messages. In our protocol, the client sends first. Both partners call Close to finish the connection. In our protocol, the client closes first. Finally, the server calls Close on its listener socket.

2.4 Libraries

Like most applications, our Monitor and Logger programs use libraries. They do not call the .NET sockets API directly. Instead, they call methods in Client and Server classes that we wrote (Figures 2.3–2.5). These classes are *wrappers* for .NET sockets that provide a similar but simplified API that is specialized for remote instrument applications. Each wrapper method Socket, Bind, and so on, calls the .NET socket method with the same name, but uses fewer parameters, or more convenient parameters. For example, the client's Receive and the server's Send methods handle floating point numbers (the temperature samples) rather than arrays of bytes, as the .NET socket API does. Although these classes are more specialized than the .NET Socket class, they still support other applications and protocols besides the ones described here (Exercise 1).

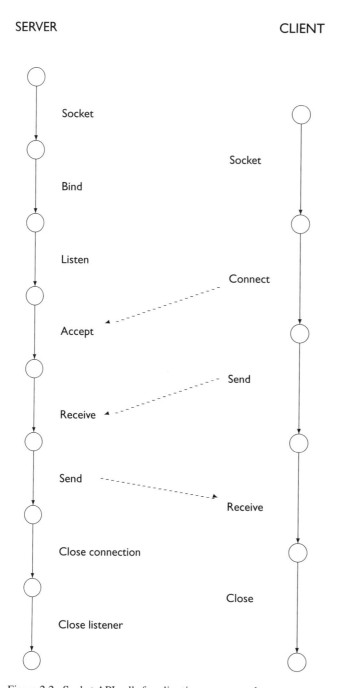

Figure 2.2. Socket API calls for client/server protocol.

```
using System;
using System.Net;
using System.Net.Sockets;

namespace ClientServerImpl
{
    // Wrapper for .NET server socket

    public class Server
    {
        Socket listenerSocket;     // assigned by Socket
        Socket connectionSocket;   // assigned by Accept, used by Send etc.

        const int BUFLEN = 40;
        byte[] receiveBuf = new byte[BUFLEN];

        // method Client.Socket assigns instance of System.Net.Sockets.Socket
        public void Socket()
        {
            listenerSocket = new Socket(AddressFamily.InterNetwork,
                                        SocketType.Stream, ProtocolType.Tcp);
        }

        public void Bind(string ipAddr, int port)
        {
            listenerSocket.Bind(new IPEndPoint(IPAddress.Parse(ipAddr), port));
        }

        public void Listen()
        {
            const int backlog = 0;
            listenerSocket.Listen(backlog);
        }

        // Socket.Accept returns connectionSocket used by Send, Receive, etc.
        public void Accept()
        {
            connectionSocket = listenerSocket.Accept();
        }

        // to be continued ...
```

Figure 2.3. Remote instrument server class (1).

We will now briefly describe how to build libraries in the .NET framework. We put each class, Client and Server, in its own file, Client.cs and Server.cs, respectively. This is a common convention but it is not required. This command invokes the C# compiler csc to compile the client library.

```
csc /target:library Client.cs
```

```
// ... continued

public string Receive()
{
    int nbytes = connectionSocket.Receive(receiveBuf);
    string command =
        System.Text.Encoding.ASCII.GetString(receiveBuf,0,nbytes);
    return command;   // command.Length = 0 means connection closed
}

public void Send(double datum)
{
    string response = String.Format("{0:F1}", datum); //1 decimal digit
    byte [] sendBuf = System.Text.Encoding.ASCII.GetBytes(response);
    connectionSocket.Send(sendBuf);
}

public void CloseConnection()
{
    connectionSocket.Close();
}

public void Close()
{
    listenerSocket.Close();
}
}
}
```

Figure 2.4. Remote instrument server class (2).

In the .NET framework, a collection of code that is compiled together (in one `csc` command) is called a *source program*. In this simple example, the source program is a single class in a single file. Usually, the source program for a library comprises several classes or other types in several files. Compiling a source program creates a binary file called an *assembly*. Assemblies are the software *components* of the .NET framework. A *library* is an assembly intended for use by applications (or other libraries); it has no main method. A library has the file type `dll`.

We create another library for the server class. We create a third library for the temperature sensor class, `Temperature` (Figure 2.6). This class provides a `Sample` method that acquires one sample from the temperature sensor, and a `ConvertToCelsius` method that converts a temperature sample from Fahrenheit to Celsius. This version of `Temperature` is a simulator; it provides a stub `Sample` method that does not require actual sensor hardware, so you can use it on any computer that provides the .NET framework.

```
using System;
using System.Net;
using System.Net.Sockets;
using System.Threading; // Thread.Sleep

namespace ClientServerImpl
{
    // Wrapper for .NET client socket

    public class Client
    {
        Socket socket;

        const int BUFLEN = 4;
        byte[] receiveBuf = new byte[BUFLEN];

        // method Client.Socket assigns instance of System.Net.Sockets.Socket
        public void Socket()
        {
            socket = new Socket(AddressFamily.InterNetwork,
                              SocketType.Stream, ProtocolType.Tcp);
        }

        public void Connect(string ipAddr, int port)
        {
            socket.Connect(new IPEndPoint(IPAddress.Parse(ipAddr), port));
        }

        public void Send(string command)
        {
            byte [] sendBuf = System.Text.Encoding.ASCII.GetBytes(command);
            socket.Send(sendBuf);
        }

        public double Receive()
        {
            int nbytes = socket.Receive(receiveBuf);
            string response =
                System.Text.Encoding.ASCII.GetString(receiveBuf,0,nbytes);
            return Double.Parse(response);
        }

        public void Close()
        {
            socket.Close();
        }

        public void Sleep(int seconds)
        {
            Thread.Sleep(1000*seconds); // convert seconds to milliseconds
        }
    }
}
```

Figure 2.5. Remote instrument client class.

```
namespace ClientServerImpl
{
    // Temperature sensor simulator

    public class Temperature
    {
        static int i = 0; // index for cycling through simulated data
        static double[] temperature = { 71.2, 71.3, 71.4 }; // simulated data

        // Simulate acquiring sample from sensor, substitute for real sensor
        public double Sample()
        {
            return temperature[i++ % temperature.Length]; // cycle through data
        }

        public static double ConvertToCelsius(double temperature)
        {
            return 5*(temperature - 32.0)/9;
        }
    }
}
```

Figure 2.6. Remote instrument temperature sensor class.

Each of our source files begins with the *namespace* declaration:

```
namespace ClientServerImpl
```

Every class (or other type) has a *fully qualified name* formed from the *simple name* that appears in its declaration and the namespace where it is declared. For example, Server is a simple name; the fully qualified name of our server class is ClientServerImpl.Server. Namespaces and fully qualified names make it possible to avoid name conflicts where other programs use the same simple names (Server, etc.). The namespace declaration is optional but should be used in code that you expect will be integrated into a larger system. The using statements identify the namespaces of other types used in the source program, so we can use their simple names (such as Socket) rather than their fully qualified names (such as System.Net.Sockets.Socket). During development, it is typical (but not required) to put files that declare different namespaces in different directories. This makes it possible to use the (short) simple names also as file names, without fear of creating file name conflicts.

2.5 Applications

Our two application programs Monitor and Logger (Figures 2.7 and 2.8) each contain a main method that calls methods in our libraries. The applications provide the

```
using System;
using System.Net; // Dns and IPHostEntry

namespace ClientServerImpl
{
    // Remote instrument standalone server program, works with Logger client

    class Monitor
    {
        #region usage method, writes help text (code not shown)

        static void Main(string[] args)
        {
            string host = "127.0.0.1";
            int port = 8000;
            int nsessions = Int32.MaxValue; // unlimited, in effect

            IPHostEntry iphe; // for checking host address string
            string command;
            double temperature;

            #region Check and process command line arguments (code not shown)

            Server server = new Server();
            Temperature sensor = new Temperature();
            server.Socket();
            server.Bind(host,port);
            Console.WriteLine("{0:u} Temperature server at {1} binds port {2}",
                             DateTime.Now, host, port);
            server.Listen();
            for (int i = 0; i < nsessions; i++)
            {
                server.Accept();
                Console.WriteLine("{0:u} Temperature server accepts connection",
                                 DateTime.Now);
                do
                {
                    command = server.Receive();
                    if (command.Length > 0) {  // command contents don't matter
                        temperature = sensor.Sample();
                        server.Send(temperature);
                    }
                }
                while (command.Length > 0); // 0 indicates connection closed
                server.CloseConnection();
                Console.WriteLine("{0:u} Temperature server connection closed",
                                 DateTime.Now);
            }
            server.Close();
            Console.WriteLine("{0:u} Temperature server exits", DateTime.Now);
        }
    }
}
```

Figure 2.7. Temperature monitor, a server application.

```csharp
using System;
using System.Net; // Dns and IPHostEntry

namespace ClientServerImpl
{
    // Remote instrument standalone client program, works with Monitor server.

    class Logger
    {
        #region usage method, writes help text (code not shown)

        static void Main(string[] args)
        {
            string host = "127.0.0.1";
            int port = 8000;
            int nsamples = Int32.MaxValue; // unlimited, in effect
            int interval = 1;
            string command = "T"; // get temperature sample
            string units = "F";

            double temperature;
            IPHostEntry iphe; // for checking host address string

            #region Check and process command line arguments (code not shown)

            Client client = new Client();
            client.Socket();
            client.Connect(host,port);
            for (int i = 0; i < nsamples; i++)
            {
                client.Send(command);
                temperature = client.Receive();
                if (units == "C")
                    temperature = Temperature.ConvertToCelsius(temperature);
                Console.WriteLine("{0:u} Temperature server at {1} " +
                            "port {2} reports {3,5:F1} {4}",
                            DateTime.Now, host, port, temperature,units);
                client.Sleep(interval);
            }
            client.Close();
        }
    }
}
```

Figure 2.8. Temperature logger, a client application.

control structure (sequences, loops, and conditional statements) that implement our protocol, and also provide data (such as IP addresses and port numbers) used by the libraries.

When an application is compiled, it *references* the libraries it uses: the compiler consults the library assemblies for information it needs. This command compiles the Monitor application, which uses the Server and Temperature libraries.

```
csc /target:exe /reference:Server.dll,Temperature.dll Monitor.cs
```

In the .NET framework, an *application* is an assembly that contains a main method. It has the file type exe. The application assembly does not contain the compiled code of the libraries it uses. Instead, it loads those library assemblies when it is executed. The referenced libraries must be available when the application is compiled, and again when it is executed.[1]

This concludes our description of the remote instrument software. Now we can describe our testing and analysis.

2.6   Unit testing

We begin our testing and analysis with unit testing. *Testing* checks software by executing it. The software that is tested is called the *implementation under test* (IUT). Different kinds of testing can be distinguished by the amount of software that is included in the IUT. *System testing* executes entire applications, such as our Logger or Monitor programs. *Unit testing* executes some of the parts, or *units*, from which applications are built. In C#, the units are classes or other types. When we are doing unit testing in the .NET framework, the IUT is a library (or libraries), such as our Client and Server libraries. Creating and running unit tests require familiarity with the source code and access to the same files and tools that the developers use. Typically, unit testing is done by the same developers who write the code.

For this example we use the NUnit testing tool, the .NET member of the xUnit family that also includes JUnit (for Java), CppUnit (for C++), and several others.[2] NUnit provides a library for writing tests, which defines several attributes and assertions. NUnit also provides *test runner* applications that execute the tests and report the results.

---

[1] There are many options for locating libraries: they can be in the same directory as the application, or in a special .NET directory called the *Global Assembly Cache* (GAC), or in a directory identified by one of the .NET .config files.

[2] Some editions of Microsoft Visual Studio include a similar unit testing tool.

```
using System;
using NUnit.Framework;

namespace ClientServerImpl
{
    // Test fixture for remote instrument Server, Client, Temperature classes

    [TestFixture]
    public class Tests
    {
        #region [SetUp], [TearDown] methods (code not shown)

        // Check Fahrenheit to Celsius conversion, one data point
        [Test]
        [Category("Convert")]
        public void Convert32()
        {
            Assert.AreEqual(Temperature.ConvertToCelsius(32), 0);
        }

        // Check Fahrenheit to Celsius conversion, several data points
        [Test]
        [Category("Convert")]
        public void ConvertMany()
        {
            Assert.AreEqual(Temperature.ConvertToCelsius(32), 0);
            Assert.AreEqual(Temperature.ConvertToCelsius(98.6), 37);
            Assert.AreEqual(Temperature.ConvertToCelsius(212), 100);
            Assert.AreEqual(Temperature.ConvertToCelsius(212), 101); //Fail!
        }

        #region Other tests (code not shown)
    }
}
```

Figure 2.9. Test fixture with test methods.

To write unit tests for NUnit, code a *test fixture* class that has *test methods*. Label them with the NUnit [TestFixture] and [Test] attributes, respectively. Each test method encodes a single test that can pass or fail; it calls a method (or methods) in the IUT (the library or libraries under test) and checks the results. Call an NUnit assertion, such as Assert.AreEqual, to check the results of each test. Our Tests class is an NUnit test fixture for testing our remote instrument libraries (Figure 2.9).

Attributes supply programmer-defined information about a type or member that is stored in the assembly, where it can be retrieved by another program. The [TestFixture] and [Test] attributes defined in the NUnit library are used by the NUnit test runner applications to identify the test classes and test methods in an

assembly. Attributes can have parameters: the attribute `[Category("Convert")]` indicates that the following method belongs to the category named `Convert`; the test
runner can be commanded to execute only the tests that belong to a particular
category.

Assertions check whether tests passed or failed. In NUnit, assertions are calls to
methods in its `Assert` class, such as the calls to `Assert.AreEqual` that appear in our
`Test` class. Each assertion checks a condition. If the condition is false, the assertion
throws an exception that is caught by the test runner, which reports a test *failure*.

To build the tests, compile your test class, referencing both the libraries you are
testing (the IUT) and the NUnit library. This creates another library that contains
your tests.

```
csc /target:library /reference:Client.dll,Server.dll,Temperature.dll ^
/reference:"%PROGRAMFILES%\NUnit-Net-2.0 2.2.8\bin\nunit.framework.dll" ^
  Tests.cs
```

To execute the tests, run one of the NUnit test runner applications, identifying
your test library on the command line or in the GUI. This command runs the comm-
and line test runner.

```
nunit-console /include=Convert Tests.dll
```

The test results appear on the console:

```
Included categories: Convert
..F
Tests run: 2, Failures: 1, Not run: 0, Time: 0.501 seconds

Failures:
1) ClientServerImpl.Tests.ConvertMany :
        expected: <100>
         but was: <101>
   at ClientServerImpl.Tests.ConvertMany()
```

This report says two tests were run and one failed, and provides some information
about the failure. In the next section we will take a closer look at those tests.

2.7   Some simple scenarios

Our `Tests` class includes two test methods, `Convert` and `ConvertMany`, for testing
the `ConvertToCelsius` method in our `Temperature` class (Figure 2.9). NUnit test

methods must be `public void` methods with no parameters, and must be labeled with the `[Test]` attribute. We have also labeled these with the optional `[Cate-gory("Convert")]` attribute so we can command the test runner to run just these tests.

Each test method tests a *run*, a sample of program behavior consisting of a sequence of method calls and other statements. `Convert32` tests a very brief run comprising a single method call. Its body is a single line:

```
Assert.AreEqual(Temperature.ConvertToCelsius(32), 0);
```

We happen to know that 32°F (the freezing point of water) corresponds to 0°C; this test method checks that the `ConvertToCelsius` method computes the conversion correctly for this case. The assertion here acts as the *oracle*, the authority that provides the correct result to determine whether the test passed or failed.

A test method can make several method calls and check several assertions, so it can test a run that is longer than a single method call. Our `ConvertMany` method checks a few other well-known conversions. Its body is several lines:

```
Assert.AreEqual(Temperature.ConvertToCelsius(32), 0);
Assert.AreEqual(Temperature.ConvertToCelsius(98.6), 37);
Assert.AreEqual(Temperature.ConvertToCelsius(212), 100);
Assert.AreEqual(Temperature.ConvertToCelsius(212), 101); // Fail!
```

If any assertion in a test method fails, the test runner considers that test a failure. Here we have deliberately put an incorrect assertion at the end of the test, in order to demonstrate how NUnit indicates test failures. This is the cause of the test failure we observed in the previous section. It also makes the point that a test failure does not necessarily indicate that the IUT is defective. It might be the test that is defective!

The `ConvertToCelsius` method is an ideal subject for unit testing because it gets all the information it needs from its argument (the temperature in Fahrenheit) and provides all of the information it computes in its return value (the temperature in Celsius). It uses no stored information, and computes no new information that must be stored from one method call to the next. The same input always produces the same output, so each method call is independent of all the others; the history of previous calls doesn't matter. Stored information is called *state*, so a method with these properties is said to be *state-independent*. It behaves like a mathematical function, so it is also said to be *functional*.

State-independent methods are ideal subjects for unit testing. Their behavior does not depend on context, so the tests can be very short. Moreover, each test is conclusive in this sense: in any context, when invoked with the same arguments, the method will always behave exactly as it did in the test. The only problem in testing a state-independent method is choosing arguments that achieve good coverage of the

```
// Client requests one temperature sample, server responds
[Test]
[Category("ClientServer")]
public void LogOneSample()
{
    const int port = 8000;
    const string host = "127.0.0.1"; // localhost
    string received, command = "T"; // get temperature sample
    double temperature = 212;
    double response;

    Client client = new Client();
    Server server = new Server();
    server.Socket();
    server.Bind(host,port);
    server.Listen();
    client.Socket();
    client.Connect(host,port); // Connect before Accept is OK
    server.Accept();           // Accept after Connect does not block
    client.Send(command);
    received = server.Receive();
    server.Send(temperature);
    response = client.Receive();
    Assert.AreEqual(command, received);
    Console.WriteLine("Server sent {0,5:F1}, client received {0,5:F1}",
                        temperature, response);
    Assert.AreEqual(temperature, response);
    client.Close();
    server.CloseConnection();
    server.Close();
} // LogOneSample
```

Figure 2.10. Test method for client/server scenario.

method's behavior. But many methods are not state-independent. This introduces complications, as we shall now see.

2.8   A more complex scenario

We would like to write tests that exercise more of the behavior exhibited by the applications. Our test method LogOneSample tests the smallest realistic run: the client requests one temperature sample and the server responds (Figure 2.10).

A realistic test of a client/server system tests one end at a time, the client or the server. From the point of view of each end, the other end is *nondeterministic*: its behavior cannot be predicted. This poses practical problems for coding tests. Here we avoid these problems by creating a *sandbox*, a testing environment where we remove the nondeterminism by controlling both client and server. Both can run on the same computer, and use the localhost IP address. In fact, we can call both client and server methods from the same test method. We call the methods in a single thread, taking care to interleave the method calls in an order that conforms to the protocol (Figure 2.2). This test exercises most of the methods in the Client and Server classes. However, it omits the Temperature class and assigns a temperature value in the test code instead. The assertions check that the command sent by the client is received by the server, and the temperature sent by the server is received by the client. The test also writes a progress message to the console, which is displayed by the test runner.

Here is a test run.

```
nunit-console /include=ClientServer Tests.dll


. . .


Included categories: ClientServer
.Server sent 212.0, client received 212.0


Tests run: 1, Failures: 0, Not run: 0, Time: 0.230 seconds
```

The test succeeds and the expected progress message appears. Can we conclude from this that the applications will work?

2.9 Failures in the field

One day we connect up our measurement system (as in Figure 2.1), start the server and the client, and leave them running. All goes well until the temperature reaches 100°. At the client, we see:

```
2006-11-07 16:07:01Z Temperature server at port 8023 reports  99.8 F
2006-11-07 16:07:11Z Temperature server at port 8023 reports  99.9 F
2006-11-07 16:07:21Z Temperature server at port 8023 reports 100.0 F
2006-11-07 16:07:31Z Temperature server at port 8023 reports   0.0 F
2006-11-07 16:07:41Z Temperature server at port 8023 reports  99.9 F
2006-11-07 16:07:51Z Temperature server at port 8023 reports  99.8 F
```

That 0.0 sample right after 100.0 looks suspicious. Perhaps there is a poor connection at the sensor? But a few minutes later we see:

```
2006-11-07 16:10:21Z Temperature server at port 8023 reports  99.8 F
2006-11-07 16:10:31Z Temperature server at port 8023 reports  99.9 F
2006-11-07 16:10:41Z Temperature server at port 8023 reports 100.0 F
2006-11-07 16:10:51Z Temperature server at port 8023 reports  99.0 F
2006-11-07 16:11:01Z Temperature server at port 8023 reports 999.0 F
2006-11-07 16:11:11Z Temperature server at port 8023 reports 899.0 F
```

That doesn't look like a bad connection. Investigating at the embedded computer confirms that the sensor and server program are working correctly.

It seems significant that troubles appear after the temperature reaches 100. But our unit test for 212 passed. What could be wrong?

2.10 Failures explained

After some investigation we discover the *defect*: the incorrect code that caused the failures.[3] The client's receive buffer is only four bytes long (BUFLEN in the Client class, Figure 2.5). We intended 40, not 4: a typographical error that was not caught by the compiler, by inspection, or by unit testing. When the server sends more than four characters, for example, 100.0, the client only reads the first four, 100. here, and then finds the remaining character(s) in the buffer the next time it calls Receive. In this way, a single sample can cause the client to become unsynchronized with the server, resulting in incorrect readings on one or more subsequent samples.[4] The unit test of Section 2.8 passed because the client Receive method uses Double.Parse to convert the buffer contents to a floating point number. This returns the same result when trailing zeroes are omitted, so the assertion did not detect that the final character was missing from the sample. This test only acquired one sample; subsequent samples that would have caused the assertion to fail were not requested.

You might object that this example is naive and unrealistic. In fact, it is a simplified account of a real experience that was too complicated to describe here in full detail.

2.11 Lessons learned

Some defects can only be revealed by realistic scenarios that resemble actual application program runs (as in Section 2.9), where we execute long sequences of

---

[3] We distinguish *defects* (flaws in the code) from *failures* (occurrences where the program does the wrong thing). Both are sometimes called *bugs*.

[4] You can observe this by instrumenting Server.Send and Client.Receive with code that shows the contents of sendBuf and receiveBuf, respectively.

different methods from several classes, and observe the effects of each method. In this example, we had to execute several methods in the correct sequence to set up the client/server connection before we could execute the defective code. Even then, executing the defective code did not cause a failure immediately. The defective code affected storage (or *state*), so the failure did not occur until later. Such defects cannot be exposed by typical unit tests (as in Section 2.6), where we only execute a short sequence of method calls (perhaps just one) and check a single result.

It is possible to code more realistic runs in unit tests, as we attempted in Section 2.8, but this requires a great deal of effort. Unit test tools only automate test execution and logging test results; they still require the tester to code every run and each assertion. Some unit testing guides recommend writing as much or more test code as implementation code.[5] Our barely realistic unit test (Figure 2.10) is almost as long as the main methods in our applications (Figures 2.7 and 2.8). It is still too short; it did not detect the defect.

We need more automation to generate and check realistic runs for testing. Simply calling methods at random would not work; we need meaningful sequences of method calls.

2.12 Model-based testing reveals the defect

Our methods automate test generation and checking, in addition to test execution and logging. The tester must describe the ordering constraints on methods and the intended results of methods by writing a model program. Our technology can then use the model program to automatically generate and check realistic runs of any desired length. Moreover, our methods can handle nondeterminism, so we can run more realistic tests where we only control one end of the client/server pair.

We develop a model program for analyzing and testing this system in Chapter 5. We automatically generate tests from this model program in Chapter 8. Here is a test run that reveals the defect:

```
TestResult(0, Verdict("Failure"),
 "Action 'ClientReceive_Finish(double(\"99\"))' not enabled in the model",
  Unexpected return value of finish action, expected:
   ClientReceive_Finish(double "99.9"))
     Trace(
         Test(0),
         ServerSocket(),
         ServerBind(),
         ServerListen(),
```

---

[5] For example, see Rainsberger (2005, p. 79).

```
        ClientSocket(),
        ClientConnect(),
        ServerAccept(),
        ServerSend(double("100")),
        ClientReceive_Start(),
        ClientReceive_Finish(double("100")),
        ServerSend(double("99.9")),
        ClientReceive_Start(),
        ClientReceive_Finish(double("99"))

    )

)
```

The message indicates that this test failed because the value 99 returned by the client's receive method differs from the expected return value 99.9 computed by the model program. The tool reports the execution of the automatically generated test run in a syntax that is easy to understand but differs from that of C#. This syntax expresses the tool's internal representation of method calls and returns as data structures called *terms*, which provide advantages that we will explain in chapters to come. Be assured that you will write model programs and program the tools in ordinary C#.

This chapter has described the effects of a trivial defect in the code, a mere typographical error. We also have analysis methods that can detect the deeper errors that arise during specification or design, as we shall see in the next chapter.

2.13 Exercises

1. (Libraries, applications). Write new server and client programs, Probe and Sampler, that use our Server and Client classes, respectively. In this protocol, the server starts first, and waits for a connection from a client. The server responds by immediately sending back the temperature, then closing the connection. The client reads the temperature, and exits. The server may wait for another client to connect, or it may also exit.

2. (Libraries). Consider the choice of the double type for the datum parameter of Server.Send and the return type of Client.Receive. Did this choice contribute to the failures (Section 2.9)? What alternatives might have been chosen? Discuss the implications of library design for unit testing.

3. (Alternatives to unit testing). The defect discussed in this chapter was not exposed by the unit tests, but evidence of failures appeared in the application program output (Section 2.9). Could you write software to detect such failures automatically? Discuss the advantages and disadvantages of unit testing, compared to analyzing log files, for detecting defects.

3 Why We Need Model-Based Analysis

This chapter demonstrates why we need model-based analysis. We exhibit a program with design errors that cause safety violations (where the program reaches forbidden states), deadlocks (where the program seems to stop running and stops responding to events), and livelocks (where the program cycles endlessly but can't make progress). We preview our analysis and visualization techniques and show how they can reveal the design errors, even before beginning any testing.

3.1 Reactive system

Suppose we are developing a process control program that runs on an embedded computer connected to sensors, timers, and a supervisor program (Figure 3.1). The temperature monitor discussed in Chapter 2 could be a component of this system; here we consider a higher level of integration. This is a *reactive system* that responds to events in its environment. In this chapter we consider just one of its features: the temperature-calibration factor. The controlled process depends on the temperature. In order to control the process accurately, the control program must obtain a temperature reading from a sensor and use it to compute the calibration factor. The calibration factor is then used in subsequent process control computations (which we do not discuss here).

The temperature in the process can change continuously, so the control program must sample the temperature often. The control program frequently polls the sensor (requests a sample). The sensor usually responds with a message that contains the most recently measured temperature. We distinguish *controllable actions* that the program commands from *observable actions* that originate in the attached equipment. All that the program can do in regard to observable actions is to wait for them (and observe them). Polling is a controllable action and message arrival is an observable action. Observable actions are prefixed with a question mark ? in Figure 3.1. A reactive system is any system that includes observable actions. Sometimes reactive

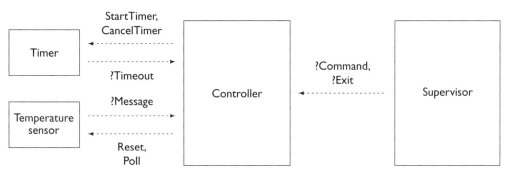

Figure 3.1. Process controller, a reactive system.

systems are called *event-driven systems*. Reactive systems include embedded control systems, operating systems, and most user interfaces. Reactive systems contrast with *closed systems*, where all actions are controllable.

The supervisor program, acting on its own schedule, frequently commands the control program to compute the calibration factor. The control program responds by computing the calibration with the most recently obtained temperature sample. The arrival of a calibrate command is another observable action. The control program cannot predict which observable action will occur next, or when it will occur. Observable actions are *nondeterministic*.

The control program schedules each polling action by starting a timer (a controllable action); when the timer times out (an observable action), the program polls the sensor (controllable) and begins waiting for a message. When the message arrives (observable), the program starts the timer again and the cycle begins over. The interval that the timer waits before timing out determines the approximate frequency at which polling occurs. It is not required that polling be exactly periodic.

The control program should continue working despite occasional faulty behavior by the sensor. It is possible that the sensor may not respond when polled. In order to prevent waiting indefinitely for an unresponsive sensor, each time the program polls, it starts the timer again (a controllable action). After some time, either a message arrives (an observable action) or the timer times out (another observable action); this is another example of nondeterminism. If the time-out occurs, the control program commands the sensor to reset, which may clear the problem. If it does, the sensor sends back a message with a temperature sample.

It is possible that a faulty sensor may report an incorrect temperature. The control program attempts to detect this. The temperature may vary over a wide range, so a simple check that the temperature lies within this range would not be sound; an incorrect temperature might be accepted. Instead, we rely on the fact that the temperature in this system cannot change too rapidly. We require that each temperature sample be close to the previous sample. If a sample differs from the previous sample by more than a particular tolerance, then the sensor is considered to be faulty and no more samples are requested. Instead, the control program commands the sensor to reset. If the sensor responds by sending back an acceptable temperature that is close to the last good sample, the sensor is considered to be working correctly again and the control program resumes polling.

The control program must not compute a calibration factor with a temperature sample that is considered erroneous, because that would result in controlling the process with an incorrect calibration factor, which could have serious consequences.

We have a *safety requirement* which stipulates that the controller must not do anything bad: the program must not compute a calibration factor with an erroneous temperature sample. We also have a *liveness requirement* which stipulates that the controller must do something good: the controller must respond to a command by calculating the calibration factor (except where this would violate the safety requirement).

3.2 Implementation

Our control program uses a typical strategy for implementing reactive programs (Figures 3.2–3.6). The observable actions are implemented by events, and the controllable actions are implemented by methods called *handlers*. The program waits for an observable action. When one occurs, the program executes a *dispatcher*, code that selects a handler, and then executes the handler selected by the dispatcher. When the handler returns, the program waits again for the next observable action.

We divide our control program into two classes. The `Controller` class is a library that contains the dispatcher and the handlers (Figures 3.2–3.4). It is largely independent of any operating system or framework.[1] We also provide a simulator application, so we can experiment with the control program design on any computer that provides the .NET framework. The simulator substitutes for the much more elaborate support (including device drivers, etc.) needed by the actual control program. The `Simulator` class is an application that generates the events that implement our observable actions (Figures 3.5 and 3.6). It also provides a rudimentary user interface so we can raise events by clicking buttons on a form.

Our simulator uses C# events and the .NET framework, in particular the event machinery provided by the `System.Windows.Forms` namespace. For example, in our `Simulator` class, `c.timer` is the .NET timer and `c.timer.Tick` is its `Tick` event (Figure 3.5). The statement

```
c.timer.Tick += new EventHandler(timer_Tick);
```

---

[1] The `Controller` class does use the .NET `Timer` class from `System.Windows.Forms`.

```
namespace ReactiveImpl
{
    using System;

    public enum ControlEvent { Timeout, Message, Command, Exit }

    public enum WaitFor { Timeout, Message }

    public enum Sensor { OK, Error }

    public class Controller
    {
        public const int MessageTimeout = 3000;   // msec, plenty of time
        public const int PollingInterval = 3000;  // msec

        ControlEvent cevent;
        WaitFor waitfor = WaitFor.Timeout;         // enable Reset
        Sensor sensor  = Sensor.Error;             // enable Reset
        string buffer;
        double previous = Double.MaxValue; // missing value flag

        public System.Windows.Forms.Timer timer =
            new System.Windows.Forms.Timer();

        public void ReceiveEvent(ControlEvent cevent, string buffer)
        {
            bool msgevent = (cevent == ControlEvent.Message);
            Console.WriteLine("?{0}{1}, {2}, {3}",
                            cevent, msgevent ? " '"+buffer+"'" : "",
                            waitfor, sensor);
            this.cevent = cevent;
            if (msgevent) this.buffer = buffer; // else ignore buffer arg.
        }

        public void DispatchHandler()
        {
            if (ResetEnabled()) Reset();
            else if (PollEnabled()) Poll();
            else if (CheckMessageEnabled()) CheckMessage();
            else if (ReportLostMessageEnabled()) ReportLostMessage();
            else if (CalibrateEnabled()) Calibrate();
        }

        // to be continued ...
```

Figure 3.2. Process controller class with dispatcher and handlers (1).

```
 // ... continued

bool ResetEnabled()
{
    return (cevent == ControlEvent.Timeout && waitfor == WaitFor.Timeout
           && sensor == Sensor.Error);
}

void Reset()
{
    Console.WriteLine(" Reset");
    ResetSensor();                  // send reset command to sensor
    StartTimer(MessageTimeout); // wait for response from sensor
    waitfor = WaitFor.Message;
}

bool PollEnabled()
{
    return (cevent == ControlEvent.Timeout && waitfor == WaitFor.Timeout
           && sensor == Sensor.OK);
}

void Poll()
{
    Console.WriteLine(" Poll");
    PollSensor();                   // send poll command to sensor
    StartTimer(MessageTimeout); // wait for response from sensor
    waitfor = WaitFor.Message;
}

bool CalibrateEnabled()
{
    return (cevent == ControlEvent.Command && waitfor == WaitFor.Timeout
           && sensor == Sensor.OK);
}

void Calibrate()
{
    Console.WriteLine(" Calibrate '{0}'", buffer);
    double data = Double.Parse(buffer);
    // compute with data (not shown)
}

// to be continued ...
```

Figure 3.3. Process controller class with dispatcher and handlers (2).

```
// ... continued

bool CheckMessageEnabled()
{
    return (cevent == ControlEvent.Message && waitfor == WaitFor.Message);
}

void CheckMessage()
{
    double tol = 5.0;
    Console.Write(" CheckMessage '{0}'", buffer);
    try {
        double data = Double.Parse(buffer);
        if (previous == Double.MaxValue) previous = data; // initialize
        Console.Write(", compare to {0}", previous);
        if (Math.Abs(data - previous) < tol) {
            previous = data;
            sensor = Sensor.OK;
        }
        else sensor = Sensor.Error; // retain old previous
        Console.WriteLine(", {0}", sensor);
    }
    catch {
        sensor = Sensor.Error;
        Console.WriteLine(", Error");
    }
    CancelTimer();                  // cancel MessageTimeout
    StartTimer(PollingInterval); // wait for next time to poll
    waitfor = WaitFor.Timeout;
}

bool ReportLostMessageEnabled()
{
    return (cevent == ControlEvent.Timeout && waitfor == WaitFor.Message
            && sensor == Sensor.OK);
}

void ReportLostMessage()
{
    Console.WriteLine(" ReportLostMessage");
    // sensor = Sensor.Error;  NOT!  Doesn't change sensor
    StartTimer(PollingInterval); // wait for next time to poll
    waitfor = WaitFor.Timeout;
}

void PollSensor() {}
void ResetSensor() {}
void CancelTimer() { timer.Enabled = false; }
void StartTimer(int interval) {
    timer.Interval = interval; timer.Enabled = true;
}
    }
}
```

Figure 3.4. Process controller class with dispatcher and handlers (3).

```csharp
namespace ReactiveImpl
{
    using System;
    using System.Drawing;
    using System.Windows.Forms;

    public class Simulator: Form
    {
        Controller c;

        Button btnMessageOK, btnMessageBad, btnCommand, btnExit;

        public Simulator()
        {
            // Controller

            c = new Controller();
            c.timer.Interval = Controller.PollingInterval;
            c.timer.Enabled = true;
            c.timer.Tick += new EventHandler(timer_Tick);

            // Panel

            Text = "Process Controller";  // caption

            btnMessageOK = new Button();
            btnMessageOK.Location = new Point(10,10);
            btnMessageOK.Size = new Size(200,50);
            btnMessageOK.Text = "MessageOK";
            btnMessageOK.Click +=
                new EventHandler(btnMessageOK_Click);

            #region Other buttons (code not shown)

            AutoScaleBaseSize = new Size(5, 13);
            ClientSize = new Size(220, 250);

            Controls.Add(btnMessageOK);
            #region  Add other buttons (code not shown)
        }

        // to be continued ...
```

Figure 3.5. Process control simulator application with events (1).

```
// ... continued

// Handlers

protected void timer_Tick(object sender, EventArgs e)
{
    c.timer.Enabled = false;  // Controller must restart timer
    c.ReceiveEvent(ControlEvent.Timeout, null);
    c.DispatchHandler();
}

#region Handlers for other buttons (code not shown)

protected void btnExit_Click(object sender, EventArgs e)
{
    c.ReceiveEvent(ControlEvent.Exit, null);
    Application.Exit();
}

// Run the simulation
public static void Main()
{
    Application.Run(new Simulator());
}
    }
}
```

Figure 3.6. Process control simulator application with events (2).

registers our method `timer_Tick` (Figure 3.6) as a handler for this event. When the timer times out, it raises its `Tick` event, which causes our handler method `timer_Tick` to execute. This machinery also ensures that events are delivered to our controller one at a time, so each event is handled before the next is delivered.

In the `Controller` class, the `DispatchHandler` method is the dispatcher that selects which handler to run after an event occurs. It contains the core logic of the controller:

```
public void DispatchHandler()
{
    if (ResetEnabled()) Reset();
    else if (PollEnabled()) Poll();
    else if (CheckMessageEnabled()) CheckMessage();
    else if (ReportLostMessageEnabled()) ReportLostMessage();
    else if (CalibrateEnabled()) Calibrate();
}
```

The dispatcher is a collection of `if` statements. In the first `if` statement, `Reset()` is the call to the handler and `ResetEnabled()` is the *guard*, a Boolean expression that must be true when the handler is invoked. A handler whose guard is true is said to be *enabled*. The design logic of the controller described in Section 3.1 is achieved by coding the guards and the bodies of the handlers. For example, here is the guard for the `Reset` handler:

```
bool ResetEnabled()
{
    return (cevent == ControlEvent.Timeout
            && waitfor == WaitFor.Timout && sensor == Sensor.Error);
}
```

This guard causes the program to invoke the `Reset` handler when the time-out event occurs, provided that the control program is waiting for a time-out and the sensor is considered to be erroneous. In contrast, here is the guard for the `Poll` handler:

```
bool PollEnabled()
{
    return (cevent == ControlEvent.Timeout
            && waitfor == WaitFor.Timeout && sensor == Sensor.OK);
}
```

This guard is similar to the previous guard, but it invokes `Poll` (instead of `Reset`) after the time-out event when the sensor is considered to be working correctly. Notice that different handlers might be invoked after the same event, depending on the values of other variables. That is why we must provide a dispatcher, instead of simply associating each handler with an event.

Each handler assigns some of the variables that are tested by the guards. Here `Reset` assigns `waitfor` to indicate that the program is now waiting for a message (instead of a time-out).

```
void Reset()
{
    Console.WriteLine(" Reset");
    ResetSensor();                  // send reset command to sensor
    StartTimer(MessageTimeout); // wait for response from sensor
    waitfor = WaitFor.Message;
}
```

Also, the call to `ResetSensor` commands the sensor to reset, which should cause another message event soon. But if no message arrives – if the sensor does not

```
// Typical trouble-free scenario
[Test]
[Category("Typical")]
public void Typical()
{
    Controller c = new Controller();
    c.ReceiveEvent(ControlEvent.Timeout, null);
    c.DispatchHandler(); // Reset expected
    c.ReceiveEvent(ControlEvent.Message, "99.9");
    c.DispatchHandler(); // CheckMessage
    c.ReceiveEvent(ControlEvent.Timeout, null);
    c.DispatchHandler(); // Poll
    c.ReceiveEvent(ControlEvent.Message, "100.0");
    c.DispatchHandler(); // CheckMessage
    // Command before Timeout scheduled by second CheckMessage
    c.ReceiveEvent(ControlEvent.Command, null);
    c.DispatchHandler(); // Calibrate
    // Exit before Timeout scheduled by second CheckMessage
    c.ReceiveEvent(ControlEvent.Exit, null);

    Console.Write("\nDid the expected handlers run? [y/n] ");
    string answer = Console.ReadLine();
    Assert.IsTrue(answer[0] == 'y' || answer[0] == 'Y');
}
```

Figure 3.7. Test method for a typical controller run.

respond to the reset command – the call to StartTimer ensures that a time-out event will occur. This will enable the ReportLostMessage handler.

In a similar way, the other guards and handlers are all coded to work together, to generate the behavior described in Section 3.1. To get the controller started, the constructor of the Simulator application starts the timer, and the variables in Controller are all initialized to enable the Reset handler when the time-out occurs.

3.3 Unit testing

The controller logic is intricate, so we suspect that it might be defective. We resolve to do some testing to check our intuitions that the controller behaves as we intend. We can test a reactive program in a *sandbox* that replaces observable events by controllable events. In our controller, we can achieve this by calling the controller's ReceiveEvent method directly from the test code, rather than invoking it from an event handler.

Figure 3.7 shows an NUnit test method that checks the typical run where the controller successfully resets, then polls, then computes the calibration factor. In this test, we do not just check a result at the end, we check that the entire run – the whole sequence of events and handler invocations – is what we intend. It is not clear how to use NUnit assertions to achieve this, so we code the test method to query the tester (the human user). The tester must watch the test output and make the judgment whether the test succeeded or failed, so this test is not fully automated.

Executing this test in `nunit-console` produces this output. The lines that begin with a question mark `?` are written by `ReceiveEvent`; they report the type of event that occured, the type of event that the controller expected (the `waitfor` variable), and whether the sensor is considered to be erroneous (the `sensor` variable). The indented lines are written by the handler methods; they indicate which handler ran, and the data the handler used. This test succeeds. The sensor status changes from `Error` to `OK` after a valid message is received. After that, the controller carries out a command to compute the calibration factor.

```
> nunit-console /include=Typical Tests.dll

...

Included categories: Brief
.?Timeout, Timeout, Error
 Reset
?Message '99.9', Message, Error
 CheckMessage '99.9', compare to 99.9, OK
?Timeout, Timeout, OK
 Poll
?Message '100.0', Message, OK
 CheckMessage '100.0', compare to 99.9, OK
?Command, Timeout, OK
 Calibrate '100.0'
?Exit, Timeout, OK


Did the expected handlers run? [y/n] y


Tests run: 1, Failures: 0, Not run: 0, Time: 2.353 seconds
```

We write a similar test method where the reported temperature differs too much from the previous sample. The controller should not calculate a calibration factor, but should reset the sensor instead. This test also succeeds. After the message with the out-of-range temperature, the command to calibrate is not executed; instead, no handler runs. But then the controller resets the sensor, and after a more reasonable temperature is received, the controller resumes carrying out calibrate commands.

```
> nunit-console /include=OutOfRangeMessage Tests.dll

...
```

```
Included categories: OutOfRangeMessage
.?Timeout, Timeout, Error
 Reset
?Message '99.9', Message, Error
 CheckMessage '99.9', compare to 99.9, OK
?Timeout, Timeout, OK
 Poll
?Message '999.9', Message, OK
 CheckMessage '999.9', compare to 99.9, Error
?Command, Timeout, Error
?Timeout, Timeout, Error
 Reset
?Message '100.1', Message, Error
 CheckMessage '100.1', compare to 99.9, OK
?Timeout, Timeout, OK
 Poll
?Message '101.5', Message, OK
 CheckMessage '101.5', compare to 100.1, OK
?Command, Timeout, OK
 Calibrate '101.5'
?Exit, Timeout, OK

Did the expected handlers run? [y/n] y

Tests run: 1, Failures: 0, Not run: 0, Time: 7.440 seconds
```

We write another test method to check that the controller reports a lost message. This test succeeds as well. After a `Timeout` event follows the `Poll` handler, the `ReportLostMessage` handler runs. The sensor status remains `OK`, so the controller still carries out the calibrate command.

```
>nunit-console /include=LostMessage Tests.dll
...

Included categories: LostMessage
.?Timeout, Timeout, Error
 Reset
?Message '99.9', Message, Error
 CheckMessage '99.9', compare to 99.9, OK
?Timeout, Timeout, OK
 Poll
```

```
?Timeout, Message, OK
 ReportLostMessage
?Command, Timeout, OK
 Calibrate '99.9'
?Timeout, Timeout, OK
 Poll
?Message '99.9', Message, OK
 CheckMessage '99.9', compare to 99.9, OK
?Command, Timeout, OK
 Calibrate '99.9'
?Exit, Timeout, OK

Did the expected handlers run? [y/n] y

Tests run: 1, Failures: 0, Not run: 0, Time: 8.606 seconds
```

These tests confirm that the controller works as intended in these runs. Can we conclude from this that the controller will always work?

3.4   Failures in simulation

We experiment with the simulator and find that the controller does not always behave as we intend. Recall that we intend that a calibrate command will be carried out if the most recent sample from the sensor is within-range, but will not be carried out if the most recent sample is out-of-range. We also intend that the controller should not experience any *generic failures* such as program crashes (unhandled exceptions in .NET), deadlocks, or endless cycles that get nowhere. Despite our intentions, we observe examples of all of these (which we can reproduce by coding unit tests).

In this run, `CommandWhenWaiting`, a calibrate command is ignored even though the sensor is OK. The command arrives when the controller is waiting for a message; no handler runs.

```
?Timeout, Timeout, Error
 Reset
?Message '99.9', Message, Error
 CheckMessage '99.9', compare to 99.9, OK
?Timeout, Timeout, OK
 Poll
?Command, Message, OK
```

```
?Message '100.0', Message, OK
 CheckMessage '100.0', compare to 99.9, OK
```

In this run, `OutOfRangeMessageWhenIdle`, the controller carries out a calibrate command using an out-of-range temperature value. The message carrying this value was late; it arrived after the time-out expired, and was not checked.

```
?Timeout, Timeout, Error
 Reset
?Message '99.9', Message, Error
 CheckMessage '99.9', compare to 99.9, OK
?Timeout, Timeout, OK
 Poll
?Timeout, Message, OK
 ReportLostMessage
?Message '999.9', Timeout, OK
?Command, Timeout, OK
 Calibrate '999.9'
```

In this run, `LostMessageWhenIdle`, the controller reaches a deadlocks. The sensor does not reply to the initial reset command. The controller does not restart the timer; polling never begins. The sensor status never becomes OK, so calibrate commands are never carried out.

```
?Timeout, Timeout, Error
 Reset
?Timeout, Message, Error
?Command, Message, Error
?Command, Message, Error
```

In this run, `InitialOutOfRangeMessage`, the controller cycles without making progress. It keeps sending reset commands but the sensor status never becomes OK. The first message in response to the initial reset command is out-of-range, so subsequent within-range messages are never accepted, and the calibrate command can never be carried out.

```
?Timeout, Timeout, Error
 Reset
?Message '999.9', Message, Error
 CheckMessage '999.9', compare to 999.9, OK
?Timeout, Timeout, OK
 Poll
?Message '99.9', Message, OK
```

```
CheckMessage '99.9', compare to 999.9, Error
?Timeout, Timeout, Error
 Reset
?Message '100.1', Message, Error
 CheckMessage '100.1', compare to 999.9, Error
?Timeout, Timeout, Error
 Reset
?Message '101.5', Message, Error
 CheckMessage '101.5', compare to 999.9, Error
?Timeout, Timeout, Error
 Reset
?Message '102.3', Message, Error
 CheckMessage '102.3', compare to 999.9, Error
```

3.5 Design defects

The defects that caused these failures are deeper than the coding defect discussed in Chapter 2. We consider these to be design errors. Recall that a design describes how a system is built up from parts and how the parts communicate. Here the controller is built up from events and handlers that communicate through variables and the timer. The design is expressed by the guard expressions that test the variables to determine which handler to run, and the statements in the handlers that assign these variables and start or cancel the timer. Each failure results from tests or assignments that do not produce the intended behaviors, when combined with the other tests and assignments in the program. All the tests and assignments cooperate to produce the behaviors, and it is necessary to consider them all to understand the failures.

All of the failures shown in Section 3.4 can be understood in this way. The CommandWhenWaiting run fails because no handler for the Command event is enabled when the controller is waiting for a message. The OutOfRangeMessageWhenIdle run fails because no handler for the Message event is enabled when the controller is waiting for a time-out. The LostMessageWhenIdle run reaches a deadlocks after a message is lost because no handler for the Timeout event is enabled when the controller is waiting for a message and the sensor is considered erroneous, and no preceding handler requested another message or scheduled another time-out. The InitialOutOfRangeMessage run cycles endlessly because none of the enabled handlers can make progress by assigning the sensor status to OK.

We designed the controller by considering some typical runs and coding tests and assignments to make them work. But many more runs are possible than the ones we considered and tested, so our design is defective. We are getting tired of experimenting with the simulator. Discovering defects by trial and error provides no confidence that we are converging on a correct design. There might be even more ways that the controller can fail. How can we be sure that we have considered enough runs? We need some systematic way to check the design thoroughly.

3.6 Reviews and inspections, static analysis

The traditional way to detect design defects is to conduct reviews or inspections where people examine design documents and code, often while consulting a checklist of likely errors. These assurance techniques are a good match to programs like ours, which have a simple, regular structure. The control program is largely built from only two kinds of methods, guards and handlers, and has a simple control structure expressed here by the `DispatchHandler` method. This makes it easy to express and check design rules that the code should observe. The design should be *complete*: there should be a handler enabled for every event in every state. The design should be *deterministic*: there should be only one handler enabled for each event in every state. The design should make *progress*: each handler should execute statements that bring the controller closer to a goal, usually by enabling a different handler. Each of the failures described in Section 3.4 is caused by a defect that violates these rules.

Considered against our design rules, the defects in this little program are obvious. But in general, reviews and inspections are time-consuming, subjective, and fallible. This little example is based on our experience with a program that has about a hundred handlers and a hundred variables, where the defects were not so obvious.

It is possible to create a program that automates some of the checking of design rules that human reviewers do, removing the tedium and subjectivity. This automated checking of source code is called *static analysis*, and can be viewed as an extension of the checking already performed by compilers and style checkers. Static analysis is a promising research area, but it is not the approach we teach in this book.

3.7 Model-based analysis reveals the design errors

Model-based analysis reveals the design errors in our controller program. We write a model program that expresses the design, and then use our mpv (Model Program Viewer) tool to explore, search, and display the finite state machine (FSM) that expresses the model program's behaviors (Figure 3.8). (It is not necessary to read the details in this figure now.) Reading the messages written by mpv, or inspecting this display while using mpv to highlight features of interest, reveals each defect. How to do this is explained in chapters to come (especially Chapters 5 and 6). For now, we just show what can be done.

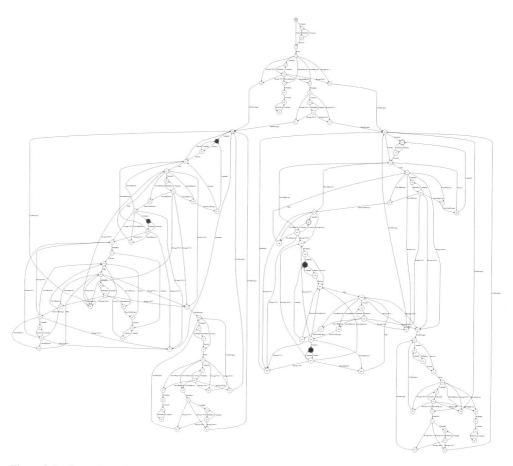

Figure 3.8. Controller FSM showing unsafe states.

Figure 3.8 shows the entire FSM of our model program. Figures 3.9–3.11 display portions of the FSM that show paths to interesting states. Each path through the FSM is a possible run of the system. The FSM represents all possible runs of this system. There are 121 states and 239 transitions between states. The model program has to have some additional methods and variables (which do not appear in the implementation) that represent the environment where the controller runs, including the timer and sensor. Therefore, the actions in the diagrams include some that do not appear in the controller implementation. For example, our implementation's Timeout event must be represented here by Timeout, TimeoutMsgLate, and TimeoutMsgLost. We also need a NoHandler action here to represent what happens when no handler is enabled.

For safety analysis, the mpv tool searches for *unsafe states* where the controller attempts to calculate the calibration factor when the temperature sample is

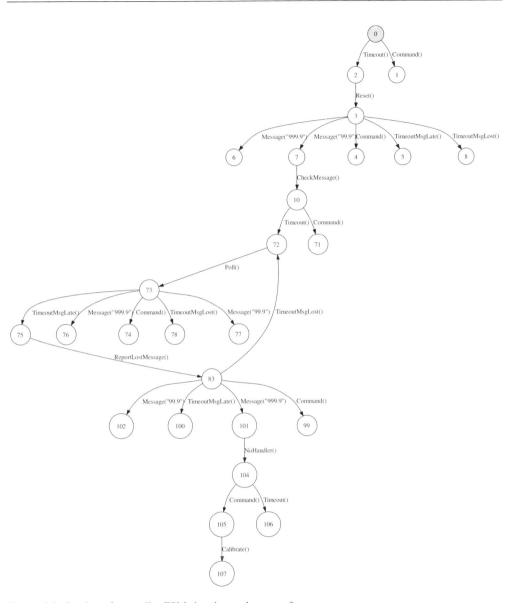

Figure 3.9. Portion of controller FSM showing path to unsafe state.

out-of-range. Figure 3.8 shows the entire FSM; the filled-in ovals are the unsafe states. (It is not necessary to search the graph visually to find out whether there are any unsafe states; the tool writes a message to report that it finds four of them.) Figure 3.9 shows the portion of the FSM that includes the path to an unsafe state traversed by the OutOfRangeMessageWhenIdle run.

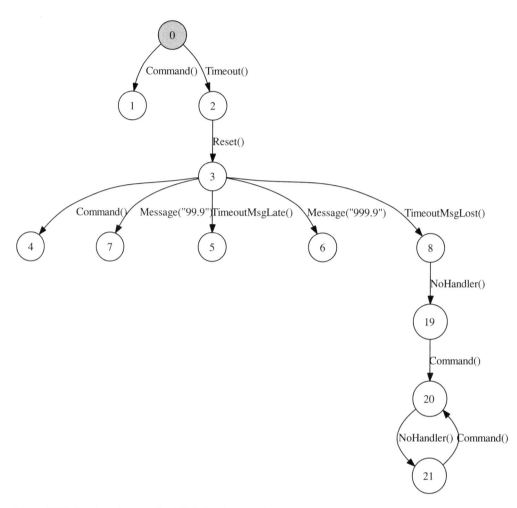

Figure 3.10. Portion of controller FSM showing deadlock.

For liveness analysis, the tool can search for *dead states* from which the controller cannot reach any *accepting states* where the program's goals have been achieved. The most obvious dead states are *deadlock* states: the program stops, as in the LostMessageWhenIdle run (Figure 3.10). The deadlock is indicated here by the loop of alternating Command and NoHandler actions, from which there is no escape. The supervisor can always command the controller, so the Command action is always enabled. But the controller can do nothing; recall that NoHandler is a dummy action that indicates no handlers are enabled. Other dead states belong to *livelocks* where the program cycles without making progress. In this FSM, we find the same cycle of actions with no escape that we found in the InitialOutOfRangeMessage run: Timeout, Reset, Message, CheckMessage (Figure 3.11).

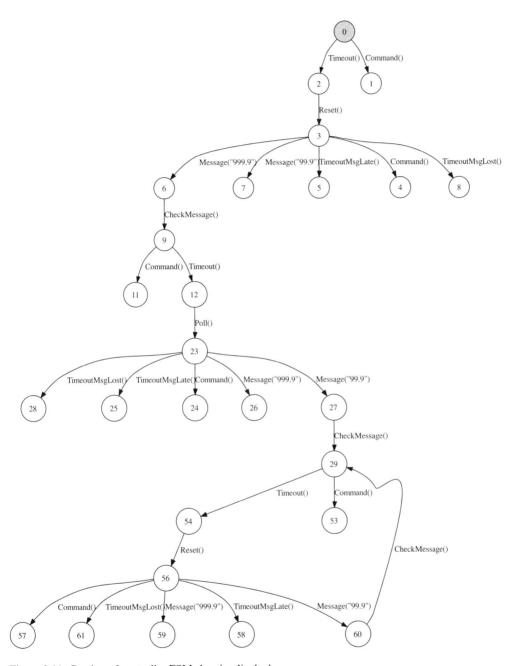

Figure 3.11. Portion of controller FSM showing livelock.

This FSM expresses all possible behaviors of the controller, so the analysis here is complete and conclusive. This is possible because our control program has only a few variables, each with just a few values, so it can be explored *exhaustively* (completely). Our techniques can also be applied to systems that cannot be explored exhaustively. We can configure exploration to achieve a degree of coverage that, although incomplete, is still capable of revealing many defects (Chapter 11).

3.8   Exercises

1. Write down another run that could be executed by the controller code, which violates the safety requirement given at the beginning of Section 3.1. Your run must be different from both the run `OutOfRangeMessageWhenIdle` in Section 3.4 and the shortest path run found by the tool in Section 3.7. Confirm your run by writing a unit test or by executing it in the simulator.

2. Write down a run that causes the controller to crash (throw an unhandled exception). Confirm your run by writing a unit test or by executing it in the simulator. Hint: see `CheckMessage`.

3. Show how to revise `Controller.cs` so the controller satisfies the safety and liveness requirements given at the end of Section 3.1. Show each difference (the contents and location of each statement that must be added, removed, or changed). Hint: use the design rules given in Section 3.6.

   Keep your revised program to use with exercises in chapters to come.

4 Further Reading

The concepts presented in this book are based on ideas from mathematics and theoretical computer science. Readers certainly do not need to understand these theoretical aspects in order to use the techniques we present. However, some may be interested in pursuing these topics in further detail, and for these readers we can point to the following sources of information.

The central idea of a model program that we present throughout the book is based on the theory of abstract state machines (ASMs) conceived by Yuri Gurevich in 1980s. An ASM is a formal way to describe the steps of an algorithm. It gives a mathematical view of program state (including the state of object-oriented systems and systems with complex structure). There is a well-developed body of scientific literature on the topic. Readers interested in ASMs may wish to see the ASM Web page maintained at the University of Michigan (ASM, 2006). Of particular interest is the "Lipari guide" (Gurevich, 1995).

We also use ideas taken from finite automata, mathematical logic, and set theory. The composition of automata for language intersection is a core concept. A classic text that describes finite automata and their properties is Hopcroft and Ullman (1979). A useful and practical introduction to logic and set theory is found in Lipschutz (1998).

A mathematically rigorous survey of assurance methods including modeling, testing, and static analysis appears in the book by Peled (2001).

The ideas in this book were developed and made practical at Microsoft Research from 1999 through 2006 in the Foundations of Software Engineering group (FSE, 2006).

Other views of model-based testing appear in the books by Utting and Legeard (2006) and by Broy et al. (2005). This is an active research area where new methods and tools appear frequently. For a sample, see the papers by Tretmans (1999) and Hartman and Nagin (2004), and the references cited therein.

Other work on particular aspects of modeling, testing, and analysis is discussed and cited in the later *Further reading* chapters (Chapters 9, 13, and 17).

The standard reference on C# is the book by Hejlsberg et al. (2006).

The most useful literature on the .NET framework is actually about the Common Language Infrastructure (CLI), the standardized subset. The standard reference is the book by Miller and Ragsdale (2004). The first chapter in the book by Stutz et al. (2003) is a good introduction to the CLI and its motivation.

The sockets API is discussed in the book by Stevens (1990).

The xUnit testing framework is the subject of the book by Hamill (2004).

The term *model program* was used by Beizer (1995), for a program written to act as an oracle.

We have tried to keep our terminology consistent with the glossaries in the IEEE standard (1983), Beizer (1990, 1995), and Binder (1999).

Part II

Systems with Finite Models

5 Model Programs

This chapter introduces model programs. We show how to code model programs that work with the tools, by using attributes from the modeling library along with some coding conventions.

In this chaper we also explain the process of writing a model program: the steps you must go through to understand the implementation and design the model program. Writing a model program does not mean writing the implementation twice. By focusing on the purpose of the model, you can write a model program that is much smaller and simpler than the implementation, but still expresses the features you want to test or analyze.

Here in Part II, we explain modeling, analysis, and testing with finite model programs that can be analyzed *exhaustively* (completely). The programs and systems we model here are "*infinite*" – perhaps not mathematically infinite, but too large to analyze exhaustively. One of the themes of this chapter is how to *finitize* (make finite) the model of an "infinite" system. Starting in Part III, the model programs are also "infinite"; we finitize the analysis instead.

In this chapter we develop and explain three model programs: a newsreader user interface, the client/server system of Chapter 2, and the reactive system of Chapter 3. We will perform safety and liveness analyses of the reactive system model in Chapter 6. We will generate and check tests of the implementation using the client/server model in Chapter 8.

5.1 States, actions, and behavior

First we must define some basic concepts and vocabulary. We will demonstrate these concepts in the sections that follow.

A *model program* is a program that describes the behavior of another program or system called the *implementation*. We say *system* here because the implementation need not be a single program. A single model program can represent a concurrent system comprising several programs, or a distributed system that includes several computers connected by a network. A model program can also represent the environment where the implementation runs, including messages in transit between networked computers, or events originating in attached hardware.

Actions are the units of behavior. In many kinds of systems, including computer systems, behaviors are made up of discrete, discontinuous steps. Each step is an action. An action can be composed of several smaller activities, but an action is *atomic*: once it begins, it runs to completion, without being interrupted or preempted by another action. For each kind of action in the implementation, there is a method in the model program. When the model program runs, each method call represents an action in the implementation.[1]

State is the information stored in a program or system at one point in time. The concept of state captures our intuition of a "situation" or "state of affairs": the important properties of a system at one moment. The state of the implementation is represented by variables of the model program. Each particular assignment of values to variables in the model program represents a particular state (a situation) of the implementation. The variables in the model program that represent implementation state are called *state variables* (to distinguish them from the model program's local variables, parameters, etc.). State variables in the model program need not correspond exactly to program variables in the implementation; they might represent information that is not stored in implementation variables (messages in transit, for example).

Every program or system starts up in an *initial state*. The initial state is usually an empty or idle state. Behavior continues until the system reaches an *accepting state*. An accepting state is usually a state where the program's goals have been achieved, where some unit of work has been completed. The system may stop in an accepting state; alternatively, it may continue, starting new work. A sequence of actions beginning in the initial state and ending in an accepting state is called a *run* or a *trace*. A run must not end in a state that is not an accepting state (if the model program does not identify any accepting states, a run may end in any state). The runs of a model program are sequences of method calls (and returns).

The *behavior* of a program or system is the complete collection of all the runs that it can execute. A *contract model program* is a *specification* that describes all of the allowed behavior of its implementation: it describes everything that its implementation must do, might do, and must *not* do. Every run that a contract model program can execute represents a run that its implementation must be able to execute. A contract model program cannot execute any run that its implementation is forbidden to execute. A contract model program often has a large collection of runs;

---

[1] This is a simplification; the relation between actions in the implementation and methods in the model program is not always one-to-one. Chapters to come and Appendix A tell the whole story.

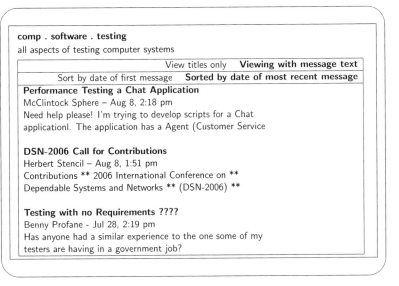

Figure 5.1. Newsreader `Topics` page in `WithText` mode.

sometimes, an infinite number. A *scenario* is a collection of runs that are pertinent to some particular situation or purpose, such as a test suite. A *scenario model program* defines a scenario; it can execute all of the runs of the scenario, but no others. A scenario model program often has a small collection of runs; sometimes, just one.

Usually a model program only models a subset or *slice* of the implementation's features. Usually a model program represents the implementation at a *level of abstraction* where many details are omitted or simplified.

5.2   Case study: user interface

We make our first model program very simple, so we can explain the process of writing it in great detail, showing the reason for every step. We will pick up the pace in the examples to come.

For our first model program we model the user interface for a Web-based news-reader, where users select a "group" (news about a particular subject), and can then read and post messages about topics in that group.

When the users first select a group, they see a list of message excerpts, each with a title line indicating the topic (Figure 5.1). By clicking on the View titles only link, they can select an alternate page that just shows a list of topics (so more topics fit on the screen, Figure 5.2). On first viewing, the topics are sorted by the date of the most recent message about that topic. Users can click on the link Sort by date of

comp . software . testing
all aspects of testing computer systems

	Viewing titles only	View with message text
Sort by date of first message	Sorted by date of most recent message	
Performance Testing a Chat Application		2:18 pm
DSN-2006 Call for Contributions		1:51 pm
Testing with no Requirements ????		1:16 pm
Software Testing		Aug 7
GUI testing using capture and playback		Aug 7
How to trace fixed bug in test case?		Aug 6
How to develop my career in software testing?		Aug 6
Need help in Performance Testing		Aug 5
Can any body explain me		Aug 5
QA Podcast		Aug 4
Testing Methods		Aug 3
Hv a query which types of errors occur		Aug 2
Automated Test Scripts		Aug 2

Figure 5.2. Newsreader `Topics` page in `TitlesOnly` mode.

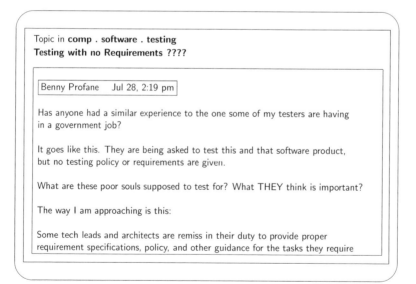

Topic in **comp . software . testing**
Testing with no Requirements ????

Benny Profane   Jul 28, 2:19 pm

Has anyone had a similar experience to the one some of my testers are having in a government job?

It goes like this. They are being asked to test this and that software product, but no testing policy or requirements are given.

What are these poor souls supposed to test for? What THEY think is important?

The way I am approaching is this:

Some tech leads and architects are remiss in their duty to provide proper requirement specifications, policy, and other guidance for the tasks they require

Figure 5.3. Newsreader `Messages` page.

first message to sort topics in that order instead. From any of these pages, the user can click on a topic title to see the list of messages about that topic (Figure 5.3; this figure just shows the first message, the others appear when the user scrolls down). From the message list, users can click on the group name link to return to the list of topics. When they do, the topic list appears the same as when last seen; any previous selections regarding message excerpts and sort order are still in effect.

5.3 Preliminary analysis

Writing a model program always begins with a *preliminary analysis* where we decide on the purpose of the model, choose the features to include in the model, select the level of abstraction, identify the actions, write some sample traces, and identify the state variables.

During preliminary analysis we study the implementation. Depending on what is available, we might study the implementation's requirements and design documents, or inspect its API or its code. In this example, we just observe its behavior.

5.3.1 Decide on the purpose

Modeling is a goal-directed activity; every model program has a purpose. We write a model program in order to answer some questions about the implementation (by testing or analysis). We have to formulate those questions before we can see how to write the model program.

In this example, our questions arise from the observation that the newsreader presents several kinds of pages that can be formatted in various styles, and several options for selecting pages and styles. Our questions are: What options are available when a particular page and style is displayed? What page and style appears when the user selects a particular option?

Our questions guide testing and analysis. To create a test suite, we express the questions this way: Are the intended options made available for each particular page and style? Does the intended page and style appear when each particular option is chosen? To perform liveness analysis, we ask: Is every option available (on some page)? Can every page and style be made to appear (by choosing some sequence of options)? Are there are any deadlocks (pages with no options) or livelocks (pages from which other pages cannot be reached)? To perform safety analysis, we ask: Are the options that are available on each page the ones that should be there? Is it possible to request some combination of page and style that doesn't make sense?

5.3.2 Select the features

We usually do not model a large system with a single model program. Instead, we select a subset of related features that comprise a self-contained package of functionality. A large implementation can be covered by several small model programs that represent different subsets of features. Choose a feature subset that makes a reasonable work assignment. For example, a tester would choose a collection of features that would be covered by a typical test suite. The chosen subset of features is sometimes called a *slice* (of the implementation's complete feature set).

For this example, we choose a very small subset of newsreader features: the screens, styles, and options described in Section 5.2. This is an unusually small collection of features for a model program that we chose to make this example brief.

5.3.3   Choose a level of abstraction

Even when we limit ourselves to a subset of features, we do not consider every implementation detail in that subset. We must decide which details to include in the model program; other details can be omitted or greatly simplified. This is called *abstraction*; our choice of which details to include defines the *level of abstraction*. A lower level shows more detail, and results in a larger, more complex model program. A higher level shows less detail, and results in a smaller, simpler model program. Working at a higher level of abstraction is easier because there is less information to deal with. You should always write your model program at the highest level of abstraction that achieves your purpose (that can answer the questions you have formulated). Much of the skill in modeling is understanding what can be left out in order to achieve the right level of abstraction.

We use three kinds of abstraction. *Data abstraction* deals with variables. A higher level of data abstraction uses fewer variables, fewer values for those variables, and simpler data types. Data abstraction is our primary technique for finitizing models: we replace a potentially "infinite"collection of values with a (usually small) finite collection. *Behavioral abstraction* deals with statements and methods. A higher level of behavioral abstraction uses fewer statements or methods, where each statement or method in the model program represents more behavior in the implementation. *Environmental abstraction* deals with control structure. A higher level of environmental abstraction removes control structure, leaving it to the tool or the environment to choose which methods to execute at run time. In other words, environmental abstraction replaces control structure with *nondeterminism*.

In this example we choose a high level of data abstraction where the variables only represent the kind of page that is displayed and its style. We do not represent the page contents (the topics and messages). We choose a high level of behavioral abstraction where each action in the model program represents a large amount of implementation behavior. Each action represents both the selection of an option that causes a new page (or a different page style) to appear, and the appearance of that page.

In every model program, we use the same high level of environmental abstraction. There is no main method, nor any other control structure that determines the sequence in which actions occur (methods are called). Instead, the model program has *enabling conditions*, which allow the sequence of method calls to be chosen at run time by the tool that executes the model program, or by the environment where the model program runs.

5.3.4 Select the actions

It is often easier to select the actions first, because we can identify them by simply observing the behavior. Recall that we choose a high level of behavioral abstraction where each action is the selection of an option that causes a new screen to appear. We select these actions:

The `SelectMessages` and `SelectTopics` actions select those pages; these are the actions that occur when users click on a topic title or the group name, respectively. `ShowTitles` and `ShowText` select the details shown on the topics page. `SortByFirst` and `SortByMostRecent` select the sort order for the topics page when the titles only are shown.

The name of an action is called an *action symbol*. The entire collection of action symbols used by a model program is called its *action vocabulary* or just its *vocabulary*.

5.3.5 Write sample traces

Now that we have identified the actions, we can describe the behavior. Drawing on our observations and understanding of how the system is supposed to behave, we write down some traces that the system can execute and that the model program must also be able to execute. Each trace is simply a sequence of (some of) the actions from the vocabulary we identified. Here is a sample trace:

```
ShowTitles(); SortByFirst(); SortByMostRecent(); ShowText();
```

Not all sequences are allowed, because not all actions are available or *enabled* in each state. It is also useful to write down some traces that the model program must *not* be able to execute. For example:

```
ShowTitles(); SortByFirst(); SortByFirst(); ShowText();
```

The system cannot execute this trace because there are two `SortByFirst` actions in succession. After the first, this action is no longer enabled.

It is helpful to refer to these sample traces as we continue the preliminary analysis and then code the model program. It can also be helpful at this stage to make a table or a diagram that summarizes many traces, as we show in Chapter 6.

5.3.6   Select the state variables

Now we can select the state variables. This is a bit more difficult because we can't simply observe them. We must infer them from the behavior; in particular, from the sample traces we wrote. (In this example we don't have access to any source code or documentation.)

The state variables in a model program serve just three purposes: first, to determine what runs are possible by selecting the actions that are enabled in each state; second, to determine the data that appear during runs by storing the arguments and return values of the actions; and third, to support safety and liveness analyses by describing the safe states and accepting states.

We select these state variables: The `page` variable indicates which kind of page is displayed, `Topics` or `Messages`. The `style` variable indicates the appearance of the entries on the topics page, `WithText` or `TitlesOnly`. The `sort` variable indicates the sort order of the topics page when titles only are shown: `ByFirst` or `ByMostRecent`.

Stored information that determines the sequencing of actions is called *control state*; other stored information is *data state*. All of our state variables store control state. For this example we chose a high level of data abstraction where we ignore the page contents (the titles and messages). Our actions have no arguments or return values. Therefore this model program has no data state, apart from what is already stored in the control state.

By limiting the state variables to the control state, we ensure that the model program is finite. In fact, it is quite small. The *state space* of a program is the set of all states that it can reach. Here we have only three state variables, each with only two values, so at most there can only be $2 \times 2 \times 2$ or eight states in this program's state space. The implementation's state space is "infinite," because it includes the topics and messages, which include strings, a data type that has an "infinite" number of values. Our choice of state variables has finitized the model program. This is an example of data abstraction.

5.4   Coding the model program

Now that we have selected the actions and state variables, we can code the model program (Figures 5.4 and 5.5). The modeling library and tools support programs that are coded in a few particular styles. In order to work with the tools, a model program must be coded in one of these styles. In this chapter we introduce the style we use for most of the examples in this book. A complete reference for writing model programs in this style appears in Appendix A. Other styles are introduced in Chapter 7, Section 7.3.2.

```
using NModel;
using NModel.Attributes;
using NModel.Execution;

namespace NewsReader
{
    static class NewsReaderUI
    {
        // Types for each state variable
        enum Page { Topics, Messages };
        enum Style { WithText, TitlesOnly };
        enum Sort { ByFirst, ByMostRecent };

        // State variables, initial state
        static Page page = Page.Topics;
        static Style style = Style.WithText;
        static Sort sort = Sort.ByMostRecent;

        // Actions: enabling condition, then action method

        static bool SelectMessagesEnabled()
        {
            return (page == Page.Topics);
        }

        [Action]
        static void SelectMessages()
        {
            page = Page.Messages;
        }

        static bool SelectTopicsEnabled()
        {
            return (page == Page.Messages);
        }

        [Action]
        static void SelectTopics()
        {
            page = Page.Topics;
        }

        // to be continued ...
```

Figure 5.4. Web-based newsreader: model program (part 1).

```
static bool ShowTitlesEnabled()
{
   return (page == Page.Topics && style == Style.WithText);
}

[Action]
static void ShowTitles()
{
    style = Style.TitlesOnly;
}

static bool ShowTextEnabled()
{
    return (page == Page.Topics && style == Style.TitlesOnly);
}

[Action]
static void ShowText()
{
    style = Style.WithText;
}

static bool SortByFirstEnabled()
{
    return (page == Page.Topics && style == Style.TitlesOnly
            && sort == Sort.ByMostRecent);
}

[Action]
static void SortByFirst()
{
    sort = Sort.ByFirst;
}

static bool SortByMostRecentEnabled()
{
    return (page == Page.Topics && style == Style.TitlesOnly
            && sort == Sort.ByFirst);
}

[Action]
static void SortByMostRecent()
{
    sort = Sort.ByMostRecent;
}
    }
}
```

Figure 5.5. Web-based newsreader: model program (part 2).

5.4.1   Program structure

A model program must include `using` statements to use the namespaces of the modeling library NModel. A typical model program uses the NModel, NModel.Attributes, and NModel.Execution namespaces. All of these are provided by the library NModel.dll. A model program is compiled to a library, for example, by a command like this one (where DEVPATH is an environment variable that stores the path to the directory that contains the library, e.g., C:\Program Files\NModel\bin):

```
csc /t:library /r:"%DEVPATH%\NModel.dll" NewsReaderUI.cs
```

We code each model program in its own namespace. A model program consists of the actions and variables defined by the types declared in its namespace. The namespace name is the model program name: NewsReader in this example. A model program can include more than one class (or other types); this simple example has just one class.

NewsReader declares some variables to store the state, some methods to implement the actions, and some methods to test when each action is enabled. That's all there is to a model program. A model program does not have a main method or any other control structure for invoking the actions.

We recommend coding model programs with no access modifiers, so most types and members have the default private access. The tools can access private types and members (using a mechanism we will describe in Chapter 6).

5.4.2   State variables

The state variables of the model program are the static fields and instance fields declared in the model program's namespace. Public and nonpublic fields are included. Fields inherited from base classes (outside of the model namespace) are included.

In our example there are only three state varables. Each has only a few values so we declare an enumerated type for each.

```
enum Page { Topics, Messages };
enum Style { WithText, TitlesOnly };
enum Sort { ByFirst, ByMostRecent };
```

In our examples all of the state variables are static variables. We declare all three, and assign the initial state in the declarations.

```
static Page page = Page.Topics;
static Style style = Style.WithText;
static Sort sort = Sort.ByMostRecent;
```

Parameters and local variables in the model program are not state variables (there are none in this example).

Sometimes it is useful to exclude a field from state for debugging or other purposes. The [ExcludeFromState] attribute can be used to annotate fields that should not be part of state. Fields excluded from the set of state variables must have no effect on the behavior of the model.

5.4.3   Action methods

The actions of the model program are methods annotated with the [Action] attribute. We call these methods *action methods*.

Each action method must express how the action changes the state (or leaves it unchanged). Usually, the body of an action method computes the next state from the current state, by assigning one or more state variables. These assignments are sometimes called *updates* and an action method is sometimes called an *update rule*.

Here is the ShowTitles action method from this example. It causes the titles only to be displayed on Topics pages by setting the style state variable to TitlesOnly.

```
[Action]
static void ShowTitles()
{
    style = Style.TitlesOnly;
}
```

In addition, an action method may consume input or produce output. It is often useful for an action method to return a value, but this is not required. An action method may have parameters. (In this example, none of the action methods performs input or output, returns a value, or has parameters.)

An action method can be a static method or an instance method (Chapter 15). (In this example, they are all static.)

Action methods cannot be overloaded; each action method must have a different name.

The action methods must all be at *top level*: the model program only defines them; it cannot call them.

A model program can also contain *helper methods* that do not represent actions. Any code in the model program can call a helper method. (There are no helper methods in this example.)

5.4.4   Enabling conditions

In addition to action methods, a model program has methods that check when each action method is *enabled* (allowed to be invoked). These are called *enabling conditions*, *preconditions*, or *guards*. Enabling conditions are the control structures of model programs. Writing enabling conditions is the only way to control the sequence of actions that can occur when a model program executes. When coding enabling conditions, it is helpful to refer to the sample traces you wrote during preliminary analysis.

An enabling condition is a Boolean method that returns a `bool` value (a Boolean method is sometimes called a `predicate`). The enabling conditions of an action method have the same name as the action method, with the added suffix `Enabled`. An action method that has no enabling condition is always enabled (as if it had an enabling condition that always returned `true`).

An enabling condition describes a set of states: all the states where it returns `true`. In this example, the enabling condition for the `ShowTitles` action method (described before) is `ShowTitlesEnabled`. It expresses that `ShowTitles` is enabled in all states where the `page` is a `Topics` page and the `style` is `WithText`. In this model program, there are two such states, where the third state variable `sort` takes on both of its two possible values.

```
static bool ShowTitlesEnabled()
{
   return (page == Page.Topics && style == Style.WithText);
}
```

Enabling conditions may have parameters, which correspond to the parameters of its action method. The parameters in the two methods are matched up by order, so the first parameter in each must have the same type (etc.), and they are always called with the same arguments (the tools ensure this). An enabling condition may have fewer parameters than its action method. An enabling condition may use its parameters, as well as the state variables, to compute its return value.

An action method may have more than one enabling condition by *overloading* (they have the same name but different parameters). All of the enabling conditions must be true to enable the action. A static enabling condition method may be used for an instance-based action method (Chapter 15).

An enabling condition must be a *pure* method: it can only return `true` or `false`; it must not have any *side effects* that update state variables or parameters. An enabling condition can include calls to helper methods, provided that those methods are also pure.

You can code the enabling conditions of several action methods such that more than one action is enabled in some states. For example, in our initial state both `SelectMessages` and `ShowTitles` are enabled. This is typical. Our model program exhibits *nondeterminism*: it is not possible to predict (from the model program itself) which of the enabled actions will be invoked. Any enabled action can be chosen at run time by the tool that executes the model program. A model program that exhibits

```
[Test]
[Category("AllowedRun")]
public void AllowedRun()
{
    Assert.IsTrue(NewsReaderUI.ShowTitlesEnabled());
    NewsReaderUI.ShowTitles();
    Assert.IsTrue(NewsReaderUI.SortByFirstEnabled());
    NewsReaderUI.SortByFirst();

    Assert.IsTrue(NewsReaderUI.SortByMostRecentEnabled());
    NewsReaderUI.SortByMostRecent();
    Assert.IsTrue(NewsReaderUI.ShowTextEnabled());
    NewsReaderUI.ShowText();
}
```

Figure 5.6. Simulation run of the newsreader model program coded as an NUnit test.

nondeterminism can execute many different runs, where actions occur in different sequences. This is what we mean by environmental abstraction.

It is an error to invoke an action method in a state where any of its enabling conditions is false. This error is handled (or prevented) differently by different tools. During simulation (Section 5.5), the enabling condition acts as a *run-time check*: if an action method is about to be invoked when its enabling condition is false, the tool reports a failure. During exploration (Chapter 6), action methods whose enabling conditions are false are simply not chosen for execution.

5.5 Simulation

Now that we have a model program, we can begin some model-based analysis. We begin with simulation: run the model program and see what happens (we should have some expectation of what should happen). Each run of the model program simulates a run of the implementation. Simulation using model programs is sometimes called animation.

It is possible to execute a model program without using any of the tools, by writing an application or a test fixture that calls its methods. (We do not recommend this, it is far more convenient to use the mpv (Model Program Viewer) tool, but here we show how it can be done, to demonstrate that a model program is just a program.) Figure 5.6 shows an NUnit test method that executes a simulation run. To make this work, we have to produce a version of our model program that declares its methods public, unlike Figures 5.4 and 5.5 and contrary to our usual recommendation to use the default private access. This version also prints progress messages from each

action method. Before calling each action method, the test method calls NUnit's
IsTrue assertion to check the enabling condition. These checks ensure that the run
will succeed only if it executes a sequence of actions that is allowed by the model
program. If it attempts to execute a forbidden sequence, it will fail.

The test method shown in Figure 5.6 programs a run that the model program
should be able to execute. It encodes this sequence of actions:

```
ShowTitles(); SortByFirst(); SortByMostRecent(); ShowText();
```

This run succeeds. It produces this output:

```
Included categories: AllowedRun
.Topics, WithText, ByMostRecent: ShowTitles
Topics, TitlesOnly, ByMostRecent: SortByFirst
Topics, TitlesOnly, ByFirst: SortByMostRecent
Topics, TitlesOnly, ByMostRecent: ShowText


Tests run: 1, Failures: 0, Not run: 0, Time: 0.080 seconds
```

We also code a run that the model program should *not* be able to execute:

```
ShowTitles(); SortByFirst(); SortByFirst(); ShowText();
```

The model program should not be able to execute this run because there are two
SortByFirst actions in succession. The second of these is not enabled (in the
implementation, this option is not available in this state). The run fails, confirming
that the model program cannot execute this run:

```
Included categories: ForbiddenRun
.Topics, WithText, ByMostRecent: ShowTitles
Topics, TitlesOnly, ByMostRecent: SortByFirst
F


Tests run: 1, Failures: 1, Not run: 0, Time: 0.080 seconds


Failures:
1) NewsReader.Tests.ForbiddenRun :
   at NewsReader.Tests.ForbiddenRun()
```

This test failure does not indicate that the model program is incorrect. We are
not testing the model program here; we are executing the model program in order
to simulate the implemention. We are only using the test tool because it is more
convenient to write two tests than to write two applications. The failure here indicates

that the sequence of actions coded in this method is not allowed by the model program. This means that the implementation is not able to execute this sequence.

Simulation is the most limited and labor-intensive model-based analysis technique because it only considers one run at a time. To perform more thorough analyses – to detect the design errors discussed in Chapter 3, for example – we need to consider many different runs. For this, we use a more powerful analysis technique called *exploration*, which we will discuss in Chapter 6.

We recommend that you simulate and explore your model program as you develop it, so you can check frequently that it behaves as you intend. There is no need to finish the model program first; you can begin analyzing as soon as you have coded a few actions. The mpv tool makes it easy, as we shall see in Chapter 6. But first, we present model programs for the two implementations in Part I.

5.6   Case study: client/server

In this section we model the client/server system discussed in Chapter 2. In this example, we have the implementation available to help us with preliminary analysis and coding.

This example shows how a single model program can represent a distributed system with programs running on two computers connected by a network.

5.6.1   Preliminary analysis

The first activity in writing a model program is always a preliminary analysis. Recall that in preliminary analysis, we decide on a purpose for the model, select the features to include, and choose a level of abstraction by identifying the actions and state variables to represent in the model.

Purpose
The purpose of this model is to automatically generate and check test runs that can detect defects like the one described in Chapter 2, Sections 2.9 and 2.10.

We will execute these tests in a configuration similar to the one where we executed the unit test described in Chapter 2, Section 2.8: a *sandbox* where both the client and server are controlled by the test runner, and both execute in a single thread, interleaving their method calls in an order that conforms to their protocol (Chapter 2, Figure 2.2).

We want a contract model that can generate all the runs that the client and server can successfully execute in the sandbox. By a "run," we mean a session where both client and server create sockets, possibly exchange some messages, and then close their sockets. By "successfully execute," we mean every method call returns, and no exceptions are thrown. Therefore, certain sequences of method calls are forbidden. If the client attempts to connect before the server is listening on its socket, the client throws an exception. If one partner attempts to receive before the other partner sends, the receive method will block and never return. The model program must not generate runs like these.

The runs that the implementation can execute depend on its configuration. If the client and server run in separate threads, then one partner could call its receive method before the other partner sends. A different model program would be needed to model that configuration. Selecting the configuration can be an important step in preliminary analysis.

The challenges in this example are to write a model program that generates all the runs we want but none that are forbidden, and that generates enough different temperatures to expose the defect while keeping the model finite.

Features
We will model all of the features of the implementation client and server classes (Chapter 2, Section 2.4). Usually, a model program only represents some of the features of the implementation. But for this example we selected a very small implementation, so we could show the complete implentation and write a complete model program.

Actions
We plan to generate test runs that call the methods of the implementation, so there must be an action in the model for each public method in the implementation. The client and server actions are distinct; the client's send is a different action from the server's send, so we have actions ClientSend and ServerSend, and so on.

Traces
We write some sample traces to make sure that the actions we chose can express the behaviors we wish to model. There are many examples in Chapter 2. For example, the run discussed in Section 2.8, which is coded in the test method in Figure 2.10, is expressed by this trace:

```
ServerSocket();
ServerBind();
ServerListen();
ClientSocket();
ClientConnect();
ServerAccept();
ClientSend();
ServerReceive();
```

```
ServerSend(212.0);
ClientReceive();    // should return 212.0
ClientClose();
ServerCloseConnection();
ServerClose();
```

Here `server.Socket` in the implementation is modeled by `ServerSocket` in the model program, and so on. The arguments of `Bind`, `Connect`, and the client's `Send` in the implementation are not needed in the model program. We use a comment to indicate the expected return value of `ClientReceive` in this trace. We explain how return values are handled in the NModel framework in Chapter 8, Section 8.2.

State variables

In the implementation, there are classes for the client and server, and particular clients and servers are instances. Any program with instances is potentially "infinite," because it can create an unlimited number of them. We must make our model program finite. In our tests, we will only have one client and one server, so instances are not needed. In our model program, the state variables are the static variables needed to model just one client and one server. This is an example of data abstraction. A model program where all variables are static can model an implementation with instances and can be connected in a test harness with that implementation (Chapter 8).

Recall that state variables can store control state that determines the sequence of actions. In this example, there are two kinds of constraints on that sequence. Sockets must be created, connected, and closed according to the protocol shown in Chapter 2, Figure 2.2. And, the send and receive actions must alternate, always beginning with a send action. Therefore we have three state variables for the control state. Two keep track of each partner's step in the protocol: `clientSocket` and `serverSocket`. The third synchronizes send and receive actions: `phase`. These three variables do not correspond closely to any variables in the implementation. In the implementation, the ordering of method calls is coded in the applications that call them.

Recall that state variables can hold data state that stores the arguments and return values of actions. In this example, the data state is the most recently acquired temperature. We store the data state in a single state variable. It turns out to be most convenient to use the client's receive buffer `clientBuffer`.

The temperature is a number. All numeric types are "infinite": not mathematically infinite, but too large to store every value. Any program that uses numbers is potentially "infinite" (i.e., it has an "infinite" state space). To finitize our model, we must limit it to a finite collection of temperatures; the smaller, the better. We decide to use just two. We suspect that there might be defects in the implementation that are sensitive to the number of digits, so we choose 99.9 and 100.0. These particular values are not important; we assume that any other numbers with the same number of digits would behave the same way. Limiting temperatures to just two values is an example of data abstraction.

There are several ways to limit the temperature to two values. We could replace the numeric type with an enumerated type. We could even replace the single ServerSend method (where the temperature is a parameter) with two parameterless methods, each coded with one particular temperature. It is more convenient for testing if the methods and parameters are similar in the model and the implementation, so we keep the single method with its numeric parameter, but limit the number of parameter values with the Domain attribute, which we will describe in the next section.

The actions and state variables we chose determine the level of abstraction of this model program. Many implementation details are left out. We do not need any actual network machinery (IP addresses, port numbers, sockets, etc.) because we model the client, the server, and the network in a single model program. Other simplifications become possible because the model program can use global information that is not available to the separate client and server programs of the implementation. This will become clear in the next section.

5.6.2   Code

The client/server model program appears in Figures 5.7–5.11. Compare this to the implementation code in Chapter 2, Figures 2.3–2.5. Usually a model program is much shorter than the implementation. That is not the case here, because the implementation is so simple (it is really just a wrapper around some methods in the .NET socket class). Much of the code in the model is enabling conditions, which describe the control structure that must be present in any applications that use the implementation (such as Monitor and Logger, Chapter 2, Section 2.5). The structure of this model program, like all model programs, is similar to the first one (Section 5.4, Figures 5.4 and 5.5). The following paragraphs explain some features that might not be obvious.

Unlike the implementation, here the client and server are not instances. The state of both client and server are static variables in one static class, and the actions of both are static methods in this class. Therefore, we use a C# *static class*. The compiler checks that all the variables and methods in a static class are declared static.

There are different methods for the actions of the client and the server, with different names. The ClientSocket and ServerSocket action methods here model the Socket methods of the client and server classes in the implementation, and so on. All of the action methods in a model (in the model namespace) must have different names. It is possible to have more than one class in a model, but even then

```
using NModel;
using NModel.Attributes;
using NModel.Execution;

namespace ClientServer
{
    public enum Socket { None, Created, Bound, Listening, Connecting,
                         Connected, Disconnected, Closed }

    public enum Phase { Send, ServerReceive, ClientReceive }

    public static class ClientServer
    {
        const double EmptyBuffer = double.MaxValue;
        const double Temp2 = 99.9;    // Temperature, 2 digits
        const double Temp3 = 100.0;   // Temperature, 3 digits

        // Control state
        public static Socket serverSocket = Socket.None;
        public static Socket clientSocket = Socket.None;
        public static Phase phase = Phase.Send;

        // Data state
        public static double clientBuffer = EmptyBuffer;

        // Server enabling conditions and actions

        public static bool ServerSocketEnabled()
        {
            return (serverSocket == Socket.None);
        }

        [Action]
        public static void ServerSocket()
        {
            serverSocket = Socket.Created;
        }

        public static bool ServerBindEnabled()
        {
            return (serverSocket == Socket.Created);
        }

        [Action]
        public static void ServerBind()
        {
            serverSocket = Socket.Bound;
        }
```

Figure 5.7. Remote instrument client/server: model program (part 1).

```
// ... continued

public static bool ServerListenEnabled()
{
    return (serverSocket == Socket.Bound);
}


[Action]
public static void ServerListen()
{
    serverSocket = Socket.Listening;
}


public static bool ServerAcceptEnabled()
{
    return (serverSocket == Socket.Listening
            && clientSocket == Socket.Connecting);
}


[Action]
public static void ServerAccept()
{
    serverSocket = Socket.Connected; clientSocket = Socket.Connected;
}


public static bool ServerReceiveEnabled()
{
    return (serverSocket == Socket.Connected
            && phase == Phase.ServerReceive);
}


// No parameter needed here, client always sends same thing
[Action]
public static void ServerReceive()
{
    phase = Phase.Send;
}

// continued ...
```

Figure 5.8. Remote instrument client/server: model program (part 2).

```
// ... continued

public static bool ServerSendEnabled()
{
    return (serverSocket == Socket.Connected
            && phase == Phase.Send);
}

// Parameter here, server can send different temperatures
[Action]
public static void ServerSend([Domain("Temperatures")] double datum)
{
    clientBuffer = datum;
    phase = Phase.ClientReceive;
}

// Domain for ServerSend parameter t
static Set<double> Temperatures()
{
    return new Set<double>(Temp2, Temp3);
}

public static bool ServerCloseConnectionEnabled()
{
    return (serverSocket == Socket.Connected);
}

[Action]
public static void ServerCloseConnection()
{
    serverSocket = Socket.Disconnected;
}

public static bool ServerCloseEnabled()
{
    return (serverSocket != Socket.None
            && serverSocket != Socket.Connected
            && serverSocket != Socket.Closed);
}

[Action]
public static void ServerClose()
{
    serverSocket = Socket.Closed;
}

// continued ...
```

Figure 5.9. Remote instrument client/server: model program (part 3).

```
// ... continued

// Client enabling conditions and actions

public static bool ClientSocketEnabled()
{
    return (clientSocket == Socket.None);
}

[Action]
public static void ClientSocket()
{
    clientSocket = Socket.Created;
}

public static bool ClientConnectEnabled()
{
    return (clientSocket == Socket.Created
            && serverSocket == Socket.Listening);
}

[Action]
public static void ClientConnect()
{
    clientSocket = Socket.Connecting;
}

public static bool ClientSendEnabled()
{
    return (clientSocket == Socket.Connected
            && phase == Phase.Send);
}

// No parameter needed here, client always sends the same thing
[Action]
public static void ClientSend()
{
    phase = Phase.ServerReceive;
}

// continued ....
```

Figure 5.10. Remote instrument client/server: model program (part 4).

```
// ... continued

public static bool ClientReceiveEnabled()
{
    return (clientSocket == Socket.Connected
            && phase == Phase.ClientReceive);
}

// Return value needed here, server sends different values
[Action]
public static double ClientReceive()
{
    double t = clientBuffer;
    clientBuffer = EmptyBuffer;
    phase = Phase.Send;
    return t;
}

public static bool ClientCloseEnabled()
{
    return (clientSocket == Socket.Created
            || clientSocket == Socket.Connected);
}

[Action] public static void ClientClose()
{
    clientSocket = Socket.Closed;
}
    }
}
```

Figure 5.11. Remote instrument client/server: model program (part 5).

all the action method names must be different (you cannot use the class names to distinguish them).

The Socket type enumerates the values of the two control state variables server-Socket and clientSocket. They represent the steps in the protocol shown in Chapter 2, Figure 2.2. The Socket type provides all of the values needed by both sockets, although each socket uses only some of them. Both variables are initialized to None to indicate no sockets have been allocated, and are intended to reach Closed at the end of every run.

The Phase type enumerates the values of the control state variable phase. They represent the alternation of send and receive actions. The initialization ensures that a send action comes first. The phase variable is updated by the send and receive actions of both partners. This would not be possible in the implementation, where the client and server execute separate programs with no shared data.

The sequences of actions that are possible are determined by the enabling conditions, boolean methods that test the values of the control state variables. Some enabling conditions test the states of both partners, which would not be possible in the implementation. For example, ClientConnectEnable and ServerAcceptEnable ensure that ClientConnect follows ServerListen and precedes ServerAccept. They prevent the sequences that would cause the client implementation to crash (if it connects before the server listens) or cause the server implementation to block (if it accepts before the client connects).

In most states more than one action is enabled, so many different runs are possible. For example, in states where phase == Phase.Send, both ClientSend and ServerSend are enabled, so either partner could send the first message.

Unlike the implmentation, here the client's send method has no command argument, and the server has no receive buffer. In the runs we wish to model, these items always have the same value (the T command), so they add no information to the state. They are only used for synchronization. In the model, synchronization is achieved by the phase variable.

Like the implementation, here the server's send method has an argument, a number that represents the temperature acquired by the server. In the model, the server's send method simply assigns this number to the client's receive buffer. This models the effect of transmission across the network.

In the model, the receive buffer is a number (a C# double), not a string as it is in the implementation. To model the situation where this buffer is empty in the implementation, we set it to a special numeric constant double.MaxValue that we name EmptyBuffer.

We limit the receive buffer to just two temperature values, the constants we call Temp2 and Temp3. We achieve this by limiting the temperatures that can be assigned to the receive buffer by the ServerSend method. We limit that method's datum parameter to the two values, by using the Domain attribute:

```
public static void ServerSend([Domain("Temperatures")] double datum)
{
    . . .
}
```

To analyze a model, or generate test cases, the arguments of every parameter of every action method must be drawn from a finite collection called a *domain*. Parameters with boolean types or enumerated types always have finite domains. Other parameters must be labeled with a Domain attribute. The argument of the attribute, "Temperatures" here, is a string that names a method in the same class that returns the set of argument values for the parameter. When a tool executes the action method, it will choose one element from this set to assign to that parameter. A domain can also be a field or a property. The domain can depend on the state (it can return different sets of values in different states).

```
static Set<double> Temperatures()
{
    return new Set<double>(Temp1, Temp2);
}
```

Here the domain method always returns the same set. A domain method can return a set that is computed from the state. Set is a C# generic collection type that is provided by the modeling library (Chapter 10). Here <double> identifies the type of the elements of the set, which must match the type of the parameter in the action method.

In this example we code the domain in the model. In Chapter 7 we show how to code the domain separately from the model (which makes it easier to use different domains with the same model).

Now that we have a model program, we must validate it. Since we intend to use it for testing, we must show that it behaves as the implementation is supposed to behave. We can do a few simulation runs as we did in Section 5.5, simulating the test run of Chapter 2, Section 2.8, for example. We will analyze this model program more thorougly in Chapter 6 and use it to generate and check tests in Chapter 8. But first we present another model program.

5.7   Case study: reactive program

In this section we model the reactive system discussed in Chapter 3. This example shows how a single model program can represent a reactive program interacting with its environment.

5.7.1   Preliminary analysis

Purpose
The purpose of this model program is to be the subject of a design analysis that can reveal the design errors that we discovered by testing in Chapter 3, Sections 3.4 and 3.5.

We also plan to use this model program for testing. After the design errors are corrected in the model program, we will be able to use the corrected model program to generate and check tests for the revised implementation (which still might have defects).

Features

We will model all of the features of the implementation `Controller` class (Chapter 3, Section 3.1).

We must also model the controller's environment: the timer, sensor, and supervisor (Chapter 3, Figure 3.1). This is necessary in order to model events realistically. In our sandbox implementation, simulated events were generated by the user (through the `Simulator` class, Figures 3.5 and 3.6) or by the test fixture (Figure 3.7). In the model, we cannot use a .NET timer as we did in the simulator, because the time-out events must be scheduled by the tools.

Actions

There is an action in the model program for every event handler in the implementation's `Controller` class: `Reset`, `Poll`, and so on. The enabling conditions for these actions are the same as the guards in the implementation: `ResetEnabled`, `PollEnabled`, and so on. There is no action in the model corresponding to the implementation's `DispatchHandler` method; its control structure is implicit in the enabling conditions.

There is also an action for each kind of event that the reactive program handles. In the implementation, there is a single method `ReceiveEvent` with a `cevent` parameter that indicates what kind of event occured. Our several event actions correspond to different invocations of `ReceiveEvent` with different values for `cevent`. In the model, it turns out to be simpler to define a different action for each type of event, because each has a different enabling condition and makes different updates to the model state. In fact, there are more of these action methods than event types. For the `Timeout` event, we have the actions `Timeout`, `TimeoutMsgLost`, and `TimeoutMsgLate`. The additional code in our several event actions (compared to `ReceiveEvent`) is necessary because the model program must model the environment that generates events, in addition to the controller.

The model program alternates between executing an event action and a handler action. We have to define a do-nothing handler `NoHandler` to model what happens when no handler is enabled in the implementation.

Traces

We write some sample traces to show how behaviors discussed in Chapter 3 are expressed in the action vocabulary we chose. The run coded in the test method named `Typical` (section 3.3) is expressed by this trace:

```
Timeout();
Reset();
Message("99.9");
CheckMessage();
```

```
Timeout();
Poll();
Message("100.0");
CheckMessage();
Command();
Calibrate();
```

Compare this trace to the test method (Figure 3.7) and the test output (Section 3.3). The calls to `ReceiveEvent` in the test method are modeled by different actions for each kind of event: `Timeout`, `Message`, and `Command` (the `Exit` event is not modeled). The calls to `DispatchHandler` are modeled by the actions for each handler: `Reset`, `Poll`, and `Calibrate`.

The simulation in Section 3.4 that shows an unsafe run, labeled `OutOfRangeMessageWhenIdle`, is expressed by this trace:

```
Timeout();
Reset();
Message("99.9");
CheckMessage();
Timeout();
Poll();
TimeoutMsgLate();
ReportLostMessage();
Message("999.9");
NoHandler();
Command();
Calibrate();
```

In this trace, two different time-out actions appear: `Timeout` and `TimeoutMessageLate`. The `NoHandler` action here indicates that no handlers are enabled after the second message.

State variables

In this example, the parts of the model program that model the `Controller` class are similar to the implementation. The model program has these control state variables, which also occur in the implementation: `cevent`, the most recent event; `waitfor`, the kind of event the controller is waiting for; and `sensor`, the inferred sensor status.

The model program has additional control state variables that are not in the implementation. `TimeoutScheduled` and `MessageRequested` model the timer and the sensor to ensure that events are modeled realistically. They are tested by the enabling conditions for the event actions, and are updated by the event actions. Finally, the `phase` variable controls the alternation of events and handlers.

The model program has two data state variables, which also appear in the implementation: `buffer` and `previous`, the most recent temperature sample and the preceding temperature sample. These are numbers, so they could generate an "infinite" state space. To finitize our model, we limit both variables to just two values that represent temperatures that are within-range and out-of-range (by the criteria explained in Chapter 3, Section 3.6: the out-of-range value differs too much from the in-range value).

5.7.2 Code

The reactive system model program appears in Figures 5.12–5.18. Compare this to the implementation code in Chapter 3, Figures 3.2–3.4. The model program includes code that models the environment (timer, sensor, and supervisor), which does not correspond to any code in the implementation `Controller` class. The following paragraphs explain some features that might not be obvious.

Both data state variables represent numbers, but `buffer` is a `string` and `previous` is a `double`. The conversion is performed by the `CheckMessage` action method.

The particular values of the two temperature values `InRange` and `OutOfRange` do not matter, but they must differ by more than `tol` in `CheckMessage`.

There are two kinds of action methods in the model program. The action methods that handle events appear first. They also appear in the implementation. The other action methods raise events. They do not appear in the implementation. The two kinds of actions alternate, using the `phase` control state variable. The events are enabled when `phase == Phase.WaitForEvent` and assign `phase = Phase.HandleEvent`. The handlers are enabled when `phase == Phase.HandleEvent` and assign `phase = Phase.WaitForEvent`.

There must be a dummy handler `NoHandler` to model what happens in the implementation when no handler is enabled. This handler's enabling condition `NoHandlerEnabled` returns `true` in states where every other handler's enabling condition returns `false`. The handler itself does nothing but assigns `phase`.

The two control state variables `TimeoutScheduled` and `MessageRequested`, which do not appear in the implementation, model the timer and the sensor. `TimeoutScheduled` is in the enabling condition for every time-out event and `MessageRequested` is in the enabling condition for the message event.

There is only one `Timeout` event in the implementation, but there are three time-out event action methods in the model. `Timeout` models a time-out that arrives when the controller is not waiting for a message; `!MessageRequested` appears in its enabling condition. `TimeoutMsgLost`, and `TimeoutMsgLate` model time-outs that arrive when a message is expected; `MessageRequested` appears in their enabling conditions. `TimeoutMsgLost` models what happens in the implementation when the message is lost; it assigns `MessageRequested = false` so the message will never be

```
using System;     // Math for Abs in CheckMessage
using  NModel;
using  NModel.Attributes;
using  NModel.Execution;

namespace Reactive
{
    static class Controller
    {
        // Types from implementation
        enum ControlEvent { Timeout, Message, Command, Exit }
        enum WaitFor { Timeout, Message }
        enum Sensor { OK, Error }

        // Types added for model
        enum Phase { WaitForEvent, HandleEvent }

        // Control state from implementation
        static ControlEvent cevent = ControlEvent.Timeout;
        static WaitFor waitfor = WaitFor.Timeout; // enable Reset
        static Sensor sensor  = Sensor.Error;      // enable Reset

        // Control state added for model

        // Alternate between waiting for events and handling events
        static Phase phase = Phase.WaitForEvent;

        // Model the timer and the sensor
        static bool TimeoutScheduled = true;
        static bool MessageRequested = false;

        // Data state from implementation
        static string buffer  = OutOfRange;
        static double previous = Uninitialized;

        // Constants
        const string InRange = "99.9";                // for buffer
        const string OutOfRange = "999.9";            // for buffer
        const double Uninitialized = double.MaxValue; // for previous

        // continued ...
```

Figure 5.12. Reactive system: model program (part 1).

```
// ... Reactive system model program, continued

// Actions and enabling conditions for Controller, from implementation

static bool ResetEnabled()
{
    return (cevent == ControlEvent.Timeout
            && waitfor == WaitFor.Timeout
            && sensor == Sensor.Error
            && phase == Phase.HandleEvent);
}

[Action]
static void Reset()
{

    ResetSensor(); // send reset command to sensor
    StartTimer();  // wait for message from from sensor
    waitfor = WaitFor.Message;
    phase = Phase.WaitForEvent;
}

static bool PollEnabled()
{
    return (cevent == ControlEvent.Timeout
            && waitfor == WaitFor.Timeout
            && sensor == Sensor.OK
            && phase == Phase.HandleEvent);
}

[Action]
static void Poll()
{

    PollSensor();   // send poll command to sensor
    StartTimer();   // wait for message from sensor
    waitfor = WaitFor.Message;
    phase = Phase.WaitForEvent;
}

// continued ...
```

Figure 5.13. Reactive system: model program (part 2).

```
// ... Reactive system model program, continued

static bool CalibrateEnabled()
{
    return (cevent == ControlEvent.Command
            && waitfor == WaitFor.Timeout
            && sensor == Sensor.OK
            && phase == Phase.HandleEvent);
}

[Action]
static void Calibrate()
{
    double data = double.Parse(buffer);
    phase = Phase.WaitForEvent;
}

static bool CheckMessageEnabled()
{
    return (cevent == ControlEvent.Message
            && waitfor == WaitFor.Message
            && phase == Phase.HandleEvent);
}

[Action]
static void CheckMessage()
{
    double tol = 5.0;
    try {
        double data = double.Parse(buffer);
        if (previous == double.MaxValue) previous = data; // initialize
        if (Math.Abs(data - previous) < tol) {
            previous = data;
            sensor = Sensor.OK;
        }
        else sensor = Sensor.Error; // retain old previous
    }
    catch {
        sensor = Sensor.Error;
    }
    CancelTimer();  // cancel messageTimeout
    StartTimer();   // wait for next time to poll
    waitfor = WaitFor.Timeout;
    phase = Phase.WaitForEvent;
}

// continued ...
```

Figure 5.14. Reactive system: model program (part 3).

```
// ... Reactive system model program, continued

static bool ReportLostMessageEnabled()
{
    return (cevent == ControlEvent.Timeout
            && waitfor == WaitFor.Message
            && sensor == Sensor.OK
            && phase == Phase.HandleEvent);
}


[Action]
static void ReportLostMessage()
{
    StartTimer();  // wait for next time to poll
    waitfor = WaitFor.Timeout;
    phase = Phase.WaitForEvent;
}


// NoHandler is enabled when no other handler is enabled
static bool NoHandlerEnabled()
{
    return (phase == Phase.HandleEvent
            && !ResetEnabled()
            && !PollEnabled()
            && !CalibrateEnabled()
            && !CheckMessageEnabled()
            && !ReportLostMessageEnabled());
}


[Action]
static void NoHandler()
{
    phase = Phase.WaitForEvent;
}


// continued ...
```

Figure 5.15. Reactive system: model program (part 4).

```
// ... Reactive system model program, continued

// Actions and enabling conditions for environment, added for model

static bool TimeoutEnabled()
{
    return (!MessageRequested
            && TimeoutScheduled
            && phase == Phase.WaitForEvent);
}

[Action]
static void Timeout()
{
    cevent = ControlEvent.Timeout;
    TimeoutScheduled = false;
    phase = Phase.HandleEvent;
}

static bool TimeoutMsgLostEnabled()
{
    return (MessageRequested
            && TimeoutScheduled
            && phase == Phase.WaitForEvent);
}

[Action]
static void TimeoutMsgLost()
{
    cevent = ControlEvent.Timeout;
    TimeoutScheduled = false;
    phase = Phase.HandleEvent;
    MessageRequested = false;
}

// continued ...
```

Figure 5.16. Reactive system: model program (part 5).

```
// ... Reactive system model program, continued


static bool TimeoutMsgLateEnabled()
{
    return (MessageRequested
            && TimeoutScheduled
            && phase == Phase.WaitForEvent);
}


[Action]
static void TimeoutMsgLate()
{
    cevent = ControlEvent.Timeout;
    TimeoutScheduled = false;
    phase = Phase.HandleEvent;
    // MessageRequested remains true, message will arrive later
}


static bool MessageEnabled()
{
    return (MessageRequested
            && phase == Phase.WaitForEvent);
}


// This action has a parameter, must have Domain
[Action]
static void Message([Domain("Messages")] string message)
{
    cevent = ControlEvent.Message;
    buffer = message;
    MessageRequested = false;
    phase = Phase.HandleEvent;
}


static Set<string> Messages()
{
    return new Set<string>(InRange, OutOfRange);
}


// continued ...
```

Figure 5.17. Reactive system: model program (part 6).

```
// ... Reactive system model program, continued

static bool CommandEnabled()
{
    return (phase == Phase.WaitForEvent);
}

[Action]
static void Command()
{
    cevent = ControlEvent.Command;
    phase = Phase.HandleEvent;
}

// Helpers for enabling events

static void PollSensor() { MessageRequested = true; }

static void ResetSensor() { MessageRequested = true; }

static void StartTimer() { TimeoutScheduled = true; }

static void CancelTimer() {  TimeoutScheduled = false; }
    }
}
```

Figure 5.18. Reactive system: model program (part 7).

delivered. TimeoutMsgLate models what happens when the message is delayed; it leaves MessageRequested == true so the message can be delivered later.

The Message event has a Domain attribute for the Messages method that returns the set containing the two message values, InRange and OutOfRange. This ensures that the buffer and previous data state variables can have only those two values.

The four helper methods PollSensor, ResetSensor, StartTimer, and CancelTimer are called by the handlers. They model commands to the sensor and timer by assigning MessageRequested and TimeoutRequested.

5.8   Other languages and tools

The concepts taught in this chapter are common to many model-based testing and analysis systems, not just the library and tools we use. Models store state and execute actions. Models are made simple by slicing and abstraction, and are often finitized before analysis. Models are written by coding action methods with enabling conditions. But other systems often use different vocabulary for the concepts. For example, an action method might be called an *update rule*, an enabling condition is a *guard* or *precondition*, the combination of an action method with its enabling conditions is a *guarded update rule*, and a model program written in this style is a *guarded update program*. Other systems also use different programming languages (or different coding conventions in the same language) for writing the model programs.

5.9 Exercises

1. Write a simple implementation of the newsreader model program of Section 5.4. Your implementation need not provide any user interface, just provide an API with a method for each action. Describe how you implemented the enabling conditions, and explain your rationale.

2. Write and execute unit tests for your implementation that execute the runs simulated in Section 5.5. How does your implementation handle the second run, where the last action is not enabled?

3. Create a version of your newsreader implementation that contains a defect in (your implementation of) an enabling condition. Write a unit test that exposes the defect.

4. Create a version of your newsreader implementation that contains a defect in (your implementation of) an action method. Write a unit test that exposes the defect.

5. Revise the reactive system model program of Section 5.7 to correct the design errors. This version should have no unsafe states and no dead states. In other words, model the implementation you wrote in Chapter 3, Exercise 3. Hint: use the design rules given in Section 3.6.

Save the programs you wrote for these exercises to use in exercises in chapters to come.

6 Exploring and Analyzing Finite Model Programs

In this chapter we introduce *exploration*, our primary technique for analyzing model programs. Exploration generates a *finite state machine* (FSM) from a model program. The FSM can then be used for visualization, analysis, and offline test generation.

In this chapter we show how model-based analysis reveals the design errors in the reactive system we discussed in Chapter 3, by exploring the model program we developed in Chapter 5, Section 5.7. We explain and demonstrate *safety analysis* that identifies *unsafe* (forbidden) states and *liveness analysis* that identifies *dead states* from which goals cannot be reached. Dead states indicate *deadlocks* (where the program seems to stop running and stops responding to events) or *livelocks* (where the program keeps running but can't make progress).

In this chapter we also introduce the mpv (Model Program Viewer) tool for visualization and analysis, and explain how to use the modeling library features that support analysis.

6.1 Finite state machines

In this section we motivate and explain FSMs.

Simulation is the most limited and labor-intensive model-based analysis technique because it only considers one run at a time (Chapter 5, Section 5.5). To perform more thorough analyses – to detect the design errors discussed in Chapter 3, for example – we need to consider many different runs. The obvious way would be to code a large number of runs, but this is not a practical solution. In order to get good coverage of program behaviors, we would usually have code a great many runs, and some would be very long. But the collection of runs would be redundant. The same sequences of actions would appear again and again in different runs, and even within a single run. We use a better representation of behaviors that removes the redundancy, representing a great many runs in a compact way: the FSM. Exploration automatically generates an FSM from a model program.

Table 6.1. *Newsreader scenario FSM: state transition table*

Current state	Action (invocation)	Next state
Topics, WithText, ByMostRecent	ShowTitles()	Topics, TitlesOnly, ByMostRecent
Topics, TitlesOnly, ByMostRecent	SortByFirst()	Topics, TitlesOnly, ByFirst
Topics, TitlesOnly, ByFirst	SortByMostRecent()	Topics, TitlesOnly, ByMostRecent
Topics, TitlesOnly, ByMostRecent	ShowText()	Topics, WithText, ByMostRecent

To describe a run of a model program, we only need to show the actions (the action method calls). More thorough analyses must use the states as well. When we consider states and actions together, we find that an action often causes a change of state: a *state transition*. FSMs are built up from state transitions, not just actions.

To completely describe each state transition, we must identify the *current state* before the transition, the *next state* after the transition (also called the *target state*), and the action. To completely describe each action, we must show the entire *invocation* (the action name and all of its arguments) and the return value (if there is one).

An FSM is simply a finite collection of state transitions described in this way, along with an identification of the *initial state* where every run begins, and optional *accepting states* where runs are allowed to end (if no accepting states are identified, runs may end in any state). A run is a sequence of state transitions, so any run can define an FSM. But a run is an ordered collection, while an FSM is unordered. It is not necessary to order the FSM because each transition identifies its current and next states.

An FSM can be represented by a state transition table or a state transition diagram. Table 6.1 shows the *state transition table* that represents the FSM for the successful simulation run of Chapter 5, Section 5.5:

```
ShowTitles(); SortByFirst(); SortByMostRecent(); ShowText();
```

We simply enter a row in the table for each transition in the run, filling in the states and the method calls from the output of the run. An FSM is an unordered collection, so we can put the rows in any order we like. In our tables, we always put the transitions that begin in the initial state in a separate section at the top of the table, separated by a double line. After that, we put all transitions that begin in the same state together in the table. These are just conventions that make the table easy to read; any other order would express the same FSM. Often, rows in our tables appear in a different order than that in which the transitions occur in our example runs.

Figure 6.1. Newsreader scenario FSM: state transition diagram.

Figure 6.1 shows a *state transition diagram* for the same run. This is another way to represent the same FSM that is shown in Table 6.1. The diagram is a picture of a data structure called a *graph*, where bubbles called *nodes* (or *vertices*) are connected by arrows called *links* (or *arcs* or *edges*). In a state transition diagram, the nodes represent states. The links represent state transitions. Each is labeled by its action (a method invocation). The diagram shows a *directed graph* because each link points in one direction, from the current state to the next state. We can reconstruct the run from the diagram by following the links. In our diagrams the initial state is usually distinguished by shading.

It is important to understand that the effects of an action only depend on the current state. To compute (or predict) the effects (the next state), it is not necessary to keep track of the history leading up to the current state.

An FSM represents behavior compactly because each transition only occurs once in the FSM, no matter how many times it occurs in the run. In a state transition diagram, each state also appears only once. If the run reaches the same state more than once, the diagram contains loops called *cycles*. In this example there are cycles through all of the states.

6.1.1 Runs and scenarios

We generated our FSM (Table 6.1, Figure 6.1) from a run of our model program. It is also possible to generate runs from an FSM. This is how we do offline test generation.

Each FSM describes every run that can be obtained by traversing a path around the nodes and links in its graph. Here is an informal description of the algorithm for generating one run: Begin in the initial state. In a state that has transitions to next states, choose any one. For example, the middle node in Figure 6.1 has two outgoing transitions, so two choices are available. If we reach a state with no outgoing transitions, the run finishes in that state. Or, if the state has been designated an accepting state, we may choose to finish the run in that state. In this example, we have have not designated any accepting states, so every state is considered an accepting state; the run may finish in any state.

We often describe this process in terms of actions, rather than transitions. An action is *enabled* in a state if it is allowed to begin in that state; otherwise, it is *disabled* in that state. Every transition out of a state is labeled with one of the actions that is enabled in that state. For example, in the middle node in Figure 6.1, two actions are enabled: `SortByFirst` and `ShowText`. The heart of the traversal algorithm can be expressed: in each state, choose an enabled action and execute it.

By this algorithm, we can obtain the original run we used to define this FSM (from Chapter 5, Section 5.5). We can also obtain many other runs from this same FSM by choosing other transitions (other enabled actions), traversing different paths around the links in the diagram (possibly repeating each cycle many times). For example, the diagram in Figure 6.1 describes many runs that begin

```
ShowTitles(); SortByFirst(); SortByMostRecent(); ShowText(); ...
```

There are many more runs that begin

```
ShowTitles(); ShowText(); ShowTitles(); SortByFirst(); ...
```

And so on. A run obtained by traversing a graph is sometimes called a *traversal* or an *unwinding*. A collection of related runs is called a *scenario*. The entire collection of runs that can be generated from an FSM is called the *scenario* defined by that FSM.

Traversing an FSM generated by exploration from a model program is our off-line test generation technique. Different traversal algorithms can achieve different measures of *behavioral coverage* (Chapter 8).

6.1.2   Scenario FSMs and the true FSM

An FSM whose purpose is to define a scenario is called a *scenario FSM*. It is possible to define many different scenario FSMs for any model program; each different scenario FSM defines a different collection of runs. There is one FSM that can generate *all* of the runs of a model program: its *true FSM*.

When the model program has a small number of states and actions, it is possible to write down its true FSM. Table 6.2 and Figure 6.2 show the state transition table and the state transition diagram, respectively, for the true FSM of our newsreader model program (Chapter 5, Figures 5.4 and 5.5). Notice that the states and transitions in Figure 6.1 also appear in Figure 6.2 (the initial state is shaded in both diagrams). Here in Table 6.2, we use a more compressed format than in Table 6.1. We merge several transitions into each row by using X to indicate "don't care" values in the current state (where any value of particular variable is handled the same way, or is simply ignored) and a dash (–) for "don't change" values in the next state (where the value of a particular variable is the same as in the current state). It turns out that here this compression results in just one row for each action. Notice that each row in Table 6.1 is also represented (in compressed format) in Table 6.2.

Table 6.2. *Newsreader true FSM: state transition table*

Current state	Action	Next state
Topics, X, X	SelectMessages	Messages, –, –
Messages, X, X	SelectTopics	Topics, –, –
Topics, WithText, X	ShowTitles	–, TitlesOnly, –
Topics, TitlesOnly, X	ShowText	–, WithText, –
Topics, TitlesOnly, ByMostRecent	SortByFirst	–, –, ByFirst
Topics, TitlesOnly, ByFirst	SortByMostRecent	–, –, ByMostRecent

X indicates "don't care" values in the current state, where any value will do
– indicates "don't change" values in the next state, where the value is the same as in the current state.
Values shown are for the variables in this order: page, style, sort
The initial state is Topics, WithText, ByMostRecent

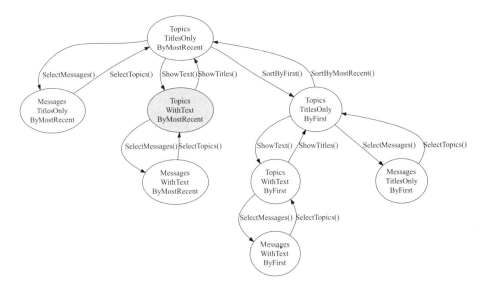

Figure 6.2. Newsreader true FSM: state transition diagram.

Compare the state transition table (Table 6.2) to the model program (Chapter 5, Figures 5.4 and 5.5). Notice that there is a row in the table for each action in the program, and notice how the current state and the next state entries in the table correspond to the enabling conditions and action methods in the program, respectively. In fact, we wrote the state transition table first, and coded the model program from it. This is often an effective way to design and code a model program that has a small number of states and actions.

Model programs need not have a small number of states and actions. State variables can be numbers, strings, objects, or other data types that can have a great many values. The actions can be method calls with arguments, which can also have a great many values. In that case, the number of states and transitions defined by the model program is effectively *"infinite"*: much too large to write down, or even to store in a computer. Then it is not possible to completely explore the true FSM. We will write and analyze such infinite model programs in Part III. In Chapter 11, we will show how to configure nonexhaustive exploration of infinite model programs, in order to perform analyses that are incomplete, but still useful (we will finitize the analysis instead of the model). But here in Part II, we only consider model programs where we can completely explore the true FSM. That is why we emphasized finitizing the model programs in Chapter 5.

6.2 Exploration

Recall that exploration automatically generates an FSM from a model program. The FSM can then be used for visualization, analysis, and offline test generation. In the following subsections we explain how to explore a model program with the library and tools.

6.2.1 Accessing the model program

To work with the library or any tool created from it (including `mpv`, `otg`, or `ct`), a model program must provide a *factory* method that creates a `LibraryModelProgram` object from the compiled model program assembly. All tools access the model program indirectly, by invoking the methods of this object.

We recommend putting the factory method in its own factory class. The factory class always has the same form; only a few identifiers must be changed for each particular model program. Figure 6.3 shows the factory class from our newsreader model program.

The factory class appears in the same namespace as the model program and must be compiled in the same assembly. For example, the code in Figure 6.3 appears in the same `NewsReader` namespace as the code in Chapter 5, Figures 5.4 and 5.5. The factory class must be declared `public static`. (The class or classes that contain the state variables and action methods of the model program need not be public; we recommend they have the default private access.) We usually name the factory class `Factory` and the factory method `Create`, but this is not required. In the body of the factory method, in the `LibraryModelProgram` constructor, the argument of the `typeof` operator must be the same class, `Factory` here. The second argument

```
public static class Factory
{
    public static ModelProgram Create()
    {
        return new LibraryModelProgram(typeof(Factory).Assembly, "NewsReader");
    }
}
```

Figure 6.3. Newsreader model program: factory class with factory method.

is a string that contains the name of the model program namespace, `NewsReader` here.

To invoke a tool on a model program, reference the assembly that contains the compiled model program, and provide the fully qualified name of the factory method in that assembly. This command invokes `mpv` on the `NewsReader` model program.[1]

```
mpv /r:NewsReaderUI.dll NewsReader.Factory.Create
```

6.2.2 Exhaustive exploration and visualization

When the `mpv` tool is invoked on a finite model program, it exhaustively explores the model program, generates its true FSM, and displays its state transition graph. For example, invoking `mpv` on `NewsReader` (as in the command earlier) displays the graph in Figure 6.4.

The graph generated by `mpv` looks similar to Figure 6.2, but not exactly the same. In Figure 6.2, each node is labeled by the values of all the state variables in that state. This does not generalize to many state variables, so `mpv` simply labels each node with a number. The initial state is always number zero but the other numbers are arbitrary. The `mpv` tool provides a state viewer panel that shows all of the state variables and their values in the selected node. This enables `mpv` to be used as a kind of debugger for model program that can be run forward or backward.[2]

Although Figures 6.2 and 6.4 do not look exactly the same, they both represent the same FSM. The positions of nodes and links can be quite sensitive to the choice of display options and other factors, so graphs that appear different at first glance can be diagrams of the same FSM. Graphs you generate (from the same model programs) might not look much like the figures in this book. It is the labels on the links and the connections between the nodes that are significant, not the positions of the nodes and links, nor the numbers on the nodes.

---

[1] A complete command reference for `mpv` and the other tools appears in Appendix B.
[2] In `mpv`, click on a node to select it. Then use the n key to step forward and p to step backward.

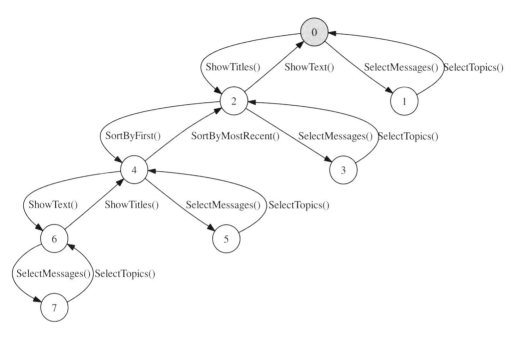

Figure 6.4. Newsreader true FSM: state transition diagram drawn by mpv tool.

It can be helpful to view the graph produced by exploration even when you do not have a precise question in mind, because it might reveal that the model program does not behave as you intend. For example, you may see many more or many fewer states and transitions than you expected, or you may see dead ends or cycles you did not expect.

We recommend that you explore and view your model program as you develop it, so you can check frequently that it behaves as you intend. There is no need to finish the model program first; you can begin exploring as soon as you have coded a few actions.

6.2.3   Interactive exploration and simulation

The mpv tool can also explore interactively, executing and displaying a few transitions at a time, under the user's control. This provides a more convenient way to simulate particular runs than coding and executing main methods or unit tests, as we did in Chapter 5, Section 5.5

Figures 6.5 and 6.6 show the interactive exploration of the first run we tested in Chapter 5. At first, only the initial state appears. At our command, mpv shows all the actions enabled in the initial state. We select ShowTitles by selecting its next state (Figure 6.5). Then we command mpv to show all the transitions enabled in that state,

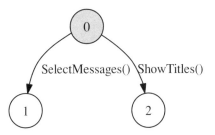

Figure 6.5. Simulation by interactive exploration (1).

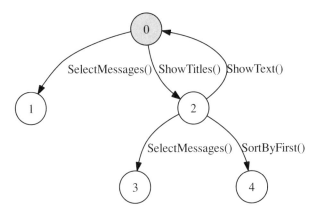

Figure 6.6. Simulation by interactive exploration (2).

and select SortByFirst by selecting its next state (Figure 6.5). Proceeding in this way, we can simulate the entire run.[3]

Interactive exploration can also show that a run is not allowed. If we attempt to explore the second run that we tested in Chapter 5, we find that after the first SortByFirst transition, the second SortByFirst transition is not enabled, so it is not possible to execute that run.

It is not always obvious whether or not a particular run (that you might write down) is allowed by a model program. As we have shown here, interactive exploration is one way to determine this. But, like any interactive procedure, it is not fully automated so it can be time-consuming and difficult to repeat. In Chapter 7 we describe another,

---

[3] In mpv, select the initial node with the mouse, press the Delete key to hide all the other states and transitions, press Enter to display the enabled transitions, press n (next) and p (previous) to select another node, and so on.

more automatic way that uses *composition* to check whether a run is allowed, which is still simpler than writing a unit test.

6.2.4   An exploration algorithm

In this subsection we explain how exploration works by presenting an exploration algorithm. You do not need to understand the algorithm in order to use the mpv tool to analyze finite model programs. But to analyze infinite model programs, you must provide additional information to guide exploration (Chapter 11). Then it becomes necessary to understand how exploration works. We prepare for that now by considering exhaustive exploration, which is the simplest case.

Exploration generates an FSM from a model program. It executes the model program, automatically selecting actions to execute, monitoring, and recording each state transition as it occurs, building a data structure that contains all the information shown in state transition tables or diagrams (Table 6.2, Figure 6.2).

Recall that we prepare for exploration by providing a factory method that creates a `LibraryModelProgram` object from the compiled model program assembly (Section 6.2.1, Figure 6.3). Exploration executes the model program indirectly, by invoking the methods of this object.

The `LibraryModelProgram` class is derived from the `ModelProgram` base class. We now provide a simplified description of this class, which omits many details. The names and members (etc.) of the types and methods in this simplified description are not the same as in the actual library. To avoid confusion with the actual modeling library, we call the class `ModelProgramSimple` here. It uses these types (which are also not exactly the same as the ones in the actual modeling library):

`State` The state of a model program, represented by a dictionary that associates each state variable name with its value.
`Action` The invocation of an action, including the action method name and all of its arguments.
`Transition` A state transition, with constructor `Transition(State current, Action a, State next)`

Our `ModelProgramSimple` class provides these properties and methods:

`State InitialState` Property that returns the model program's initial state
`Set<Action> GetActions(State s)` Method that returns the set of actions that are enabled in state s.
`State GetTargetState(State s, Action a)` Method that returns the next state reached by executing action a in the current state s.

```
ModelProgramSimple m = ModelName.Factory.Create(); // factory method
Sequence<State> frontier = new Sequence<State>(m.InitialState);
Sequence<State> explored = new Sequence<State>();      // empty
Set<Transition> transitions = new Set<Transition>();   // empty
while (!frontier.IsEmpty)
{
    State current = frontier.Head; // choose first element of frontier
    frontier = frontier.Tail;      // all but first element of frontier
    explored = explored.AddLast(current); // append current to explored
    foreach (Action a in m.GetActions(current))
    {
        State next = m.GetNextState(current, a);
        if (!frontier.Contains(next) && !explored.Contains(next))
        {
            frontier = frontier.AddLast(next); // append for breadth-first
        }
        transitions = transitions.Add(Transition(current, a, next));
    }
}
```

Figure 6.7. An exhaustive exploration algorithm.

The exploration algorithm also uses these types, which are defined in the modeling library (Chapter 10):

Set<T> The unordered collection of elements of type T, with constructors Set<T>(), Set<T>(x,y,z), and so on, and method Add, where s.Add(x) returns a new set that contains all the elements of set s and the element x.

Sequence<T> The ordered collection of elements of type T, with properties Head (the first element), Tail (all but the first element), and methods AddFirst (which pushes an element on the head), and AddLast (which appends an element to end).

Figure 6.7 shows an exhaustive exploration algorithm. (This simplified version is not the actual code used by the mpv tool.) The *frontier* is the collection of states that have been reached but whose enabled transitions have not yet been executed. (In Figure 6.5, states 1 and 2 are on the frontier; in Figure 6.6, states 1, 3, and 4 are on the frontier.) When exploration begins, only the initial state is on the frontier. Exploration proceeds by executing transitions that are enabled on the frontier. When executing, a transition reaches a state that has not already been reached, that state is added to the frontier. When all of the transitions that are enabled in a state have been executed, that state is removed from the frontier and added to the collection of explored states. (In Figure 6.5, state 0 has been explored; in Figure 6.6, states 0 and 2 have been explored.) The algorithm terminates when the frontier is empty.

If the model program is finite, this algorithm always terminates. When it does, the collection of transitions is the true FSM. Variations are possible. In Figure 6.7 the frontier is a sequence and new states are appended to the tail. This results in breadth-first exploration of the graph of the FSM. If new states were pushed on the head, depth-first exploration would occur instead. When exploration is exhaustive, as it is here, the final result is the same; otherwise, the two strategies explore different subsets of the true FSM.

Interactive exploration works almost the same way. Instead of working through the frontier sequentially until it is empty, interactive exploration allows the user to choose elements from the frontier in any order, and to exit at any time. Where exhaustive exploration has this:

```
while (!frontier.IsEmpty)
{
   State current = frontier.Head;  // choose first element of frontier
   frontier = frontier.Tail;      // all but first element of frontier
   ...
```

Interactive exploration has something like this:

```
while (!frontier.IsEmpty && still_interested)
{
   State current = frontier.Choose(i);  // choose an element of frontier
   frontier = frontier.Remove(current); // remove that element
   ...
```

This same algorithm can be easily extended to explore infinite model programs, because it is *lazy*: it delays computing each next state until it is needed, growing the FSM on the frontier as it goes, always adding to an incomplete subset of the true FSM. To limit exploration it is only necessary to add a *stopping rule* to exit before the frontier is empty. In fact, the mpv tool already provides one stopping rule: exploration stops after a certain number of transitions, MaxTransitions, has been found. It could be coded this way:

```
while (!frontier.IsEmpty && transitions.Count < MaxTransitions)
   ...
```

In mpv, MaxTransitions can be set on the command line, in a configuration file, or in the graphical user interface.

In this simplified description we have not discussed *parameter generation*, which assigns values to the parameters of action methods. Recall that parameter values are drawn from a set called a *domain*. In each state, exploration executes each action method repeatedly, using as many different values as it can from the domains of all its parameters. Each combination of parameter values defines a different action, so larger domains result in more actions and more transitions. Enabling conditions can depend on parameters as well as state variables, so each combination of parameter values must be checked; some combinations may not be enabled in some states.

6.3 Analysis

It can be helpful to simply view the graph of the FSM, but it is more useful to investigate particular issues. Exploration can provide the answers to several kinds of specific questions.

Several statistics are computed during exploration, including the number of states and transitions found (this is not shown in the algorithm of Figure 6.7). These statistics can provide useful diagnostic information. For example, they reveal whether exploration did in fact generate the true FSM. The default for the limit `MaxTransitions` is quite small, only 100. If exploration reaches this limit, it does not generate the true FSM, but only some portion of it. When this happens, the number of transitions found equals `MaxTransitions`. You may also notice unexpected dead ends in the graph. In that case, you should increase `MaxTransitions` and explore again.

Many analysis questions can be expressed in terms of *safety* or *liveness*. In the following subsections we use safety and liveness analyses to reveal design errors in the reactive system we discussed in Chapter 3, whose model program we developed in Chapter 5, Section 5.7.

6.3.1 Safety

Safety analysis checks whether anything bad can happen. It searches for unsafe states that violate safety requirements. We express *safety requirements* by writing a Boolean expression called an *invariant*, which is supposed to be true in every state that can be reached. An *unsafe state* is a state where an invariant is false. For the tools, an invariant is a Boolean field, property, or method labeled with the `[StateInvariant]` attribute.

Safety analysis depends on writing an invariant that expresses the safety property we wish to check. We must consider which states are allowed (that make the invariant true) and which are forbidden (that make the invariant false). Identifying the safe states requires judgment and understanding the program's purpose.

Recall that the purpose of our reactive system is to perform a calibration with a valid temperature sample. Performing a calibration with an invalid temperature sample would be bad. Here the bad thing is an action (performing a calibration) but

```
[StateInvariant]
public static bool CalibrateInRange()
{
    return (!CalibrateEnabled()
            ||  buffer == InRange);
}
```

Figure 6.8. Reactive system: state invariant for safety analysis.

safety analysis requires that we identify states. We resolve this by describing the states where the action is enabled, instead of the action itself. In the unsafe states, the calibration action is enabled but the temperature is invalid. This Boolean expression is true in the unsafe states:

```
CalibrateEnabled() && buffer != InRange     // unsafe states
```

It is often easier to describe the unsafe states first, as we did here. Negate the expression for unsafe states to obtain the safety condition.[4]

```
!CalibrateEnabled() || buffer == InRange    // safety condition
```

We wrap this expression in a static method, label it with the [StateInvariant] attribute, and place it in the Controller class in the Reactive model program namespace (Figure 6.8).

Now that we have defined the state invariant, exploration can find all of the unsafe states in the generated FSM. We command the mpv tool to explore the reactive system model program, and to count and display unsafe states:

```
mpv /r:Controller.dll Reactive.Factory.Create /safetyCheckIsOn+ ...
```

Figure 6.9 shows the generated FSM. We had to increase MaxTransitions to 300 to generate the true FSM. The mpv tool finds 239 transitions and 121 states, including 4 unsafe states. The unsafe states are marked but they are hard to find in Figure 6.9. They are easier to find in the mpv session, where we can magnify and scroll the graph.

To check that the unsafe states found by exploration include the one we expect, we explore interactively. We reproduce the OutOfRangeMessageWhenIdle run we found by experimenting with the implementation (Chapter 3, Section 3.4). The FSM we generate shows a path to one of the unsafe states (Figure 6.10). This FSM contains the second trace we wrote in Chapter 5, Section 5.7.1. The unsafe state is the state labeled 105 near the bottom of the diagram, where *Calibrate* is enabled.

---

[4] Here we apply *De Morgan's Law*, which shows how to negate expressions involving *and* and *or*: ! (p && q) == !p || !q.

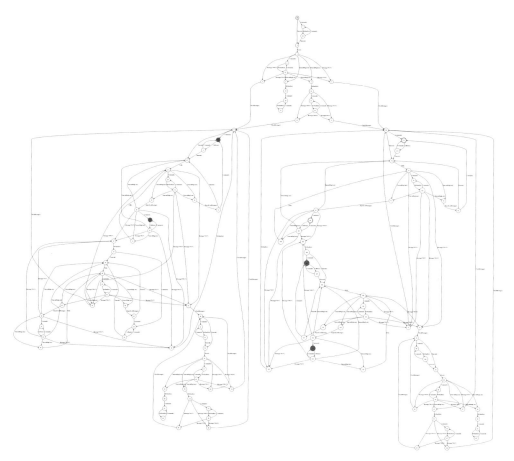

Figure 6.9. Reactive system: true FSM showing unsafe states.

This example confirms that model-based analysis reveals one of the design errors we originally discovered by executing the implementation.

6.3.2   Liveness

Liveness analysis checks whether something good will happen. It searches for dead states from which goals cannot be reached. We express *liveness requirements* by identifying *accepting states*, where goals have been reached. We define accepting states by writing an *accepting state condition*, a Boolean expression that is supposed to be true in every accepting state. A *dead state* is a state from which an accepting state cannot be reached. For the tools, an accepting state condition is a Boolean field, property, or method labeled with the [AcceptingStateCondition] attribute.

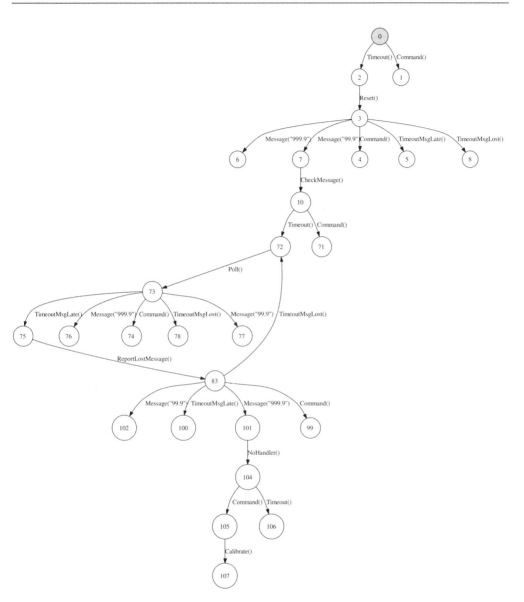

Figure 6.10. Reactive system: interactive exploration showing path to unsafe state.

Liveness analysis depends on writing an accepting state condition that expresses the goal we intend the program to achieve. An *accepting state* is often defined to be a state where the program is allowed to stop. However, many programs including embedded controllers (like the one in this example) are never supposed to stop. In order to use liveness analysis with such systems, we must broadenour definition. We

```
[AcceptingStateCondition]
public static bool SafeCalibrateEnabled()
{
    return (CalibrateEnabled()
            && buffer == InRange
            && previous == double.Parse(InRange));
}
```

Figure 6.11. Reactive system: accepting state condition for liveness analysis.

now say that an *accepting state* is a state where a program goal has been achieved, where some unit of work has been finished, where there is not a portion of work left undone, where a task has been completed, and where there is not some task left unfinished. Some judgment and understanding of a program's purpose is required in order to identify its accepting states.

Recall that the purpose of our reactive system is to perform a calibration with a valid temperature sample. Also recall that a temperature sample is considered valid when it does not differ too much from the preceding sample. Therefore, the goal of the program has been achieved when two successive within-range temperatures have been sampled, and a Calibration action occurs. Liveness analysis requires that we express this in terms of a state, not an action, so once again we subsitute the action's enabling condition for the action itself. The accepting state condition is

```
CalibrateEnabled() && buffer == InRange
&& previous == double.Parse(InRange)
```

We wrap this expression in a static method, label it with the `[AcceptingStateCondition]` attribute, and place it in the `Controller` class in the `Reactive` model program namespace (Figure 6.11).

Now that we have defined the accepting state condition, exploration can find all of the accepting states and dead states in the generated FSM. We command the `mpv` tool to explore the reactive system model program, and to count and display unsafe states:

```
mpv /r:Controller.dll Reactive.Factory.Create /livenessCheckIsOn+ ...
```

Figure 6.12 shows the generated FSM. We had to increase `MaxTransitions` to 300 to generate the true FSM. The `mpv` tool finds 239 transitions and 121 states, including 2 accepting states and 61 dead states. The accepting states are marked but they are hard to find in Figure 6.12. They are easier to find in the `mpv` session, where we can magnify and scroll the graph.

The dead states are easier to find, because there are so many of them. Near the initial state, the FSM divides into two regions, each with many interior links but no

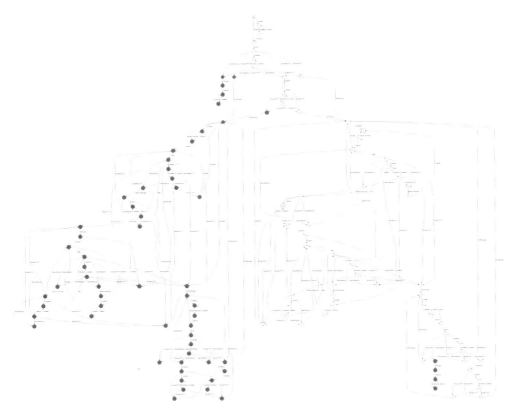

Figure 6.12. Reactive system: True FSM showing accepting states and dead states.

links connecting outside (lower left and lower right in Figure 6.12). This indicates that, depending on the first several actions at startup, the program permanently enters one or the other of two modes. In one of these modes, all of the states are dead states (lower left in Figure 6.12). Inspecting the FSM closely (magnifying and scrolling in mpv) reveals that the program enters this mode when the first temperature sample is out-of-range. After that the program cannot escape. This is the same behavior we observed in the InitialOutOfRangeMessage run we found by experimenting with the implementation, where an out-of-range temperature sample at startup is followed by a *livelock* where the program resets endlessly without making progress (Chapter 3, Section 3.4). Exploring interactively, we reproduce the InitialOutOfRangeMessage run (Figure 6.13). The cycle including the Reset action appears in the lower right of the diagram. Exploration finds that all of states on the frontier at lower left in this diagram are also dead states. They offer no escape; they only lead to longer cycles.

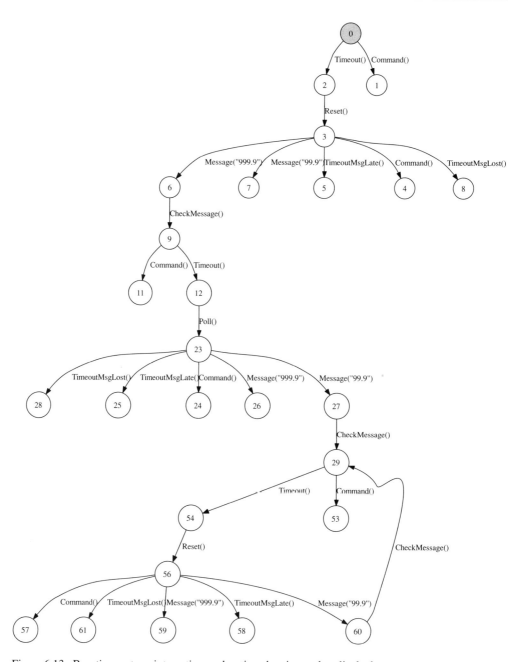

Figure 6.13. Reactive system: interactive exploration showing path to livelock.

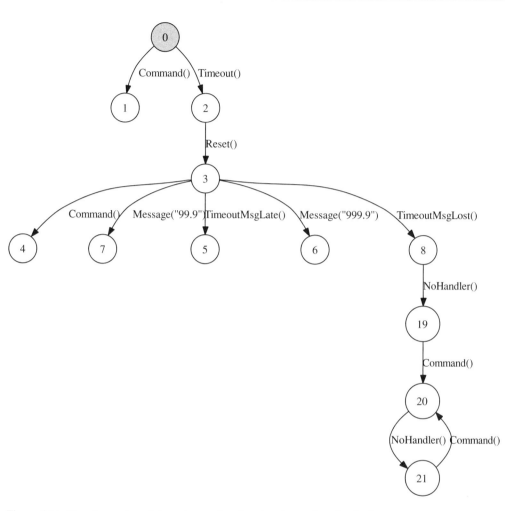

Figure 6.14. Reactive system: interactive exploration showing path to deadlock.

We also reproduce the `LostMessageWhenIdle` run, where the program reaches a deadlocks (Figure 6.14). The deadlock is indicated by the loop of alternating `Command` and `NoHandler` actions, from which there is no escape. The deadlock here is a loop rather than a dead end. The supervisor can always command the controller, so the `Command` action is always enabled. But the controller can do nothing; recall that `NoHandler` is a dummy action that indicates no handlers are enabled.

These examples confirm that model-based analysis reveals the design errors we originally discovered by executing the implementation.

In Chapter 7 we will discuss another kind of analysis. Instead of searching for unsafe states or dead states, that analysis checks *temporal properties* defined by sequences of actions.

6.4 Exercise

1. Explore a program with mpv, with MaxTransitions set low enough so that the FSM is not completely explored. Try several different values for MaxTransitions. Does it appear that mpv explores the FSM depth-first, breadth-first, or in some other way?

7 Structuring Model Programs with Features and Composition

In this chapter we describe two mechanisms for structuring model programs at a large scale: *features* and *composition*. Each provides a way to combine model programs in order to create a new one, or to write a model program as a collection of parts that are themselves complete (or nearly complete) model programs.

Both mechanisms are so versatile that they can be used in many ways. In Chapter 14 we use them to model interacting features. In this chapter we use them to limit analysis and testing to particular scenarios of interest. We also show how composition can be used in analysis to check *temporal properties* defined by sequences of actions.

7.1 Scenario control

The problem of limiting analysis and testing to particular runs of interest is called *scenario control*. Scenario control is necessary because we usually write a model program to act as a specification or *contract*, so it describes everything the implementation must do, might do, and must not do. As a result, the model program usually describes a large number of runs. When we analyze, and especially when we test, we usually do not want to consider all of these runs. We would like to limit our consideration to a particular *scenario*: a collection of runs (perhaps just one) that are pertinent to some issue.

Here is an example that shows why we need scenario control. Figure 7.1 shows the true FSM we obtained by exploring the client/server model program we developed in Chapter 5, Section 5.6. There are many paths through this FSM; each path describes a different run. But is it useful to consider every run? In other words, does every run have a different effect? Let's look more closely. Figure 7.2 shows the first few transitions of all the runs, where the client and server each perform the initial actions of the protocol shown in Chapter 2, Figure 2.2: the server executes Socket, Bind,

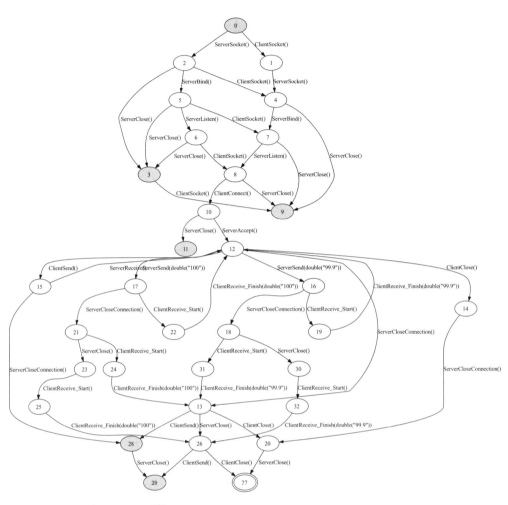

Figure 7.1. Client/server: true FSM.

and Listen, and the client executes Socket. There are several runs where the client Socket action is *interleaved* between different server actions. We know that all of these runs have to be equivalent because the client and server do not even begin to interact until the client's Connect action. Before that, the order of the interleaving of client and server actions cannot make any difference. Indeed, all of these runs reach the same state. There are several other runs where the server executes Close before the client connects. Nothing interesting can happen after that, so these runs end in dead states. In the usual case where we want to see what happens after the client and server connect, we could replace all of the runs in Figure 7.2 by a single run without losing any useful information.

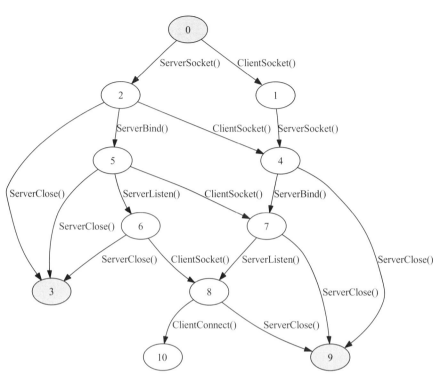

Figure 7.2. Client/server: the first few transitions of all runs.

This example shows that we often know a priori – before any exploration or testing – that we do not want to consider certain runs. We need a way to use this a priori knowledge – or other preferences – in automated analysis and testing. But we do not want to put limitations into the model program itself. We want to separate the *contract model program* that describes all allowed behaviors from *scenario control*, the limitations we introduce to focus on interesting runs. Then we can use the same contract model program to analyze or test many different scenarios. Features and composition make this possible.

7.2 Features

A *feature* is a cluster of related state variables and actions that can be selectively included or excluded from a model program. Features make it possible to define different configurations for a model program, which include different subsets of features, in a single source program file (or collection of files). In addition, features can be combined for purposes of scenario control.

7.2.1   Defining features

To define a feature, declare its state variables, action methods, and enabling methods in a class. The feature name is the class name. Label the class with the [Feature] attribute.

Each feature can be selectively included or excluded from the model program. Classes that are not labeled with the [Feature] attribute are always included. State variables that are declared within a feature should only be used by that feature. State variables that are used by more than one feature should be declared in a class that is not a feature, so they will always be included.

Figure 7.3 shows excerpts from a version of the client/server model program where the client and server are separate features (compare to the original version in Chapter 5, Figures 5.7–5.10). All of the state variables are used by both the client and the server, so they remain in the ClientServer class, which is not a feature. The state variables are declared internal to make them accessible in the feature classes. The action methods and enabling conditions of the client and server are declared in the new Client and Server classes, which are features.

7.2.2   Including or excluding features

Features are included in a model program by naming them in the LibraryModel-Program constructor (Chapter 6, Section 6.2.1). This constructor has an optional third argument, a set of strings that name the features to include. If this argument is omitted, all features are included. You can write several factory methods, where each one names a particular combination of features. When you invoke a tool, use the factory method that names the features you want to include.

In Figure 7.3, the factory method CreateServerOnly names the server feature but not the client. This command runs mpv on the client/server model program with just the server feature included.

```
mpv /r:ClientServer.dll ClientServer.Factory.CreateServerOnly
```

Figure 7.4 shows the diagram that mpv displays. The client feature was excluded from the model program, so only a few server actions are enabled (the ones that do not involve communication with the client).

7.2.3   Combining features

Features can be combined to model interacting features in the implementation, or to achieve scenario control. To combine features, give some of their action methods the same names. Action methods in classes that are not features (which are always included in the model program) can also have the same names. All of the action methods that have the same name are parts of the same action; they are executed together. The combined action is enabled only when all the enabling conditions for

```
namespace ClientServer
{
    ...
    static class ClientServer
    {
        // State variables used by all features
        internal static Socket serverSocket = Socket.None;
        ...
    }

    [Feature]
    static class Server
    {
        // Server action methods and enabling conditions
        ...
        public static bool ServerSocketEnabled()
        ...
        [Action]
        public static void ServerSocket()
        ...
    }

    [Feature]
    class Client
    {
        // Client action methods and enabling conditions
        ...
     }

    // Factory class, several factory methods select different features
    public static class Factory
    {
        // No features argument in constructor, include all features
        public static ModelProgram Create()
        {
            return new LibraryModelProgram(typeof(Factory).Assembly,
                                    "ClientServer");
        }

        // Features argument in constructor, include just that feature
        public static ModelProgram CreateServerOnly()
        {
            return new LibraryModelProgram(typeof(Factory).Assembly,
                                    "ClientServer",
                                    new Set<string>("Server")); //feature
        }
    }
}
```

Figure 7.3. Client/server: model program with features (excerpts).

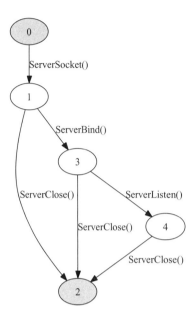

Figure 7.4. Client/server: server feature included, client feature not included.

all of its action methods are true (in all the included features and other classes). During exploration, the combined action is executed repeatedly in each state, with each combination of parameter values that is enabled in all of the features. When the combined action executes, all of the action methods for that action execute, as if in parallel (actually, in some order that cannot be predicted). This only makes sense if the next state after executing all the action methods is the same for any order of execution. This is assured if none of the action methods assigns state variables that are used by other action methods in the same action.

Here we show how to combine features to control *parameter generation*, an aspect of scenario control. Recall that each parameter of each action method must be provided with a *domain*, a set of argument values for that parameter. In each state, exploration executes each action method repeatedly, using as many different values as it can from the domains of all its parameters, so larger domains result in more transitions and more runs. Therefore, selecting domains can limit or select runs. In our examples in Chapter 5, each domain is coded directly into the contract model program. In the client/server example, one particular domain Temperatures is always used for the datum parameter of the ServerSend action method:

```
[Action]
static void ServerSend([Domain("Temperatures")] double datum)

    . . .

static Set<double> Temperatures()

    . . .
```

This code is inflexible. It is often better to separate the domains from the contract model program, so the same model program can be configured with different domains for different scenarios. Figure 7.5 shows how to use features to achieve this. In the contract model program, code the action method without a domain. Then, in a feature, code an action method with the same name, but include the domain. Leave the body of this action method empty. To select that domain, include that feature. When the combined action executes, the domain from the selected feature is used, and the body of the action method in the contract model program executes with a parameter value from that domain. (In this example the feature has no enabling conditions; the ones in the contract model program are sufficient.) Create different features that use different domains and include the one that generates the scenario you want. You must include one of these features; a model program cannot be explored (is not *explorable*) if there are parameters without domains.

7.3 Composition

Composition combines separate model programs into a new model program called the *product*. The product formed by composing model programs M1 and M2 is written M1 × M2 or M1*M2. Composition is performed automatically by the analysis and testing tools when multiple model programs are named on the command line; the tools can then analyze or test from the product. You can also do composition in programs you write by calling the library. Composition can be used to build up complex model programs by combining simpler ones (as we shall see in Chapter 14). In this chapter we use it for scenario control.

The next section explains how composition is done. The section after that describes some additional styles for coding model programs that make it easy to write scenarios for composition. In Section 7.3.3 we will return to using composition for scenario control.

7.3.1 Understanding composition

Recall that features are classes in the same model program (the same namespace), which may use the same state variables and are compiled into the same assembly. In contrast, we compose separate model programs, which can be in separate namespaces and can be compiled into separate assemblies. All of the tools accept any number of model programs; they form the product of all of them. No special coding is needed to prepare model programs for composition (no attributes, etc.). Any two (or more) model programs can be composed (although the product is not always useful, of course).

The product of two or more model programs has all the state variables and all the actions of each of the composed programs. The key idea in composition is that

```
namespace ClientServer
{
    ...
    static class ClientServer
    {
        // State variables, methods used by all features
        ...
        [Action]
        static void ServerSend(double datum) // No [Domain], use features instead
        ...
    }

    [Feature]
    static class TemperatureX2
    {
        readonly static Set<double> Temperatures = new Set<double>(99.9, 100.0);

        [Action]
        static void ServerSend([Domain("Temperatures")] double datum) {}
    }

    [Feature]
    static class TemperatureX4
    {
        readonly static Set<double> Temperatures =
                            new Set<double>(98.8, 99.9, 100.0, 101.1);

        [Action]
        static void ServerSend([Domain("Temperatures")] double datum) {}
    }

    // Factory class, factory methods select features with different domains
    public static class Factory
    {
        public static ModelProgram CreateWithTemperatureX2()
        {
            return new LibraryModelProgram(typeof(Factory).Assembly,
                                    "ClientServer",
                                    new Set<string>("TemperatureX2"));
        }

        public static ModelProgram CreateWithTemperatureX4()
        {
            ...
        }
    }
}
```

Figure 7.5. Client/server: model program with features that select domains (excerpts).

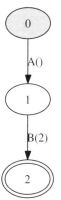

Figure 7.6. Model program M1.

shared actions that have the same name in two or more of the composed programs are one action in the product. They execute together, and can only execute when all of the actions are simultaneously enabled in each of their programs.

The requirement in composition that shared actions must be enabled simultaneously in every composed program where they occur often has the effect of restricting behavior, eliminating some runs. That is why composition is useful for scenario control. Composition restricts behavior to the intersection of the runs of each composed program. In other words, the runs of the product are the runs that are allowed by every one of the composed programs.[1]

However, there is an important exception: Actions that are not shared can interleave in any order in the product, and can execute whenever they are enabled in their own programs. If you wish to suppress this interleaving, you must add those actions to the other model programs (so there are no longer any unshared actions), and disable those actions in every state in the other model programs.

To summarize: Under composition, model programs synchronize steps for shared actions and interleave actions not found in their common action vocabulary.

Here is a small example. M1 and M2 are model programs; for this discussion it is most helpful to show the FSM of each program. M1 has actions A() and B(2) that make transitions from the initial state 0 to state 1 to the accepting state 2 (Figure 7.6). M2 has actions B() and C() that make transitions from state 0 to 1 and back again; here state 0 is both the initial state and the accepting state (Figure 7.7). Their product M1 × M2 appears in Figure 7.8. All three actions appear in the product.

---

[1] Composition of model programs is a generalization of the construction of finite automata for the intersection of regular languages. For example, see the discussion following Theorem 3.3 on pp. 59–60 of Hopcroft and Ullman (1979).

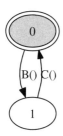

Figure 7.7. Model program M2.

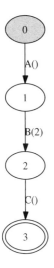

Figure 7.8. Model program M1 × M2, the product of M1 and M2.

Let us explain exactly how the FSM of the product M1 × M2 in Figure 7.8 was obtained. There is a systematic method for generating the product of two model programs. First, identify the action vocabulary for each program, and the unshared actions from the other program. For M1 the action vocabulary is A, B and there is one unshared action, C; for M2 the action vocabulary is B, C and the unshared action is A. Then, form the *loop extension* of each program: at each state, add a self-loop transition for each of the unshared actions. The two loop extensions now have the same action vocabulary. Moreover, in the loop extensions, actions with the same action symbol are made to have the same *arity* (number of parameters) by extending them with *placeholder* parameters indicated by _ (underscore). Here the action B() from M2 becomes B(_) in the loop extension of M2, so it has the same arity as B(2) in M1. Figures 7.9 and 7.10 show the loop extensions of M1 and M2, respectively. The product is generated from these loop extensions.

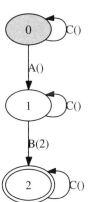

Figure 7.9. Loop extension of model program M1.

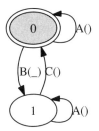

Figure 7.10. Loop extension of model program M2.

Each state in the product is a *pair state* formed from a state in M1 and a state in M2 (Figure 7.11). Form the initial pair state (0, 0) from the initial states of M1 and M2. Generate the rest of the product by exploring from the initial pair state. Each action that is enabled in a pair state must be enabled in both corresponding states in the loop extensions of both programs. Here action A() is the only action which is enabled in the initial states of both programs; C() and B(_) are only enabled in M1 and M2, respectively. Executing action A() makes the transition to state 1 in M1 and makes a self-loop transition back to state 0 in M2, so in the product A() makes the transition to the pair state (1, 0). In this state, B(2) is enabled in M1 and B(_) is enabled in M2. These two actions *match* because their names are the same, and a placeholder matches any argument; here the placeholder in B(_) matches the argument in B(2). These actions make transitions to states 2 and 1 in M1 and M2 respectively, resulting in the pair state (2, 1) in the product. The action which appears in the product is B(2), not the action B(_) with the placeholder. In the pair state (2, 1), C() is enabled in both programs, making a final transition to the pair state (2, 0) in the product. In that pair state, there are no actions that are enabled in both programs, so exploration stops;

Table 7.1. *Pair states, enabled actions, and matched actions in M1 × M2*

Pair state	M1 enabled actions	M2 enabled actions
(0, **0**)	**A**(), C()	**A**(), B(_)
(1, **0**)	**B**(2), C()	A(), **B**(_)
(2, 1)	C()	A(), C()
(**2, 0**)	C()	A(), B(_)

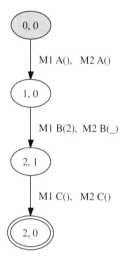

Figure 7.11. Model program M1 × M2, showing pair states and matched actions.

the product is complete. The pair state (2, 0) is an accepting state in the product because both states in the pair are accepting states in their own programs.

   Table 7.1 summarizes this procedure. For each pair state, it shows the actions that are enabled in each loop extension, with the matching actions printed in bold type. Accepting states are also printed in bold type.

   There are a few additional complications that did not arise in this simple example, concerning the arguments of actions. When actions have the same name but different arguments (other than the placeholder), they do not match. For example, if M2 in this example had action B(3) instead of B(_), it would not match B(2) in M1 and no B action would appear in the product. Moreover, it is possible to define actions that have placeholders in any position, so the action D(_,4) in one program would match D(3,_) in another, resulting in D(3,4) in the product. More complex examples and explanations of composition appear in Chapter 14, especially Section 14.3.

   Sometimes it is useful to view the *projection* of a product onto one of the composed programs. Figure 7.12 shows the projection of the product M1 × M2 onto M2. The projection is generated by exploring the product. Each time the product

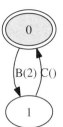

Figure 7.12. M1 × M2 projected onto M2.

```
FSM(0, AcceptingStates(), Transitions(t(0,A(),1), t(1,B(2),2)))
```

Figure 7.13. M1 as an FSM text file.

executes an action of M2, that transition is added to the projection onto M2. In this example the projection of M1 × M2 onto M2 looks like the original M2 (Figure 7.7), except the action B() from M2 is replaced by the action B(2) from the product. Sometimes the projection has fewer transitions than the original program. This is significant when composition is used for analysis (Section 7.5).

7.3.2   FSMs for scenario control

We often write a *scenario model program* to compose with a contract model program for scenario control. It is often convenient to express a scenario model program as an FSM. The library and tools support several styles for coding model programs. All of the examples so far have used just one of these styles, the style introduced in Chapter 5 and described in Appendix A. In this section we introduce two more styles that make it easier to code FSMs for scenario control.

First we show how to code an FSM in the familiar style. Figure 7.13 shows program M1 from Section 7.3.1, coded in C#, in the same style as the other model programs we have seen. There is just a single state variable, which corresponds to the state numbers shown in the state bubbles in Figure 7.6. We call a program coded in this style a *library model program*. There is a factory method that invokes the constructor for the LibraryModelProgram class, which is derived from the ModelProgram base class. To display the FSM, compile the program and invoke mpv:

```
mpv /r:M1.dll M1.Factory.Create
```

To compose and display two model programs, for example, M1 and M2 as in Figure 7.8, invoke mpv with both:

```
mpv /r:M1.dll /r:M2.dll M1.Factory.Create M2.Factory.Create
```

Now we introduce another style, the *FSM model program*. Figure 7.12 shows M1 coded in this style. It also uses C#, but instead of coding state variables and action methods, we code the FSM as an array of strings where each string describes one transistion, in the format `"t(current state, action, next state)"`. The current state in the first transition is the initial state. In the factory method, the array of strings is passed to the `FSM.Create` method, which returns an instance of the FSM class. Another method in this class can be used to identify the accepting states, if any. The FSM instance is passed to the constructor for the `FsmModelProgram` class, which is also derived from `ModelProgram`. An FSM model program is compiled and displayed in exactly the same way as a library model program.

Now we introduce a third style, the *FSM text file*, which is the most compact (Figure 7.13). This style dispenses with C# and assemblies altogether and just puts the FSM in a text file, in a parenthesized format. The first element inside the outer parentheses is the initial state. The second element is a sequence of accepting states (which is left empty here, which indicates there are no accepting states). It is not necessary to compile an FSM file. To display the FSM in the file, invoke mpv with the `/fsm` option and name the file:

```
mpv /fsm:M1.txt
```

In practice, we rarely write an FSM model program, we just write an FSM text file instead. When you invoke a tool with the `/fsm` option, it reads the FSM from the file and constructs a `FsmModelProgram` instance in much same way as shown in Figure 7.12. The tools do require you to write a factory method for library model programs (rather than just invoking the constructor automatically) because this is where you identify the features you want to include.

The tools do not depend on the source form of model programs. They access every model program in a uniform way through an instance of the `ModelProgram` class, which always provides certain properties and methods, including `InitialState`, `GetActions`, `GetTargetState`, and so on. (Chapter 6, Section 6.2.4). As a result, every style of model program can be composed, explored, viewed, and used for testing in the same way. From the tools' point of view, the differences between model program styles are hidden by derived types such as `LibraryModelProgram` and `FsmModelProgram`. It is possible to support model programs written in other styles and languages by coding additional types derived from `ModelProgram`. For example, you could support model programs that are expressed as diagrams rather than text.

7.3.3   Scenario model programs

Now that we understand composition and know how to write scenario model programs easily, we are ready to use composition for scenario control.

Recall that the purpose of scenario control is to eliminate runs allowed by a contract model program that are not pertinent to the particular issue we wish to analyze or test. The unwanted runs can be eliminated by composing the contract model program with a scenario model program that encodes the runs we wish to see. It is often convenient to code the scenario model program as an FSM. Recall that composition has the effect of selecting only the runs that are allowed by both composed programs. If there is a particular sequence of actions you want to see in the product, put that sequence in the scenario model program. If there are other actions you would allow to interleave in the product, do not mention those actions in the scenario model program. If there are actions you want to eliminate from the product, include those actions in the vocabulary of the scenario model program but do not write any transitions that use them. This has the effect of disabling those actions in all states.

There is a typical scenario that we often want to use for testing: first, a sequence of setup actions, then several (or many) interleaved test actions, and finally, a sequence of cleanup actions. Figure 7.14 shows a model program for generating such a scenario from the client/server model program. Compare this to the true FSM for the contract model program (Figures 7.1, and 7.2). The setup and cleanup sequences in the scenario model program select one run through the many paths allowed by the contract model program. The scenario model program does not mention the send and receive actions; those are the test actions that are allowed to interleave.

This command displays the test scenario model program composed with the contract model program:

```
mpv /fsm:Scenario.txt /r:ClientServer.dll ClientServer.Factory.Create
```

Figure 7.15 shows the result. The setup and cleanup sequences from the scenario model program also appear in the product. The loops in the middle of the diagram represent the interleaving of the test actions, send and receive. We will use this product in Chapter 8 to generate and check tests that reveal the defect we discussed in Chapter 2.

7.4   Choosing among options for scenario control

There are three ways to control the scenarios of a model program: enabling conditions, features, or composition. We recommend that the model program should be a specification or contract, so its enabling conditions should permit all allowed runs, not just particular scenarios. Scenario control should be separated out with features or composition, so the same contract model program can analyze or test different scenarios. Features can access the model program state, so use features for

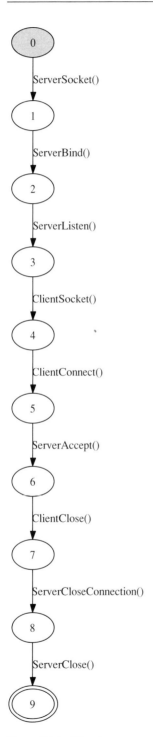

Figure 7.14. Client/server: test scenario.

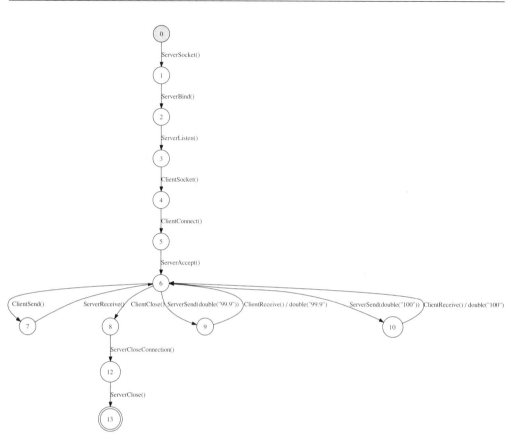

Figure 7.15. Client/server: test scenario composed with contract model program.

state-dependent parameter generation, or when enabling conditions must depend on the contract model program state in other ways. Composed programs cannot share state, so use composition when you can describe the scenario you want in terms of sequences of actions, without refering to the contract model program state. In particular, use composition when the scenario can be expressed as an FSM.

7.5 Composition for analysis

We now show how composition can be used for analysis. Recall that the analysis methods discussed in Chapter 6 require you to write Boolean expressions that identify unsafe states (for safety analysis) or accepting states (for liveness analysis). But sometimes it is easier to express requirements in terms of actions, rather than states. For example, in the reactive system, we can express the safety requirement this way: the calibrate action should not follow the arrival of a message containing an out-of-range temperature. And, the liveness requirement is: the calibrate action should follow the arrival of a command. A property expressed in this way, by describing the ordering of actions, is a *temporal property*.

Scenario model programs can express temporal properties, and composition can check them. Compose the contract model program with the scenario model program that expresses the property. Examine the projection of the product onto the scenario. If the projection is complete (it contains all of the transitions of the original scenario model program), then the contract model program can execute that scenario, and you will be able to find the runs of the scenario in the product. If the projection is incomplete (if it is missing some transitions), then the contract model program cannot execute that scenario, and you will not find any runs of the scenario in the product.

Notice how this use of composition differs from scenario control, where we write a scenario that we want the contract model program to execute, that we assume it *can* execute. For analysis, we write a scenario that the contract model program may *not* be able to execute; that is what we want to find out.

Let's look at some examples. First, we consider an example where the scenario model program describes exactly one run. The analysis tells us whether the contract model program can execute that run; it provides the same information as simulation (Chapter 5, Section 5.5) or interactive exploration (Chapter 6, Section 6.2.3), but may be easier to set up and repeat.

To make this easy to understand, we return to the simple news reader example. Let us see what happens when the contract model program *cannot* execute the scenario. We choose the run that we simulated in Chapter 5:

```
ShowTitles(); SortByFirst(); SortByFirst(); ShowText();
```

We encode this run as a scenario in an FSM text file with these contents:

```
FSM(0, AcceptingStates(), Transitions(
    t(0,ShowTitles(),1), t(1,SortByFirst(),2), t(2,SortByFirst(),3),
        t(3,ShowText(),4)),
    Vocabulary("ShowTitles","ShowText","SelectMessages","SelectTopics",
            "SortByFirst","SortByMostRecent"))
```

This FSM text file contains an entry at the end that defines the vocabulary of the scenario machine, the names of all its actions. If this entry is omitted, the vocabulary is understood to be the actions that appear in the transitions. Here we need to list the vocabulary because it includes actions that do not appear in any of the transitions of this particular scenario. When we use composition to check whether the contract model program can execute a particular run, we must include the whole vocabulary of the contract model program in the scenario model program. In the product, any actions of the contract model program that do not appear in the scenario vocabulary

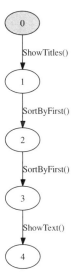

Figure 7.16. Newsreader scenario FSM for analysis by composition.

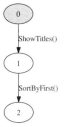

Figure 7.17. News reader scenario FSM, incomplete projection after composition.

might interleave anywhere among the actions of the scenario. Defining the scenario vocabulary as we do here prevents these unwanted interleavings from confusing the analysis.

    Figure 7.16 shows the FSM for this scenario. We compose this with the contract model program (whose FSM is shown in Chapter 6, Figure 6.2). Figure 7.17 shows the projection of the product onto the scenario. The projection is incomplete; it only includes the first two transitions of the scenario. This shows that the contract model program cannot execute this scenario, because the third transition of the scenario is not enabled in the contract model program. It was at this point that the simulation failed (Chapter 5, Section 5.5). The FSM of the product shows the same thing, but the product sometimes contains additional transitions that make it harder to interpret, so we recommend inspecting the projection for this analysis.

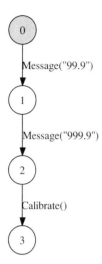

Figure 7.18. Reactive system: scenario FSM for safety analysis.

The preceding example resembles simulation or interactive exploration in checking just one run. But a scenario model program can describe more than one run. In the next example we take advantage of this to reveal the safety violations in the reactive system that we exposed by a different technique in Chapter 6, Section 6.3.1. Recall that we had to write a Boolean expression that described the safe states. Now we will describe the safety violation in terms of actions, not states.

A safety violation occurs if the program performs a calibration after it receives a message that contains an out-of-range temperature. In order to enable the calibration, the program must first receive an in-range temperature. The safety violation can be described by a scenario that contains just those three actions:

```
FSM(0,AcceptingStates(),Transitions(
    t(0,Message("99.9"),1),
    t(1,Message("999.9"),2),
    t(2,Calibrate(),3)))
```

It is not necessary to include any other action in the scenario, because they will be filled-in by interleaving when we compose the scenario with the contract model program. Recall that any actions that are not explicitly included in the vocabulary of the scenario model program can interleave among its actions when it is composed. Here we make use of that fact to complete the runs. Many interleavings are possible, so this scenario describes many runs.

We compose this scenario machine (whose FSM appears in Figure 7.18) with the contract model program (whose FSM, with unsafe states highlighted, appears in Figure 6.9 in Chapter 6). The projection of the product onto the scenario resembles

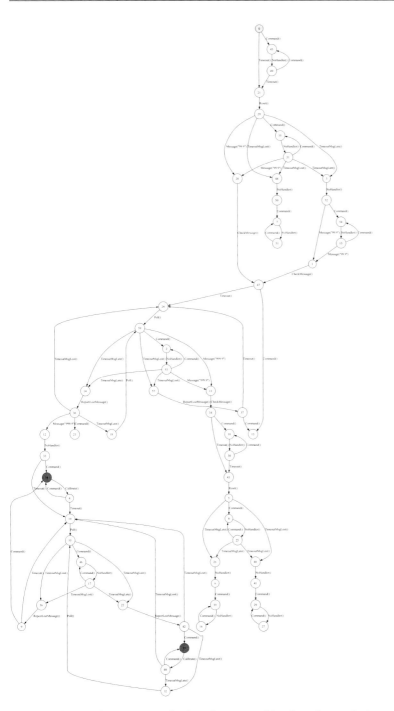

Figure 7.19. Reactive system: projection after composition for safety analysis.

Figure 7.18; it includes all the transitions of the scenario. This indicates that the contract model program can execute the scenario; there are some unsafe runs. The projection of the product onto the contract model program appears in Figure 7.19 (the product itself is similar but includes some distracting complications). Many runs described by the scenario machine appear in the projection, including the unsafe run shown in Figure 6.10 in Chapter 6. (We can confirm this by magnifying and inspecting the graph, or by exploring it interactively.)

It is important to understand that here we did not have to identify any unsafe states in order to perform this analysis; we only had to write the scenario. Moreover, we did not have to describe any paths completely in our scenario, we only had to identify what is common to the unsafe runs: a few actions and their ordering.

This analysis takes a somewhat different view of safety than does the analysis of Chapter 6. Here, a run is unsafe if it includes the actions of our scenario (in that order); in Chapter 6, a run is unsafe if it reaches an unsafe state (that violates an invariant defined by a Boolean expression). To compare the two analyses, in Figure 7.19, we have highlighted the states that are unsafe according to the analysis in Chapter 6.

Two of the four unsafe states identified in Chapter 6 appear in the projection here. These two states are highlighted in the right lobe of the FSM of the contract model program (Figure 6.9 in Chapter 6). Notice how a portion of that contract FSM appears here in the projected FSM. The left lobe of the contract FSM does not appear in the projection because in all the paths to that lobe, the out-of-range message reporting temperature 999.9 precedes any in-range message reporting 99.9 (see Figure 6.12 in Chapter 6 and the accompanying discussion). Therefore, those paths do not match our scenario and are excluded from the product. Two of the unsafe states appear in that lobe, so they are not reachable by the scenario we specified.

The two analyses produce results that are similar but not identical. For the temporal analysis we performed here, we chose a scenario that is a bit more selective (considers fewer runs to be unsafe) than the state-based analysis we performed in Chapter 6.

7.6 Exercises

1. We say we want to keep contract model programs free of limitations intended to reduce the number of runs. Is the client/server model program in Chapter 5 entirely free of such limitations? If not, show an example of such a limitation.
2. In the example in Section 7.3.1, the true FSM of the product contained all of the states and actions of the true FSM of each of the programs that were composed. Is this always true? If not, provide a counterexample.

8 Testing Closed Systems

In this chapter we introduce model-based testing. We test the client/server implementation we described in Chapter 2, and reveal the defect we discussed there. We generate the test suite and check the results with the model program we developed in Chapter 5, Section 5.6. We introduce our test generator tool `otg` and our test runner tool `ct`, and show how to write a test harness that connects an implementation to the `ct` tool.

In this chapter we describe *offline* test generation, where test suites are generated before running the tests. Offline test generation works best with finite model programs that can be explored completely. In Chapter 12 we introduce *on-the-fly testing*, where the test case is generated as the test executes. On-the-fly testing is an attractive alternative for "infinite" model programs that cannot be explored completely.

In this chapter we test *closed systems* where the tester controls every action. In Chapter 16 we test *reactive systems*, where some actions are invoked by the environment.

8.1 Offline test generation

The offline test generator `otg` explores a model program to create a finite state machine (FSM), traverses paths through the FSM, and saves the paths in a file so they can be used later. The paths define a collection of program runs. The collection is called a *test suite*; each run in the collection is a *test case*. Later, the implementation can execute the test suite, under the control of a test runner.[1]

The `otg` tool has one traversal algorithm built in. The algorithm eliminates all paths to dead states, then traverses the remaining paths using a *postman tour* that covers the entire graph of the FSM in the minimum number of steps, visiting each state and taking each transition at least once.

---

[1] A complete command reference for `otg` appears in Appendix B.2.

Instead of explaining the traversal algorithm here, we simply exhibit the results.[2] Figure 8.1 shows the test suite generated by otg from the client/server contract model program developed in Chapter 5, Section 5.6, whose true FSM is shown in Chapter 7, Figure 7.1. This test suite was generated and stored in the file ContractTest.txt by the command:

```
otg /r:ClientServer.dll ClientServer.Factory.Create ^
    /file:ContractTest.txt
```

This test suite is itself an FSM; in fact, Figure 8.1 was created by this mpv commmand:

```
mpv /testSuite:ContractTest.txt
```

It is clear from Figure 8.1 that the test suite describes a collection of six sequences. Each sequence is a test case. The ct tool can interpret the contents of the test suite file, and, when harnessed to the implementation, can execute and check all the test cases.

The test suite in Figure 8.1 describes many similar runs because it was generated from the true FSM of the contract model program, without using any scenario control. It is likely that a smaller test suite would be as effective in detecting defects, for the reasons explained in Chapter 7, Section 7.1.

We can generate a smaller test suite by using scenario control. Let us generate a test suite from the client/server contract model program composed with the scenario machine developed in Chapter 7, Section 7.3.3. The FSM of the composition is shown in Figure 7.15. This command generates the test suite.

```
otg /r:ClientServer.dll ClientServer.Factory.Create ^
    /fsm:Scenario.txt ^
    /file:ScenarioTest.txt
```

Figure 8.2 shows the generated test suite. There is just a single run, because all the states and transitions in the FSM of the composition can be visited by traversing a single path from the initial state to the accepting state, including each of the loops in the middle of the FSM (Figure 7.15 in Chapter 7).

Other traversal algorithms are possible. In addition to the postman tour, model-based offline test generators sometimes provide random traversals, traversals that cover the shortest path to an accepting state (or some other interesting state), or traversals that achieve transition coverage but with an upper limit on the length of each test case (which generates more runs, but shorter runs, than does the postman tour). At the time of this writing, the otg tool provides none of these, but the modeling library could be used to write a custom offline test generator.

---

[2] The traversal algorithm is explained in several references cited in Further Reading (Chapter 9).

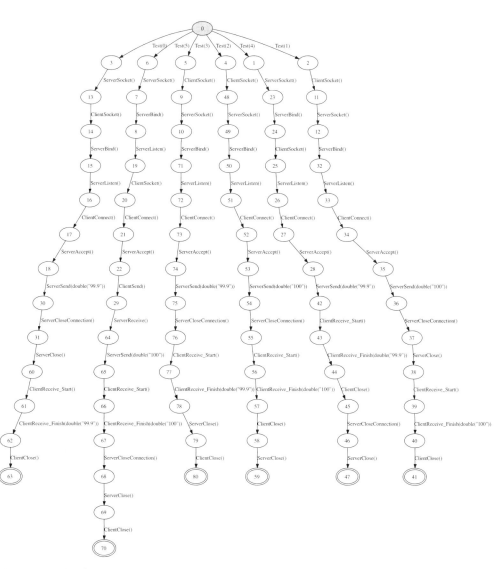

Figure 8.1. Client/server: test suite generated from contract model program.

8.2 Traces and terms

In order to write the test harness that connects the implementation to the test runner, you must understand how test suites are represented in the files written by the test generator.

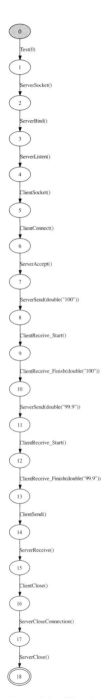

Figure 8.2. Client/server: test suite generated with scenario control.

```
TestSuite(

    TestCase(

            ServerSocket(),

            ServerBind(),

            ServerListen(),

            ClientSocket(),

            ClientConnect(),

            ServerAccept(),

            ServerSend(double("100")),

            ClientReceive_Start(),

            ClientReceive_Finish(double("100")),

            ServerSend(double("99.9")),

            ClientReceive_Start(),

            ClientReceive_Finish(double("99.9")),

            ClientSend(),

            ServerReceive(),

            ClientClose(),

            ServerCloseConnection(),

            ServerClose()

    )

)
```

Figure 8.3. Client/server: test suite file contents, showing a trace with terms.

The otg tool saves test suites in text files. Figure 8.3 shows the contents of ScenarioTest.txt, which describes the test suite with one test case whose FSM is displayed in Figure 8.2. Each test case in a test suite file is a *trace*, text that represents a program run. A trace is not expressed in C# code, although it resembles code (compare the trace in Figure 8.3 to the unit test in Chapter 2, Figure 2.10, and also to the trace we wrote in Chapter 5, Section 5.6.1). A trace is a sequence of actions. Each action is expressed as a *term*, a data structure that the tools use to represent actions. The syntax of terms is easy to understand, but differs from the syntax of C# method calls. The tools use terms because they are easier to work with than program text. You must work with terms in your test harness code.

Actions are not exactly the same as method calls. Most of the actions in Figure 8.3 correspond to a method call, but not all. Each client Receive method call corresponds to *two* actions, for example:

```
ClientReceive_Start(),
ClientReceive_Finish(double("100")),
```

The first action, called the *start action*, is the method call. The second action, the *finish action*, is the method return including the expected return value computed by the model program, which appears in parentheses in the term. The pair of actions is called a *split action*. Any action method that has outputs (a return value or C# `out` or `byref` parameters) must be modeled as a split action. You do not have to code both actions in your model program; the tools automatically create split actions from every action method with outputs (use the `mpv` option `combineActions-` to display both actions in each pair).

It is necessary to model the two actions separately because the implementation might not execute the finish action. The start action is *controllable*; the test harness can always cause the implementation to execute the method call. But the finish action is *observable*; the test harness can only wait for the method return. If the implementation crashes or hangs, the method will not return and the finish action will not occur. The test runner indicates that these are failures.

Actions (with no outputs) that are not split actions are called *atomic actions*.

Actions are not exactly the same as method calls, and (e.g., with split actions) there is not always a one-to-one relation between method calls and actions. Therefore, we must distinguish between method names and *action symbols*, the names of actions. The default behavior of the library and tools is to automatically derive the action symbols from method names, but you can also assign your own action symbols in the action attributes (Appendix A). The entire collection of action symbols used by a model program is called its *action vocabulary* or just its *vocabulary*.

8.3 Test harness

A *test harness* is code that enables a test runner to execute an implementation. You must write a test harness for each implementation. Figures 8.4 and 8.5 show the test harness that connects the client/server implantation to the `ct` tool. The implementation appears in Chapter 2, Figures 2.3–2.5.

You can write the harness to accommodate differences between the model and the implementation. The harness in Figures 8.4 and 8.5 drives an implementation where sockets are objects, but in the model they are static variables. Although the library and tools use .NET, you can write a harness for an implementation that does not use .NET.

Write the test harness in the same namespace as the implementation. The test harness implements the modeling library's `IStepper` interface, so we often call a test harness a *stepper*; it "steps" the implementation through the actions of each test case. To implement the `IStepper` interface you must write two methods, `Reset` and `DoAction`. The stepper must also provide a factory method that returns the stepper object.

The `Reset` method executes after each test case to reset the implementation to its initial state.

```csharp
using System;
using NModel.Conformance;
using NModel.Terms;

namespace ClientServerImpl
{
    public class Stepper: IStepper
    {
        const int port = 8000;
        const string host = "127.0.0.1"; // localhost

        Server s = new Server();
        Client c = new Client();

        public Action DoAction(Action action)
        {
            switch (action.Name)
            {
                case("Tests"): return null; // first action in test seq.

                case("ServerSocket"):
                    s.Socket(); return null;
                case("ServerBind"):
                    s.Bind(host,port); return null;
                case("ServerListen"):
                    s.Listen(); return null;
                case("ServerAccept"):
                    s.Accept(); return null;
                case("ServerReceive"):
                    s.Receive(); return null;
                case("ServerSend"):
                    // s.Send sends a double, not a string
                    s.Send((double)action[0]);
                    return null;
                case("ServerCloseConnection"):
                    s.CloseConnection(); return null;
                case("ServerClose"):
                    s.Close(); return null;

                // continued ...
```

Figure 8.4. Client/server: test harness (stepper) (1).

```
                    // ... continued

              case ("ClientSocket"):
                    c.Socket (); return null;
                    case ("ClientConnect"):
                    c.Connect (host,port); return null;
              case ("ClientSend"):
                    c.Send ("T"); return null;
              case ("ClientReceive_Start"):
                    // c.Receive returns a double, not a string
                    return Action.Create ("ClientReceive_Finish", c.Receive ());
              case ("ClientClose"):
                    c.Close (); return null;


                    default: throw new Exception ("Unexpected action " + action);

              }
        }

        public void Reset ()
        {
              s = new Server ();
              c = new Client ();
        }

        // Factory method
        public static IStepper Create ()
        {
              return new Stepper ();
        }
    }
}
```

Figure 8.5. Client/server: test harness (stepper) (2).

The DoAction method is the core of the test harness. It invokes the implementation's controllable actions, monitors the implemenation's observable actions, collects the output from the implementation, and checks the implementation against
the model.

To invoke each controllable action, the test runner passes DoAction a term that
represents the action. There is a case in DoAction for each action symbol. The code
in the case branch invokes the corresponding method in the implementation. In the
simple case where the action has no outputs, DoAction returns null.

Here is an example from Figure 8.4, the case where DoAction handles the server's Bind action. Here the socket s and the host and port have been declared and assigned in the stepper.

```
case ("ServerBind") :
    s.Bind(host,port);
    return null;
```

Here is a more complex case, where DoAction handles the server's Send action. This code extracts the argument from the action term using the indexer expression a[0], casts it to double, and passes it to the implementation. The modeling library provides action arguments through a C# *indexer*, which accesses elements by subscripts. (Appendix A.3 explains this and other facilities for working with action terms.)

```
case ("ServerSend") :
    // s.Send sends a double, not a string
    s.Send((double) action[0]);
    return null;
```

The most complex cases occur where there is a split action (that has outputs). The test runner passes DoAction a term that represents the start action. DoAction invokes the corresponding method in the implementation. When that method returns, DoAction collects the output, constructs a term that represents the finish action using Action.Create, and returns the finish action to the test runner. Here is an example, the case where DoAction handles the client's Receive action:

```
case ("ClientReceive_Start") :
    // c.Receive returns a double, not a string
    return Action.Create("ClientReceive_Finish", c.Receive());
```

The DoAction code could also read implementation state variables, and include their values in the term for the finish action. To make use of this information, the corresponding action method of the model would have to return the values of model state variables in out parameters.

The test runner indicates a test failure if the finish action returned by DoAction does not match the finish action generated by the model program (e.g., if the implementation returns a different value than the model program computed). That is, how the model program acts as a test oracle.

The test runner also indicates a test failure if DoAction throws an exception. For this reason, DoAction usually does not handle exceptions thrown by the implementation.

Compile the stepper to a library. Reference the implementation in the compilation:

```
csc /t:library /out:Stepper.dll ^
    /r:Server.dll /r:Client.dll ^
    /r:"%DEVPATH%\NModel.dll" ^
    Stepper.cs
```

8.4 Test execution

To execute a test suite, invoke the test runner tool `ct`, naming the stepper and the test suite. You do not need to name the model program; all of the information needed from the model program is already represented in the test suite. This command executes the test suite generated from the contract model program (Figure 8.1).[3]

```
ct /r:Stepper.dll
    /iut:ClientServerImpl.Stepper.Create  /testSuite:ContractTest.txt
```

When we execute this command, all of the tests succeed:

```
TestResult(0, Verdict("Success"), "",
    Trace(
        Test(0),
        ServerSocket(),
        ...  etc.
        ClientClose()
    )
...
...  etc.
...
TestResult(5, Verdict("Success"), "",
    ...
    )
)
```

Next we execute the test suite generated from the client/server contract model program composed with the scenario machine (Figure 8.2):

```
ct /r:Stepper.dll /iut:ClientServerImpl.Stepper.Create ^
    /testSuite:ScenarioTest.txt
```

---

[3] A complete command reference for `ct` appears in Appendix B.3.

When we execute this command, the test fails:

```
TestResult(0, Verdict("Failure"),
 "Action 'ClientReceive_Finish(double(\"99\"))' not enabled in the model",
  Unexpected return value of finish action, expected:
   ClientReceive_Finish(double "99.9"))
     Trace(
            Test(0),
            ServerSocket(),
            ServerBind(),
            ServerListen(),
            ClientSocket(),
            ClientConnect(),
            ServerAccept(),
            ServerSend(double("100")),
            ClientReceive_Start(),
            ClientReceive_Finish(double("100")),
            ServerSend(double("99.9")),
            ClientReceive_Start(),
            ClientReceive_Finish(double("99"))

      )

 )
```

The output shows the trace of the actual test run through the action that failed (compare to the trace of the test case in Figure 8.3). The message indicates that this test failed because the return value 99 in the last finish action is not the same as the expected return value 99.9 computed by the model program and stored in test case.

8.5 Limitations of offline testing

The five test cases in the first test suite all pass; they do not reveal the defect in the implementation that we discussed in Chapter 2, Section 2.10. Recall that the defect causes a failure after the server sends the client more than four characters (e.g., "100.0"), but the client only fails when it receives the message *after* the first message with four characters. At least two messages must be sent and received to expose the defect (where the first message contains more than four characters). Each of the test cases in the first test suite only send and receive one message, so they cannot expose the defect.

The single test case in the second test suite does expose the defect, because two messages are sent and received, and the first message contains more than four characters.

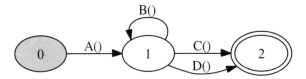

Figure 8.6. Transition coverage versus path coverage.

The number of messages sent by each test case is a consequence of the traversal algorithm used by the offline test generator tool, otg. The postman tour algorithm achieves full *transition coverage*: every transition in the FSM is taken at least once. The postman tour is *minimal*: the total number of transitions in the test suite is the minumum needed to achieve transition coverage; the algorithm avoids traversing the same transition more than once, if that is possible. This explains the shapes of the test suites displayed in Figures 8.1 and 8.2. (In the second test suite, it is pure luck that the longer message happens to be sent first.)

These examples confirm that minimal transition coverage is not sufficient to expose some defects. Consider the simple example in Figure 8.6. Minimal transition coverage will generate two test cases: A(),B(),C() and A(),D(). The assumption is that the model state really does determine the behavior; there is no need to cover every path; D() will not be affected by B() preceding it. This assumption can be false if the implementation has *hidden state* that is not represented in the model. In that case, we should also attempt some amount of *path coverage* by also testing the paths A(),B(),D(), and maybe even A(),B(),B(),D(). In our client/server implementation, the hidden state is the client's receive buffer.

These are limitations of minimal transition coverage, not offline test generation in general. We can imagine an offline test generator with a more thorough traversal algorithm. But the requirement in offline testing that the entire test suite must be computed in advance discourages thorough coverage. Moreover, it is not feasible to explore the true FSM of many "infinite" model programs at all. And, when the implementation exhibits nondeterminism, it is wasteful to compute paths that may never be taken. For these reasons, the tools emphasize on-the-fly testing, where the tests are computed as the test executes. In contrast with the limited choice of traversal algorithms built into the otg tool (just one at this writing), the ct tool provides rich opportunities for testers to program their own on-the-fly testing strategies, as we shall see in Chapters 12 and 16.

8.6 Exercises

1. Write a stepper for the three newsreader implementations you wrote for the problems in Chapter 5. Generate a test suite from the newsreader model program

in Chapter 5, and execute it on all three implementations (the correct one and the two defective ones).

2. Write another model program, implementation, and stepper for the newsreader, where each action returns the value of the page state variable at the time the action exits. Write the stepper to check the return values. Make versions of this implementation with the same two defects as in Exercises 3 and 4 in Chapter 5. Generate a test suite from the model program. Execute the test suite on all three of these implementations. Are the defects revealed earlier in the execution of the test suite?

3. Write another model program, implementation, and stepper for the newsreader, where each action returns the value of all three state variables as C# out parameters at the time the action exits. Write the stepper to check the out parameters. Make versions of this implementation with the same two defects as in Exercises 3 and 4 in Chapter 5. Generate a test suite from the model program. Execute the test suite on all three of these implementations. Are the defects revealed earlier in the execution of the test suite?

4. Generate a test suite from the revised version of the reactive system model program (without unsafe states or dead states) that you wrote for Exercise 5 in Chapter 5. Execute this test suite on the implementation from Chapter 3 (with unsafe states and dead states) and on the revised implementation you wrote for Exercise 3 (without unsafe states and dead states) in Chapter 3.

5. Could you use ct as a unit testing tool, as an alternative to NUnit? How? What would correspond to a test and a test fixture?

9 Further Reading

There are many modeling languages based on guarded update rules (or something similar), including Alloy (Jackson, 2006), ASMs (Gurevich, 1995; Börger and Stärk, 2003), B (Abrial, 1996), Promela (Holzmann, 2004), TLA (Lamport, 2002), Unity (Chandy and Misra, 1988), VDM (Fitzgerald and Larsen, 1998), and Z (Woodcock and Loomes, 1989; Spivey, 1992; Davies and Woodcock, 1996; Jacky, 1997). Case studies in these languages show how different kinds of systems can be described in modeling styles similar to ours.

The immediate predecessors of the modeling library and tools described in this book are the AsmL language and the AsmL-T tool (Barnett et al., 2003), and more recently, the Spec# language and the Spec Explorer tool (Veanes et al., in press; Campbell et al., 2005a). Development on Spec Explorer continues.

Peled (2001) presents an exhaustive exploration algorithm similar to ours. Grieskamp et al. (2002) describe a more complex exploration algorithm.

Exploration has some similarities to *model checking*, which also generates and explores a finite state machine (FSM), but usually emphasizes verifying (or providing counterexamples to) properties expressed as formulas in temporal logic. This is similar to our checking of temporal properties, but we express them with FSMs instead of formulas. Model checking was originally described by Clarke et al. (1986) in a classic paper and later described in a survey article (Clarke et al., 1994) and a book (Clarke et al., 1999). Some other model checkers are described in the books by Peled (2001) and Holzmann (2004).

Composition of model programs is a generalization of the construction of finite automata for the intersection of regular languages. For example, see the discussion following Theorem 3.3 on pp. 59–60 of Hopcroft and Ullman (1979).

The classic books on testing are by Myers (1979) Myers et al. (2004), and Beizer (1984, 1990, 1995). Poston (1996) surveys and collects some early papers on what we now call model-based testing. Binder (1999) adds special consideration for object-oriented programs. Kaner et al. (1993) emphasize the pragmatics of testing desktop applications, including business considerations. Peled (2001) also discusses testing. All of these books have voluminous bibliographies up to their publication dates.

The review article by Lee and Yannakakis (1996) discusses generating tests from FSMs, including the postman tour. Peled (2001) also discusses the postman tour. Thimbleby (2003) presents a complete implementation of the postman tour.

Part III

Systems with Complex State

10 Modeling Systems with Structured State

In the previous chapters we saw model programs that could be exhaustively explored into their corresponding finite state machines. In this chapter, we will show how the concept of a model program can cover larger, even infinite, numbers of states and transitions.

10.1 "Infinite" model programs

To understand this we can introduce data types like integers and strings to our model program. Unlike the data types we have considered up to this point, numbers and strings are drawn from very large, or even infinite, domains.

Here is an example of a model program that has a number of states bounded only by the size of the integer data type:

```
namespace Counter1
{
    static class Contract
    {
        static int counter = 0;

        [Action]
        static void Increment() { counter = counter + 1; }

        [Action]
        static void Decrement() { counter = counter - 1; }
    }
}
```

What's interesing here is that even with just two actions and no parameters, the number of states may grow without limit, or at least without a computationally feasible limit.

This kind of model program is *finitely branching*. In other words, there are only a finite number of transitions available in each state. As the example shows, even a finitely branching model may have a computationally infeasible number of states. We will show in Chapter 11 how to adapt our analysis techniques to cases like this. In this chapter we'll focus on how to write model programs that benefit from the descriptive power of richer structural data types.

It is also possible to write model programs that are not finitely branching. Surprisingly, this does not necessarily mean that the number of states is unbounded. For example, here is a model program with only five states that has (computationally) infinite branching:

```
namespace Counter2
{
    static class Contract
    {
        static int counter = 0;

        [Action]
        static void ModularIncrement(int x)
        { counter = (counter + x) % 5; }
    }
}
```

This model program is infinitely branching because in every state there are an "infinite" (very large) number of integer values for the parameter x. There are only five states because the modulus operator % in this example limits the counter to five values.

The previous two examples illustrate one of the main differences between model programs and finite state machines (FSMs). FSMs always have a finite number of states and transitions, while model programs may represent systems with an unbounded number of states and transitions.

You can understand this difference by analogy. Consider the relationship between the string array type string[] and an enumerator of strings IEnumerator<string>. Conceptually, the two types are similar, but the string array is a finite type that provides a Length operation and random, indexed access. The enumerator, on the other hand, has a more limited interface that does not support querying for the number of elements or for random access. Instead, the enumerator allows you to get the first element in the enumeration and each successive element in turn. There is no requirement that the number of elements in the enumerator be finite.

Similarly, a data structure for an FSM provides operations that allow you to query for the number of states and transitions. A model program, in contrast, has a more limited interface. The model program allows you to get the initial state and produce transitions that take you to subsequent states. Like an enumerator, you can't find out how many states a model program has without exploring it step by step.

Model programs with large numbers of states and transitions are not just a theoretical curiosity. Using values with large domains like strings and integers turns out to be very useful for modeling real world systems. Data types like int and string provide descriptive power. We'll see this with an example later in this chapter. For now, let's review the kinds of data types that can be used in writing model programs.

10.2 Types for model programs

You may only use certain types for state variables and action parameters in model programs that work with the tools we describe.[1] This is necessary because exploration using these tools can only determine whether two states are equal when the state variables belong to these types.

Any of the following .NET-provided types may be used for state variables and action parameters: bool, byte, char, double, float, int, long, short, string as well as any enum type defined by the model program.

In addition to these built-in types, you may also use the structured types and collection types described in the rest of this chapter and the object types that we will introduce later in Chapter 15.[2]

10.3 Compound values

Extending our model program with strings and integers doesn't change the way we do state comparison. Just as in the previous chapters, two states are equal if their variables contain the same values. The string data type is compatible with this kind of equality: two strings are equal if they contain the same characters. Whether the two strings share the same location in memory doesn't matter when asking if they are equal. This kind of equality is called *structural equality*. It is the kind of equality that matters for state comparison.

---

[1] For the purposes of this chapter we use the term *model program* to mean a model program written in C# source, compiled into a .NET assembly and loaded as a LibraryModelProgram data type. The NModel package allows extenders to implement other kinds of model programs that need not rely on .NET types for internal state.

[2] The modeling framework provides an interface called IAbstractValue for extending the range of types permitted in model programs. This is documented in the NModel package. Most users will not need to do this kind of extension. Creating subclasses of CompoundValue is the easiest way to add data types.

Structural equality may be contrasted with *reference equality* where two objects are equal if they occupy the same location of the computer's memory. In object-oriented programming languages, reference equality is the default. However, structual equality may be explicitly provided by an implementation. For example, the `string` type in .NET languages provides structural equality.

Sometimes we want to use data structures that go beyond the built-in value types.[3] We can do this with custom data types. But in order to preserve the desirable property of state comparison, we need to use custom data types with structural equality.

The C# language provides a keyword `struct` that may be used to declare data types with structural equality. There are some technical limitations here – for example, C# structs must be of a fixed length in memory. The NModel framework uses classes instead of structs for implementing structural data types.

In order for equality of states to be well defined, we use *compound values*. Compound values are data types distinguished by their use of structural equality and their ability to handle variable-length and tree-structured data in addition to records of fixed size.

The NModel modeling framework includes a mechanism that makes it easy to define custom structural types with a built-in base class called `CompoundValue`. This data type is a useful building block for many kinds of data structured data values.

For example, a binary tree of integers could be defined in this way:

```
class IntTree : CompoundValue
{
    public readonly int value;
    public readonly IntTree left;
    public readonly IntTree right;

    public IntTree(int value, IntTree left, IntTree right)
    {
        this.value = value;
        this.left = left;
        this.right = right;
    }
}
```

All fields of a type that derives from `CompoundValue` must be marked `readonly`. This is because structural data types are immutable values, like strings and integers.

---

[3] The `string` type isn't technically a value type in .NET terminology, but for simplicity we will use that term because strings are immutable and use structural equality. We ignore the issue of whether a value is stack-allocated.

The data fields of a value are not variable locations of memory like typical instances of class types.

Note that compound values, although they may be tree-structured, are by construction not allowed to contain circular references.

The `CompoundValue` base class provides the necessary support for structural equality, hash coding, and several other services required by the modeling framework.

The NModel framework includes several families of compound values as built-in types. These are documented in Appendix A and in the NModel package itself. These types are used frequently in software models. In the following sections, we will describe these built-in types for sets, maps, sequences, bags, pairs, and triples. All of these built-in types are immutable value types, like the `string` type. If you can program using strings, you should be able to master the modeling collection types.

10.3.1 Sets

A *set* is an unordered collection of distinct elements. Sets are immutable values but you can construct new sets by operations such as union and intersection, just as you can construct .NET string values by concatenation. Appendix A.2.2 provides a list of set operations provided by the NModel library.

You will find that sets, which are unordered, are preferable to ordered sequences in many modeling examples because they reduce the number of states that must be considered for design analysis and testing. States that use sets are more abstract than states that use ordered data structures like sequences.

Two sets that contain the same elements are equal, regardless of the order in which their elements were added. Sequences, on the other hand, are not equal if their elements appear in different orders.

For example, consider a network model where there are some clients communicating with a server. Clients may join and leave the session at any time. If the model of the server state uses a set to keep track of active clients, then the order in which clients arrive will not matter. This is a useful abstraction, especially if no operations of the system depend on the order of client entry.

```
static Set<string> clients = Set<string>.EmptySet;


[Action]
static void AddClient(string client)
{
    clients = clients.Add(client);
}
```

```
[Action]
static void RemoveClient(string client)
{
    clients = clients.Remove(client);
}
```

This model program shows the basic operation of sets. The expression `Set<string>`. `EmptySet` is a way to denote the empty set of strings. This is analogous to the expression `string.Empty` provided by the .NET framework that returns the empty string. We say "the" empty string because all empty strings are equal.[4] It is useful to think that there is just one empty string value, just as there is only one value for `0` or `1`. Similarly, there is just one empty set of strings.

We should point out that in the set implementation provided by NModel, the values `Set<string>.EmptySet` and `Set<int>.EmptySet` are not equal. You can think of each set as having a subscript based on the type parameter inside the angle brackets. This is true even for subtypes: values of type `Set<object>` and `Set<int>` are never equal, even if they contain the same elements.

Another thing to point out is that the `Add` and `Remove` operations return new set values. This is because set values, like .NET strings, are immutable. There is no way to change their values. However, we can update a state variable with the new value that results from adding or removing an element:

```
clients = clients.Add(client);
```

If you were to explore the model program shown above for the client/server system, you would notice that the following two traces result in the same end state:

```
Trace 1                 Trace 2

AddClient("alice")  AddClient("bob")
AddClient("bob")    AddClient("alice")
```

Modeling complex state often needs mathematical data structures like sets. Using sets whenever order doesn't matter can dramatically reduce the number of states you will have to consider for design analysis and testing. Sets are the bread and butter of experienced software modelers. They appear very often.

Creating sets

The easiest way to create a set is to list its elements in the constructor. The order in which arguments appear doesn't matter and duplicates will be ignored:

---

[4] When we use the word "equals," we mean equality in the sense of the `Object.Equals` method.

```
Set<string> cities = new Set<string>("Athens", "Rome", "Athens",
                          "Paris", "New York", "Seattle");
Assert.AreEqual(cities.Count, 5);
```

You can also create a set from an IEnumerable object. Many .NET data types support enumeration by means of IEnumerable, and this can act as an interface between the data types used for modeling and system data types. Here is an example:

```
static Set<string> ConvertToSet(IEnumerable<string> list)
{
    return new Set<string>(list);
}
```

The order of elements in the enumeration doesn't matter, and duplicate elements will be ignored.

Note that sets themselves implement the IEnumerable interface, so they can be used iteratively:

```
static int CountOdd(Set<int> s)
{
    int result = 0;
    foreach(int i in s)
      if (i % 2 == 1) result += 1;
    return result;
}
```

You can expect iteration over sets to occur in an arbitrary order.

Set properties and queries

There are several properties defined for sets. You can use IsEmpty to determine if the set has no elements. The Count property returns the number of elements contained in a set.

You can use the Contains method to see whether a given element is in the set.

```
Set<string> cities = new Set<string>("Athens", "Rome", "Athens"};

Assert.IsFalse(cities.IsEmpty);
Assert.AreEqual(cities.Count, 2);
Assert.IsTrue(cities.Contains("Rome"));
Assert.IsFalse(cities.Contains("New York"));
```

Union, intersection, and difference

Any two sets of the same type can be combined by union, intersection, and difference. *Union* produces the set with all of the elements. *Intersection* is the set of elements shared by the two sets. *Difference* is the set of elements from the first set that are not found in the second set.

```
Set<int> s1 = new Set<int>(1, 2, 3, 4, 5, 6);
Set<int> s2 = new Set<int>(1, 3, 5, 7, 9, 11);
Set<int> s3 = s1.Union(s2);
Set<int> s4 = s1.Intersect(s2);
Set<int> s5 = s1.Difference(s2);
Assert.AreEqual(s3, new Set<int>(1, 2, 3, 4, 5, 6, 7, 9, 11));
Assert.AreEqual(s4, new Set<int>(1, 3, 5));
Assert.AreEqual(s5, new Set<int>(2, 4, 6));
```

You can write union as +, intersection as *, and difference as -.

```
Set<int> s1 = new Set<int>(1, 2, 3, 4, 5, 6);
Set<int> s2 = new Set<int>(1, 3, 5, 7, 9, 11);
Set<int> s3 = s1 + s2;
Set<int> s4 = s1 * s2;
Set<int> s5 = s1 - s2;
Assert.AreEqual(s3, new Set<int>(11, 3, 2, 9, 6, 5, 7, 4, 1));
Assert.AreEqual(s4, new Set<int>(3, 1, 5));
Assert.AreEqual(s5, new Set<int>(6, 4, 2));
```

10.3.2 Maps

Maps associate unique keys with values. This is similar to the .NET `Dictionary` type, except that a map is an immutable value. Operations to add and remove elements result in new maps instead of making changes to the map given as the argument.

Another difference between maps and the .NET dictionary type is structural equality. Two maps of the same type are equal if they contain the same key/value pairs. Dictionaries in .NET use reference equality instead of structural equality.

Also, unlike the .NET dictionary type, the value `null` may be used as a key in a map.

Appendix A.2.3 provides a list of map operations provided by the NModel library.

Maps appear often in models with structured state. Maps may be used to represent *dynamic functions*, or key/value relationships that evolve during the run of the system. For example, a server may have an operation that assigns integer priorities to its active clients:

```
static Map<string, int> priority = Map<string, int>.EmptyMap;

[Action]
static void SetPriority(string client, int p)
{
    priority = priority.Override(client, p);
}
```

The Override method produces a new map by substituting a key/value pair. If the key given as the argument is not in the map, then a new key/value pair is added. In this example we set the variable priority to contain the value of the new map.

Creating maps

If your map contains five or fewer key/value pairs, you can use a map constructor that takes keys and values as arguments:

```
Map<string, int> cityId = new Map<string,int>("Athens", 1, "Rome", 2,
                                "Paris", 3, "New York", 4);
Assert.AreEqual(cityId["Paris"], 3);
```

A common way to build a map is to start with the empty map and add elements programmatically:

```
Map<int, string> idCity = Map<int, string>.EmptyMap;
string[] cities =
    new string[]{"Athens", "Rome", "Paris", "New York"};
for(int i = 0; i < cities.Length; i += 1)
    idCity = idCity.Add(i + 100, city[i]);
Assert.AreEqual(idCity[102], "Paris");
```

Map lookup operations

The lookup operations for a map are very similar to those of a .NET dictionary. If you need to look up the value of a key, you may use the C# indexer syntax:

```
Map<string, string> cityState =
        new Map<string, string>("Athens", "GA", "Paris", "TX"};
Assert.AreEqual(cityState["Paris"], "TX");
```

An exception will be thrown if the requested key is not in the map. Normally, you will want to use the `ContainsKey` method to check that the key is in the map before doing the lookup.

You can combine the `ContainsKey` check and lookup into a single operation using `TryGetValue`.

```
static string LookupState(string city)
{
  Map<string, string> cityState =
      new Map<string, string>("Athens", "GA", "Paris", "TX"};
  string state;
  return (cityState.TryGetValue(city, out state) ? state
                                      : "Unknown state");

}
```

Iterating through maps

Maps support iteration through keys, values, or key value pairs:

```
Map<string, int> cityLength =
    new Map<string, int>("Athens", 6, "Paris", 5};

foreach(string city in cityLength.Keys) /* ... */

foreach(int length in cityLength.Values) /* ... */

foreach(Pair<string, int> keyValuePair in cityLength) /* ... */
```

The `Keys` and `Values` properties return sets. This means that when iterating through values of a map, values associated with more than one key will only be encountered once. The `Pair` data type is decribed in Section 10.3.6.

10.3.3 Sequences

A *sequence* is an ordered collection of (possibly repeating) elements. This is similar to the .NET `List` type, except that a sequence is an immutable value. Operations to add and remove elements result in new sequences instead of making changes to the sequence given as the argument.

Another difference between sequences and the .NET list type is structural equality. Two sequences are equal if they contain the same elements, in the same order. Lists in .NET use reference equality instead of structural equality.

Appendix A.2.4 provides a reference of sequence operations provided by the NModel library.

Sequences appear in models where it is important to distinguish elements based on order. For example, you could model a variable-length stack (LIFO) with operations Push and Pop using a sequence:

```
static class Stack
{
    static Sequence<int> contents = Sequence<int>.EmptySequence;

    [Action]
    static void Push(int value)
    {
        contents = contents.AddFirst(value);
    }

    static bool PopEnabled() { return !contents.IsEmpty; }

    [Action]
    static int Pop()
    {
        int result = contents.Head;
        contents = contents.Tail;
        return result;
    }
}
```

Order matters in this example: Pop must produce the value given by the most recent Push action.

Creating sequences

You can create a sequence by listing its elements as arguments to the constructor:

```
Sequence<string> ratings = new Sequence<string>("Poor", "Average",
                                                "Excellent")
```

You can also start with the empty sequence and add elements to the beginning or end programmatically:

```
Sequence<int> squares = Map<int>.EmptySequence;
for(int i = 0; i < 5; i += 1)
    squares = squares.AddLast(i * i);
```

You can construct a sequence from any value that supports IEnumerable:

```
static Sequence<string> ConvertToSequence(IEnumerable<string> list)
{
    return new Sequence<string>(list);
}
```

Sequence queries

You can access the first and last element of a sequence using the Head and Last properties.

The subsequence of all elements except the first is the Tail. The subsequence of all elements except the last is the Front of the sequence.

```
Sequence<int> squares = new Sequence<int>(0, 1, 4, 9, 16, 25, 36);
Assert.AreEqual(squares.Head, 0);
Assert.AreEqual(squares.Last, 36);
Assert.AreEqual(squares.Tail.Head, 1);
Assert.AreEqual(squares.Front.Last, 25);
Assert.AreEqual(squares.Tail.Tail.Head, 4);
```

Sequences also provide for random access using the C# indexer. However, if your primary mode of access is random, you should consider using the ValueArray type instead of a sequence.

10.3.4 Value arrays

A *value array* is an ordered collection of (possibly repeating) elements. It is similar to the .NET Array type, except that a value array is immutable. Unlike a .NET array, a value array uses structural equality.

Sequences and value arrays are similar in the way that .NET lists and arrays are similar. In other words, sequences are best for list-like iterative construction and access. Value arrays work best when random access is the most common form of access and when incrementally adding elements is not common.

Sequences appear more often than value arrays in most models, especially when small numbers of elements are involved. Value arrays are useful for larger data sets that require a lot of random access. Most models will not require them.

Appendix A.2.5 lists value array operations provided by the NModel library. Value arrays are created from a .NET array:

```
string[] ratingsArr = new string[]{"Poor", "Average", "Excellent"};
ValueArray<string> ratings = new ValueArray<string>(ratingsArr);
Assert.AreEqual(ratings[2], "Excellent");
```

Random access is supported through the C# indexer.

10.3.5 Bags or multisets

A *bag*, or multiset, is an unordered collection of possibly repeating elements. Unlike sets, an element may appear in a bag more than once. Bags are immutable values, but you can construct new bags by operations such as union and intersection.

Appendix A.2.6 provides a list of bag operations provided by the NModel library.

Like sets, bags are unordered. Two bags are equal if they contain the number of occurrences of the same elements. The number of occurrences of a given element is called its *multiplicity*.

Bags are useful as a way to abstract the order of a sequence while still allowing for duplicate values.

For example, you might use a bag to model reference counting. In reference counting, operations track whether an element may be deleted based on the number of references.

```
static class ReferenceCounting
{
    static Bag<string> references = Bag<string>.EmptyBag;
    static Set<string> allocated = Set<string>.EmptySet;

    [Action]
    static void AddReference(string obj)
    {
        references = references.Add(obj);
        allocated = allocated.Add(obj);
    }

    static bool RemoveReferenceEnabled(string obj)
    {
        return references.Contains(obj);
    }
    [Action]
    static void RemoveReference(string obj)
    {
        references = references.Remove(obj);
    }

    static bool DeleteObjectEnabled(string obj)
    {
        return allocated.Contains(obj) && !references.Contains(obj);
    }
}
```

```
[Action]
static void DeleteObject(string obj)
{
    references = references.Remove(obj);
}
}
```

If you were to explore this model program you would notice that the following two traces result in the same end state:

```
Trace 1                     Trace 2

AddReference("objA")        AddReference("objA")
RemoveReference("objA")     AddReference("objA")
AddReference("objA")        RemoveReference("objA")
RemoveReference("objA")     RemoveReference("objA")
DeleteObject("objA")        DeleteObject("objA")
```

Creating bags

The easiest way to create a new bag is to list the elements in the constructor. The order in which arguments appear doesn't matter, and duplicates will be used as many times as they appear:

```
Bag<string> cities = new Bag<string>("Athens", "Rome", "Athens",
                          "Paris", "New York", "Seattle");
Assert AreEqual(cities.Count, 6);
```

You can also create a bag from an IEnumerable object:

```
static Bag<string> ConvertToBag(IEnumerable<string> list)
{
    return new Bag<string>(list);
}
```

Like sets, bags implement the IEnumerable interface, so they can be used iteratively. If an element appears in a bag more than once, iteration will include it more than once. If you want to get access to the unique values found in a bag, you can use the Keys property.

Iteration over bags occurs in an arbitrary order.

Bag properties and queries

Bags support all of the set operations. The behavior of these operations is similar to that of sets, except that multiplicity is respected. For example, the `Union` operation for a bag adds the multiplicities of each element.

Bags have a few operations that are not available on sets. For example, you can find out the multiplicity of an element in a bag with the `CountItem` method. You can find out the number of distinct elements in the bag using the `CountUnique` property. The `Count` property returns to total number of elements, including multiples.

10.3.6 Pairs and triples

A *pair* is a data record with two elements. A pair is an immutable value with structural equality.

```
Pair<int, string> nameId = new Pair<int, string>(1, "Alice");
Assert.AreEqual(nameId.First, 1);
Assert.AreEqual(nameId.Second, "Alice");
```

The pair constructor takes the paired values as its argument. The properties `First` and `Second` give access to contents of the pair.

A *triple* is a data record with three elements. Like pairs, triples are immutable values with structural equality.

```
Triple<int, string, double> nameIdPay =
            new Triple<int, string, double>(1, "Alice", 2000.0);
Assert.AreEqual(nameId.First, 1);
Assert.AreEqual(nameId.Second, "Alice");
Assert.AreEqual(nameId.Third, 2000.0);
```

The triple constructor takes three values as its arguments. The properties `First`, `Second`, and `Third` give access to contents of the data record.

Pairs and triples work well with sets, maps, sequences, and bags. For example, a set of pairs represents a *binary relation*. Binary relations occur often in systems with dynamic relationships between entities.

10.4 Case study: revision control system

In this section we present a case study for a revision control system that uses some of the data types introduced in the preceding sections.

A *revision control system* is a distributed software application that helps programmers work together on a common source base. Each user edits a *local copy* of the source files in the repository. Changes made to this local copy affect the global repository of source code only when the user *commits* changes. Changes are always applied as an atomic transaction.

An important feature of a revision control system is the handling of *conflicts*, or cases when two users have made simultaneous updates to the same source file. The system provides operations that identify the conflicts and allow users to choose how to resolve them.

In our case study, we have not modeled any particular revision control system; instead, we have abstracted features that are common to typical revision control systems. If you want to compare the model with an implementation, you might want to look at the Subversion revision control system that is available as open source.

10.4.1   Vocabulary of actions

We view a revision control system as a model program with the following vocabulary of user actions:

- Synchronize updates a given client's local copy to include the latest revisions in the global repository. However, changed files will not be overwritten; instead, they will be marked as conflicts to be resolved before committing.
- Edit represents a file change in the client's local view of the repository.
- Revert undoes a previous edit, restoring a file's state to the version of the last Synchronize operation.
- Commit propagates local file changes to the global repository.
- Resolve reconciles conflicts between a local version of a file and changes to the global repository made in parallel by another user. All files with conflicts must be resolved before a set of changes may be propagated to the global repository.

The server has two actions that represent the server's possible repsonses to a client's request to commit changes:

- MustResolve occurs after a Commit action for a client with unresolved file conflicts. No changes to the global repository are made.
- CommitComplete occurs when changes have been successfully propagated to the repository.

Here is a trace of a sample session for two clients.

```
Synchronize("alice")
Edit("alice", "file1", Op("Add"))
Commit("alice")
CommitComplete("alice", 1)
Synchronize("bob")
```

```
Edit ("bob", "file1", Op("Change"))
Edit ("alice", "file1", Op("Change"))
Commit ("alice")
CommitComplete ("alice", 2)
Commit ("bob")
MustResolve ("bob", Set<string>("file1"))
Resolve ("bob", "file1")
Commit ("bob")
CommitComplete ("bob", 3)
```

This trace shows a scenario where client `alice` adds a file named `file1` to the repository and commits her change. Client `bob` synchronizes against the repository and begins to edit `file1`. Alice, in the meantime, edits `file1` and commits her changes.

When client `bob` commits, the system tells him that there is a conflict to resolve. He resolves the conflict with the `Resolve` action and commits again. The system responds with `CommitComplete`, indicating that the change has been incorporated into the repository. The repository increments its global revision number and reports it in the `CommitComplete` action.

10.4.2 State and derived state

We introduce just enough state to accurately determine which traces of the system are possible and which are not. For ease of understanding, we can separate state into the state of the repository and the state of the users of the repository.

Global version

```
namespace RevisionControl
{
    partial static class Repository
    {
        public static int currentRevision = 0;
    }
}
```

In C# the keyword `partial` may be used to break up a class definition into several blocks. We use this here to indicate that blocks of code separated by explanatory text all belong to the same class.

The state of the revision control system includes a global version number `currentRevision`. This represents number of times any change has been committed to the repository.

In the code snippets that follow, we will omit for brevity the `RevisionControl` namespace declaration that defines the model's scope, but this can be assumed.

Revision data type

In addition to the `int` and `string` data types, we will use an additional data record to define the concept of a "revision."

```
enum Op { Add, Delete, Change }

class Revision : CompoundValue
{
    public readonly Op op;
    public readonly int revisionNumber;

    public Revision(Op op, int revisionNumber)
    {
        this.op = op;
        this.revisionNumber = revisionNumber;
    }
}
```

The enumeration `Op` defines the kind of edit operations provided by the revision control system. Edits may consist of adding a file, changing the contents of an existing file, or deleting a file.

We define a new compound value type `Revision` that is a pair of values: an operation and a revision number that says in which version of the repository the change appears. This lets the repository keep accurate information about all previous versions.

Repository file state

The repository maintains a per-file record of each revision that been made. We can model the change list as a sequence of revisions. The database of changes is a map associating file names to change lists.

```
partial static class Repository
{
    static Map<string, Sequence<Revision>> db =
            Map<string, Sequence<Revision>>.EmptyMap;
}
```

The first element of a change log is the most recent revision.

Client state

Clients of the revision control system have several elements of state. Since these occur on a per-client basis, we can use maps whose keys are client names.

```
partial static class User
{
    static Map<string, int> version
                = Map<string, int>.EmptyMap;

    static Map<string, Map<string, Op>> revisions
                = Map<string, Map<string, Op>>.EmptyMap;

    static Map<string, Set<string>> conflicts
                = Map<string, Set<string>>.EmptyMap;

    static Set<string> commitPending  = Set<string>.EmptySet;
}
```

The `version` state variable records the version of the global repository that corresponds with the most recent commit operation. This is a per-client element of state because clients may synchronize with the global repository at different times. The ability of clients to take a snapshot of the repository's state is an important feature of the revision conrol system.

The `revisions` state variable records for each client which files contain pending edits for that client. The value is a map of file names to the current edit operation.

The `conflicts` state variable is used when committing changes to the database. It contains a set of files with version conflicts. Such files must be *resolved* before a change may be committed to the repository.

The `commitPending` state variable records whether a client is in the process of perfoming a commit operation. Client operations are disabled when there is a pending commit operation.

Derived state

The C# model program includes several elements of *derived state*. These are methods or properties that query the state but do not change it.

```
partial static class User
{
    static bool CommitPending(string user)
    { return commitPending.Contains(user); }
```

```
static bool IsUser(string user)
{ return version.ContainsKey(user); }

static bool CanStep(string user)
{ return IsUser(user) && !CommitPending(user); }

static Set<string> Users()
{ return version.Keys; }
}
```

The `CommitPending` method says whether a given user is waiting for a `Commit` action to respond.

The `IsUser` method determines whether the string given as its argument has appeared in at least one `Synchronize` action.

The `CanStep` method says whether the client actions `Commit`, `Resolve`, `Edit`, and `Revert` can be taken. This is true if the user has performed at least one checkout action and is not waiting for a pending commit action.

Synchronize action

The `Synchronize` action brings a client's view of the repository up to date with respect to the server. The practical effect of this is to set the version number of the client to be equal to the repository's revision number.

```
partial static class User
{
    static bool SynchronizeEnabled(string user)
    {
        return !CommitPending(user);
    }

    [Action]
    static void Synchronize(string user)
    {
        int newVersion = Repository.currentRevision;

        if (IsUser(user))
        {
            IdentifyConflicts(user, version[user]);
            version = version.Override(user, newVersion);
        }
        else
```

```
        {
            version = version.Add(user, newVersion);
            revisions = revisions.Add(user, Map<string,Op>.EmptyMap);
            conflicts = conflicts.Add(user, Set<string>.EmptySet);
        }
    }
```

Synchronize may occur at any time except when there is a pending commit action for the given user. It is also possible to use Synchronize for a new user.

A Synchronize action may occur after some files have been edited but before they have been committed to the repository. If the version of a file in the repository is more recent (i.e., is larger) than the version already modified, then a *conflict* occurs. The following method checks for such conflicts.

```
partial static class User
{
    static void IdentifyConflicts(string user, int currentVersion)
    {
        Set<string> userConflicts = conflicts[user];
        foreach (Pair<string, Op> revision in revisions[user])
        {
            string file = revision.First;
            Op op = revision.Second;

            if (!userConflicts.Contains(file) &&
                currentVersion < Repository.FileVersion(file) &&
                Repository.FileExists(file, currentVersion) &&
                op != Op.Delete)
                userConflicts = userConflicts.Add(file);
        }
        conflicts = conflicts.Override(user, userConflicts);
    }
}
```

When checking for conflicts, two helper methods are used to detect whether the repository has seen an update that conflicts with the currently edited version in the client.

The FileVersion method returns the version number of the most recent checkin of a given file:

```
partial static class Repository
{
```

```
public static int FileVersion(string file)
{
    Sequence<Revision> revisions;
    return (db.TryGetValue(file, out revisions) ?
                revisions.Head.revisionNumber : -1);
}
}
```

The `FileExists` method checks whether a given file is in the repository, and if so, whether the last operation for that file was `Add` or `Change`.

```
partial static class Repository
{
    public static bool FileExists(string file, int version)
    {
        Sequence<Revision> revisions;
        if (db.TryGetValue(file, out revisions))
            foreach (Revision r in revisions)
                if (r.revisionNumber <= version)
                    return (r.op != Op.Delete);
        return false;
    }
}
```

Edit action

The `Edit` action represents a local, pending change created on the client. Edits do not affect the state of the repository until a `Commit` action occurs.

```
partial static class User
{
    static bool EditEnabled(string user, string file, Op op)
    {
        return (CanStep(user) &&
                !revisions[user].ContainsKey(file) &&
                (Repository.FileExists(file, version[user]) ?
                                op != Op.Add : op == Op.Add));
    }

    [Action]
    static void Edit([Domain("Users")] string user,string file,Op op)
    {
        Map<string, Op> userRevisions = revisions[user];
```

```
            revisions = revisions.Override(user, userRevisions.Add(file,
                      (op == Op.Delete ? Op.Delete : Op.Add)));

    }
}
```

Revert action

Edits may be undone using the Revert action. This restores the client's view a given file to be consistent with the last update (checkout) operation.

```
partial static class User
{
    static bool RevertEnabled(string user, string file)
    {
        return CanStep(user) && revisions[user].ContainsKey(file);
    }


    [Action]

    static void Revert([Domain("Users")] string user, string file)
    {
        revisions = revisions.Override(user,
                              revisions[user].RemoveKey(file));

    }
}
```

Commit action

The Commit action begins the process of recording edits made by a client in the global repository.

```
partial static class User
{
    static bool CommitEnabled(string user)
    {
        return CanStep(user);
    }


    [Action]
    static void Commit([Domain("Users")] string user)
    {
        commitPending = commitPending.Add(user);
```

```
                    IdentifyConflicts(user, version[user]);
                    version = version.Override(user, Repository.currentRevision);
            }
      }
```

Commit checks for update conflicts and marks the user as "pending." This will allow either of two possible actions to complete: MustResolve and CommitComplete.

MustResolve action
A client's request to commit changes can only be propagated to the repository if there are no conflicts.

```
partial static class User
{
    static Set<Set<string>> ResolveSets()
    {
        Set<Set<string>> result = Set<Set<string>>.EmptySet;
        foreach (string user in Users())
            if (commitPending.Contains(user))
            {
                Set<string> fileConflicts = FileConflicts(user);
                if (!fileConflicts.IsEmpty)
                    result = result.Add(fileConflicts);
            }
        return result;
    }

    static Set<string> FileConflicts(string user)
    {
        Set<string> result = conflicts[user];

        foreach (Pair<string, Op> revision in revisions[user])
        {
            string file = revision.First;
            Op op = revision.Second;

            if (version[user] < Repository.FileVersion(file) &&
                Repository.FileExists(file) &&
                op != Op.Delete)
                result = result.Add(file);
        }
    }
```

```
            return result;
    }


    static bool MustResolveEnabled(string user, Set<string> files)
    {
        return IsUser(user) && CommitPending(user) &&
                !files.IsEmpty && Object.Equals(files,
                                             FileConflicts(user));
    }


    [Action]
    static void MustResolve([Domain("Users")] string user,
                           [Domain("ResolveSets")] Set<string> files)
    {
        commitPending = commitPending.Remove(user);
        IdentifyConflicts(user, version[user]);
        version = version.Override(user, Repository.currentRevision);
    }
  }
}
```

Resolve action

The Resolve action reconciles differences between a local edited version of a file
and a parallel update on the server. Of course, in the model we don't deal with the
actual contents of the file; instead, we examine the conditions that must occur in
order for the resolve operation to occur.

```
partial static class User
{
    static bool ResolveEnabled(string user, string file)
    {
        return (CanStep(user) && conflicts[user].Contains(file));
    }


    [Action]
    static void Resolve([Domain("Users")] string user, string file)
    {
        Set<string> remainingFiles = conflicts[user].Remove(file);
        conflicts = conflicts.Override(user, remainingFiles);
    }
}
```

CommitComplete action

If a `Commit` action is pending and there are no conflicts, then the repository is able to incorporate the proposed changes. The successful update is represented by the `CommitComplete` action.

```
partial static class User
{
    static Set<int> NextVersion()
    {
        return new Set<int>(Repository.currentRevision,
                            Repository.currentRevision + 1);
    }

    static bool CommitCompleteEnabled(string user, int newVersion)
    {
        return IsUser(user) && CommitPending(user)
            && conflicts[user].IsEmpty
            && newVersion == (revisions[user].IsEmpty
                ? Repository.currentRevision
                : (Repository.currentRevision + 1));
    }

    [Action]
    static void CommitComplete([Domain("Users")] string user,
                               [Domain("NextVersion")] int newVersion)
    {
        Map<string, Op> userRevisions = revisions[user];

        version = version.Override(user, newVersion);
        revisions = revisions.Override(user, Map<string,Op>.EmptyMap);
        commitPending = commitPending.Remove(user);
        Repository.Commit(user, "Check in", userRevisions);
    }
}
```

In later chapters we will show how the model of revision control system can be used to predict behavior. For now, let's just consider one scenario.

If you look at the scenario given above in Section 10.4.1, you may notice that user `bob` had other ways to resolve the conflict. We can use the model to enumerate what the possible outcomes might have been. These are shown in Figure 10.1. The

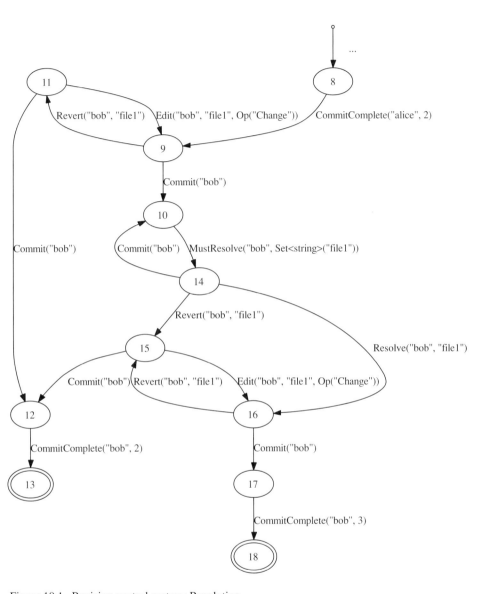

Figure 10.1. Revision control system: Resolution.

figure starts with the CommitComplete("alice", 2) action of the scenario and shows all possible completions for user bob.

10.5 Exercises

1. In what ways is a .NET array different from a Sequence?

2. An object graph is a directed, possibly cyclic, graph that arises from relations among values. For example, the instance fields of objects in an object-oriented program represent an object graph. How can a cyclic object graph be represented using the data types described in this chapter?

3. Extend the repository control system to account for forking. Forking divides the source files of the repository into independently updated branches.

11 Analyzing Systems with Complex State

In Chapter 6 we saw how a technique known as exploration can enumerate the possible states and transitions of a finite model program. We saw how exploration can "unwind" a model program into its corresponding finite state machine. We showed how the finite state machine could be used for safety and liveness analysis, as well as for generating test cases that cover all model behaviors.

In Chapter 7 we showed techniques that limit exploration to scenarios of interest. This allowed us to choose behavioral aspects to explore, instead of always considering the full space of possibilities.

In this chapter we show how these ideas apply to model programs that have larger, even unbounded, numbers of states and transitions. We will also introduce some additional techniques for handling large search spaces. After reading about these techniques you might even be inspired to invent a few of your own.

11.1 Explorable model programs

We say that a model program is *explorable* if the domain of every action parameter is "finite" (feasible to enumerate).[1] You might recall from Section 10.1 that a model program may be "large" in several ways. Either the number of states may be large or the number of transitions may be large, or both.

Consider the model program that uses modular arithmetic to increment a counter:

```
namespace Counter
{
    static class Contract
```

---

[1] As in the previous chapters, we use the term finite to mean the case where it is computationally feasible to enumerate all of the values. Although the number of 32-bit integers is fixed, we don't consider it feasible to enumerate all 32-bit integers during exploration.

```
{
    static int counter = 0;

    [Action]
    static void ModularIncrement(int x)
    { counter = (counter + x) % 5; }
}
}
```

This model program is not explorable because the parameter x could take an "infinite" (very large) number of values. We sometimes call a model program like this a *contract model program* because it defines all possible behaviors of a system, even when those behaviors are too complex to be encoded as a finite state machine. In fact, many contract model programs will not be explorable.

After thinking about the problem, we might say that it would be sufficient to explore the Counter model program with just five input values 0, 1, 2, 3, and 4. We might justify this by saying that these values are representative of typical inputs and that after examining the logic, we see that other values would not produce additional states.

If we are willing to restrict the scope of our analysis in this way then we can use the Domain attribute that was introduced on page 81 to create a finitely branching model program:

```
namespace Counter
{
    static class Contract
    {
        static int counter = 0;

        static readonly Set<int> inputs = new Set<int>(0, 1, 2, 3, 4);

        [Action]
        static void ModularIncrement([Domain("inputs")] int x)
        { counter = (counter + x) % 5; }
    }
}
```

Adding a Domain attribute gives us an explorable model program with five possible actions in each state.[2] Unfortunately, this approach introduces a new problem. What

---

[2] Although we don't make use of it in this example, it is possible to make the domain depend on the current state. To do this, you would just give the domain as a static method that references one or more state variables to compute the set of values returned.

relation does the modified model program have to the original? Mixing parameter restrictions inline with our model confuses the contract (the system's specified behavior) with a scenario (a particular situation of interest for analysis or testing).

A better way to deal with this case would be to use the Feature attribute we saw in Section 7.2. To do this, we create a new class within the same namespace:

```
namespace Counter
{
    [Feature]
    static class SmallDomain
    {
        readonly Set<int> inputs = new Set<int>(0, 1, 2, 3, 4);

        [Action]
        static void ModularIncrement([Domain("inputs")] int x)  { }
    }
}
```

We can combine the SmallDomain feature with the contract model program by means of a factory method. Factory methods were introduced in Section 6.2.1.

```
namespace Counter
{
    public static class Factory
    {
        public static ModelProgram Create()
        {
            return new LibraryModelProgram(typeof(Factory).Assembly,
                        "Counter", Set<string>.EmptySet);
        }

        public static ModelProgram CreateFinite()
        {
            return new LibraryModelProgram(typeof(Factory).Assembly,
                        "Counter", new Set<string>("SmallDomain"));
        }
    }
}
```

The factory contains methods that create either of two versions of the Counter model. The model program produced by CreateFinite includes the feature that restricts the domain to five elements. The advantage of this approach is that it keeps an understandable separation between scenario and contract model program. It also makes it possible for there to be several scenarios, not just one. Also, even though it is not explorable, the full contract model program is useful for other purposes, such as determining whether a trace taken from a log file is valid.

11.2 Pruning techniques

Once you have made your model program explorable by using the technique described in the previous section, you may still notice that it has an unbounded number of possible states. In this section we introduce some techniques for managing this proliferation of states.

11.2.1 State and transition limits

A simple way of limiting the number of transitions is to impose a limit and then halt exploration after the maximum number has been reached. You can do this by providing a maxTransitions command-line argument to the mpv tool.

Although this technique is simple, it isn't very systematic. Still, it is a useful stop gap when other pruning techniques haven't been applied yet.

11.2.2 State filters

Sometimes it's useful to consider only a subset of the possible states. For example, consider the following explorable, but infinite, model program:

```
namespace Counter2
{
    static class Contract
    {
        public static int counter = 0;

        [Action]
        static void Increment() { counter = counter + 1; }

        static bool DecrementEnabled() { return counter > 0; }

        [Action]
        static void Decrement() { counter = counter - 1; }
    }
}
```

We might want to consider only states where the counter is 0, 1, or 2. Clearly, this is a small subset of the possible states for this model program, but it is a good place to start when trying to analyze the behavior of the system.

To do this we can use a state filter. A *state filter* is a Boolean condition that must be satisfied in the end state of a transition in order for the transition to be included in the exploration. State filters say which states are "interesting" for analysis.

We can keep the contract separate from the "small state" scenario limitation by putting the state filter in a feature:

```
namespace Counter2
{
    [Feature]
    static class SmallState
    {
        [StateFilter]
        static bool WithinCounterLimit()
        { return Contract.counter < 3; }
    }
}
```

If you include the SmallState feature in your model program factory, then exploration via the mpv tool will include only transitions that result in a state in which the WithinCounterLimit method returns true.

11.2.3 Strenghening enabling conditions

Sometimes it is useful to omit certain kinds of transitions that are allowed by the contract model program but are of less interest for a test purpose or analysis goal.

A general technique that can be used here is to *strengthen enabling conditions*. With this technique, you can add additional constraints that depend on the state of the system and the action parameters.

```
namespace Counter2
{
    static class PreconditionLimits
    {
        static bool IncrementEnabled()
        { return Contract.counter < 2; }

        [Action]
        static void Increment() { }
    }
}
```

Including this feature limits possible transitions by adding a state-based requirement to the Increment action. The effect of strengthening the precondition of Increment is the same as the state filter we described in the previous section.

11.2.4 Scenarios and composition

We showed how to use model program composition as a means of scenario control in Section 7.3. This technique works well for models that have complex state because it is a very general way to control exploration that can finitize parameter domains and strengthen preconditions.

For example, we could make the infinitely branching Counter model program shown in Section 11.1 explorable using composition. To do this, we would create a finite state machine with only one state and five self-looping transitions.

```
FSM(0, AcceptingStates(0),
    Transitions(t(0, ModularIncrement(0), 0),
                t(0, ModularIncrement(1), 0),
                t(0, ModularIncrement(2), 0),
                t(0, ModularIncrement(3), 0),
                t(0, ModularIncrement(4), 0)))
```

If we compose this FSM with the Counter model program using the technique described in Section 7.3.2, the result is a model program that is explorable. To do this, we could put the FSM into a text file CounterArgs.txt and include it as an argument to the mpv tool:

```
mpv /r:Counter.dll Counter.Factory.Create /fsm:CounterArgs.txt
```

Note that the FSM in this example had only one state. Its effect was the same as the Domain attribute shown in Section 11.1.

In general, it is possible to consider scenarios provided by arbitrary model programs. For example, we could consider the scenario where the modular counter is incremented by even numbers and odd numbers in alternation.

```
FSM(0, AcceptingStates(0),
    Transitions(t(0, ModularIncrement(0), 1),
                t(1, ModularIncrement(1), 0),
                t(0, ModularIncrement(2), 1),
                t(1, ModularIncrement(3), 0),
                t(0, ModularIncrement(4), 1)))
```

This is a contrived example, just for the purposes of demonstrating the idea.

11.2.5 State grouping

State grouping is a pruning technique that limits exploration to unique representatives of user-provided state properties. If during exploration a state is encountered that does not produce a new value of one of the desired properties, it is pruned away. In other words, state exploration with grouping seeks to produce distinct examples of the abstracted state values, rather than distinct states. This can reduce the number of states greatly while still uncovering "interesting" traces.

An attribute in the form [StateProperty("*name*")] can be placed on a method, property or field to define a state property named *name*. The value of the property in a given state is the return value of the method, or the value of the field or property in that state. State properties are sometimes called *abstraction functions* because they remove detail.

Here is an example.

```
namespace Stack
{
  static class Contract
  {
      static Sequence<int> contents = Sequence<int>.EmptySequence;

      static readonly Set<int> elements = new Set<int>(0,1,2,3,4,5);

      [Action]
      static void Push([Domain("elements")] int x)
      { contents = contents.AddFirst(x); }

      static void PopEnabled() { return !contents.IsEmpty; }

      [Action]
      static void Pop() { contents = contents.Tail; }

      [StateFilter]
      static bool SizeLimit() { return contents.Count < 6; }

      [StateProperty("Count")]
      static int Count() { return contents.Count; }
  }
}
```

If we explore this model program using the mpv tool without state grouping, we notice that it branches quickly. However, if we use the Count property as a state grouping, then the branching is eliminated. Instead, we explore an action only if it leads to a state with a Count value that has not previously been seen. The idea in this example is that the size of the stack is the interesting property and that the particular choice of elements may be ignored for the purposes of analysis.

The mpv tool supports state grouping over state property *state-property* with the /group:*state-property* switch. More than one /group switch may be supplied. If grouping is specified then each state must produce a new value for at least one of the given state properties in order to be included in the exploration.

11.3 Sampling

Up to this point we have discussed pruning techniques that eliminate some transitions from an exhaustive search. In effect, we are "cutting away" (pruning) choices.

Another category of techniques is *sampling*. Here we focus on selecting a desirable path to explore, rather than excluding undesired transitions as with pruning. Exploration via sampling is a *stochastic* algorithm because it combines random and directed aspects.

We present exploration via sampling in Chapter 12 in the context of testing. However, stochastic techniques may be appropriate for design analysis in some cases where the state space is large.

11.4 Exercises

1. Use the Domain attributes and StateFilter attributes in a feature that makes the revision control system a finite model program. Which state variables must be mentioned in your state filter expressions? Which action parameters must be given finite domains?
2. Use a Domain attribute in a feature to limit the number of users of the revision control system to two. Then, use state grouping to create two properties that represent the state of each client. Can you use these properties with state groupings to eliminate some interleavings? You will also need a property that represents the state of the repository.
3. Create a scenario for the state repository system that shows all of the ways that Revert can affect the behavior of the system for one user.

12 Testing Systems with Complex State

This chapter discusses various approaches to on-the-fly testing of closed systems. (We discuss on-the-fly testing of reactive systems in Chapter 16.)

The main difference between on-the-fly testing and offline testing is that in the case of on-the-fly testing, action sequences are not known beforehand; that is, there is no pregenerated test suite.

The use of on-the-fly testing is most relevant when the state space of the model is too large to be covered comprehensively. It may still be possible to use various finitization techniques discussed in earlier chapters to cope with this problem; on-the-fly testing is an alternative approach that may be more suitable in some situations, for example, when existence of a test suite is not relevant, or when it is not clear how to finitize or abstract the model.

Another case when on-the-fly testing is useful is when implementation under test (IUT) has *hidden* states that are not distinguished by the model. In other words, if a state is revisited in the model, the corresponding state in the implementation may be new. In such a case a test suite that provides transition coverage of the model might not expose an error because a transition in the model has to be traversed multiple times before the IUT is in a state where the error occurs. The error discussed in Chapter 2 is an example.

The key concept of on-the-fly testing is a *strategy*. Intuitively, a strategy is a function that during each step of testing selects which action to apply next. A strategy may be very cheap; for example, it may make a random choice of what action to take, or it may be very expensive and try to compute the best possible choice according to some optimization criterion. A strategy can use additional memory besides the model state to record prior action selection history, or it can be memoryless and forget prior choices. Strategies can use *coverage points* to help exercise the implementation thoroughly. There is a whole spectrum of possible strategies. We illustrate how one can use the basic strategy that is supported by the library and how one can define customized strategies for on-the-fly testing.

On-the-fly testing with a programmable strategy is the testing technique supported by the ct tool. Internally, it even handles offline testing (as demonstrated in Chapter 8) as a special case of this.

12.1 On-the-fly testing

First let us demonstrate on-the-fly testing with the client/server example from previous chapters. On-the-fly testing is the easiest way to begin testing with the ct (Conformance Tester) tool. It is not necessary to generate a test suite or create a scenario. All you need is an implementation (Chapter 2), a model program (Chapter 5), and a test harness or *stepper* (Chapter 8). The built-in strategy of the ct tool is random testing: in each state, select an enabled action at random. (The strategy is not completely random; it uses the model program to rule out actions that are not enabled in the current state.) We know that this model program will always reach a deadlock state or an accepting state, so we don't have to make any arrangements to stop the test runs. Let's see if random testing can reveal the defect we know is there. We issue this command:

```
ct /r:ClientServer.dll ClientServer.Factory.Create
   /r:Stepper.dll /iut:ClientServerImpl.Stepper.Create
   /runs:1
```

One test run executes:

```
TestResult(0, Verdict("Failure"),
            "Run stopped in a non-accepting state",
     Trace(
         ClientSocket(),
         ServerSocket(),
         ServerClose()
     )
)
```

The tester randomly chose one of the many paths to a deadlock state (state 9 in Figure 7.2 in Chapter 7). This happens again and again, so we give ct some guidance by providing a scenario machine (Figure 7.14 in Chapter 7).

```
ct /r:ClientServer.dll ClientServer.Factory.Create
   /r:Stepper.dll /iut:ClientServerImpl.Stepper.Create
   /runs:1
   /fsm:Scenario.txt
```

This test run executes:

```
TestResult(0, Verdict("Success"), "",
    Trace(
        ServerSocket(),
        ServerBind(),
        ServerListen(),
        ClientSocket(),
        ClientConnect(),
        ServerAccept(),
        ServerSend(double("99.9")),
        ClientReceive_Start(),
        ClientReceive_Finish(double("99.9")),
        ServerSend(double("99.9")),
        ClientReceive_Start(),
        ClientReceive_Finish(double("99.9")),
        ClientSend(),
        ServerReceive(),
        ServerSend(double("100")),
        ClientReceive_Start(),
        ClientReceive_Finish(double("100")),
        ClientSend(),
        ServerReceive(),
        ClientSend(),
        ServerReceive(),
        ClientClose(),
        ServerCloseConnection(),
        ServerClose()
    )
)
```

This test succeeded because the server didn't send 100 until the last message.
After a few more random test runs, ct executes a run that fails, revealing the
defect.

   This example shows that a random test strategy generates a lot of test runs easily;
it is no more work for us to set /nruns:1000. But many of those randomly generated
runs do not exercise the implementation thoroughly, so in this example the built-in
random strategy does not achieve good *coverage* rapidly. We can often do better
by programming our own strategy, which we can load into ct with the /strategy
option. The following sections show how.

12.2 Implementation, model and stepper

For the example in this chapter we use an implementation of a *bag*, shown in Figure 12.1, as a sample IUT throughout this section to illustrate various techniques that can be used for on-the-fly testing. This example is small and easy to understand while it naturally leads to a model program with complex state and infinite behavior. It helps to illustrate on a smaller scale many of the properties of more complex model programs that use state variables with unbounded data types.

12.2.1 Implementation

A bag is an unordered collection of elements. An element can be added to the bag, deleted from the bag, and looked up in the bag. The multiplicity of an element is the number of times it occurs in the bag. Looking up an element in the bag returns the multiplicity of that element. An element is not in the bag if and only if its multiplicity is zero. You can also count the total number of elements in the bag. Unlike the bag data type in the modeling library, the bag implementation is not a value type.

12.2.2 Model

The bag model has an action vocabulary that corresponds to the methods of the bag implementation. The model program is shown in Figure 12.2. The following action trace is an example of a correct behavior of the bag:

```
Add("elem1")
Add("elem1")
Count_Start()
Count_Finish(2)
Lookup_Start("elem1")
Lookup_Finish(2)
Lookup_Start("elem2")
Lookup_Finish(0)
Delete("elem1")
Lookup_Start("elem1")
Lookup_Finish(1)
```

The content variable is the only state variable of the model program. In the initial state, the value of content is the empty bag. The bag model program defines an infinite state machine because the input parameter domains of the actions are unbounded and the size of the bag is unbounded. One way to constrain the set of

```
using System.Collections.Generic;
namespace BagImpl
{
    public class BagImpl
    {
        Dictionary<string, int> table = new Dictionary<string, int>();
        int count = 0;

        public int Lookup(string element)
        {
            int c = 0;
            table.TryGetValue(element, out c);
            return c;
        }

        public void Add(string element)
        {
            if (table.ContainsKey(element))
                table[element] += 1;
            else
                table[element] = 1;
            count += 1;
        }

        public void Delete(string element)
        {
            if (table.ContainsKey(element))
            {
                table[element] -= 1;
                count -= 1;
            }
        }

        public int Count
        {
            get
            {
                return count;
            }
        }
    }
}
```

Figure 12.1. Bag implementation.

```
using System.Collections.Generic;
using NModel;
using NModel.Attributes;

namespace BagModel
{
    static class Contract
    {
        static Bag<string> content = Bag<string>.EmptyBag;

        [Action]
        static void Add(string element)
        {
            content = content.Add(element);
        }

        [Action]
        static void Delete(string element)
        {
            content = content.Remove(element);
        }

        [Action]
        static int Lookup(string element)
        {
            return content.CountItem(element);
        }

        [Action]
        static int Count()
        {
            return content.Count;
        }
    }
}
```

Figure 12.2. Bag model.

possible input parameters is to provide a separate *feature* of the model that allows only a fixed set of elements to occur as input arguments to the respective actions. Such a feature is shown in Figure 12.3. This feature restricts the set of possible elements to null, "", and "b". It uses the Domain attribute to associate a fixed set of elements with each input parameter.

```
using System.Collections.Generic;
using NModel;
using NModel.Attributes;

namespace BagModel
{
    [Feature]
    static class ElementRestriction
    {
        readonly static Set<string> E = new Set<string>(null,"","b");

        [Action]
        static void Add([Domain("E")]string e)\verb+{}+

        [Action]
        static void Delete([Domain("E")]string e)\verb+{}+

        [Action]
        static void Lookup_Start([Domain("E")]string e)\verb+{}+

        [AcceptingStateCondition]
        static bool IsAcceptingState() {return Contract.content.IsEmpty;}
    }


    public static class Factory
    {
        public static ModelProgram CreateScenario()
        {
            return new LibraryModelProgram(typeof(Contract).Assembly,
                "BagModel", new Set<string>("ElementRestriction"));
        }
    }
}
```

Figure 12.3. A feature of the bag model and a scenario including the feature.

The factory method CreateScenario creates a *restricted model* where the input parameters to the actions are restricted to the given elements. The method uses the LibraryModelProgram constructor that takes an assembly, a namespace that identifies a model program in the assembly, and a set of feature names within that model program as arguments. Notice that the `ElementRestriction` feature has a void `Lookup_Start` method as opposed to a `Lookup` method that returns an integer. This is because the feature does not need to restrict the return values. Using features to restrict parameter domains is one possible use of features. We discuss more about the use of features in forthcoming sections. The scenario model produced by `CreateScenario` is still infinite because the size of the bag is unbounded. However, unlike the `Contract` model program, the model program created by `CreateScenario` is *explorable* because all parameter domains are finite.

Often it is useful to identify a particular set of states of a model program or a restricted model program as *accepting states*. A legal run must terminate in an accepting state. What states are considered as accepting states may depend on what features are considered. The feature in Figure 12.3 defines that the accepting state condition for this feature is that the bag is empty; thus, the initial state is the only accepting state in this case. If no accepting state condition is provided then all states are considered as accepting states. If multiple features are considered then the accepting state condition is the conjunction of all the accepting state conditions present in the included features.

12.2.3 Stepping the implementation

Recall that an IUT is exposed through a *stepper* (Section 8.3). The stepper "steps" through the IUT one action at a time. It has a current state that corresponds to the current state of the IUT. Initially, the stepper's current state corresponds to the IUT's initial state.

When the stepper performs an action, it calls the IUT with the corresponding input arguments. The inputs encoded in the action are abstract and are not necessarily the concrete values required by the IUT. However, there must be a well-defined mapping from abstract input actions to concrete input values. This mapping is an integral part of the stepper.

Performing an action in the stepper may cause the stepper to return an output action as a return value. This action either corresponds to the immediate return value of a method or represents an abstraction of the resulting state of the IUT. There must be a well-defined mapping from the concrete return values of the IUT to the abstract actions returned by the stepper.

Steppers are implementations of the modeling library's `IStepper` interface.

```
public interface IStepper
{
    Action DoAction(Action action);
    void Reset();
}
```

The DoAction method makes a step according to the given input action. It may return either an output action or the special value null, which indicates that there is no immediate output action. You should implement the DoAction method to throw an exception if the input action fails. The Reset method should reset the implementation to its initial state. If the stepper cannot reset the implementation from its current state, it should throw an exception.

Since we are not interested in testing multiple instances of BagImpl, we assume that the initial state of the stepper references a fixed instance of BagImpl that has been created initially.

These are the action symbols that the stepper must handle:

- An Add symbol that takes a string as an argument.
- A Delete symbol that takes a string as an argument.
- A Lookup_Start symbol that takes a string as an argument, and a Lookup_Finish symbol that takes an integer as an argument. The action Lookup_Start(e) represents the invocation of the bag implementation's Lookup method with input parameter e, and the action Lookup_Finish(k) represents the return value k of the invocation.
- A Count_Start symbol and a Count_Finish symbol that take an integer as an argument. The action Count_Start() represents the invocation of the bag implementation's implicit get_Count method, and the action Count_Finish(k) represents the return value k of the invocation.

A stepper for BagImpl is shown in Figure 12.4. In order to map the stepper's input actions to concrete inputs for the bag implementation, the stepper must extract the first argument of the input action a, using the indexer expression a[0] and a cast to string. The modeling library provides action arguments through a C# *indexer*, which accesses elements by subscripts. In order to construct the output actions that correspond to the return values of the lookup and count operations, the stepper uses the utility function Action.Create to create an output action from a given action name and arguments given as .NET values. (Appendix A.3 explains these and other facilities for working with action terms.)

12.3 Strategies

In a typical model, there are multiple possible actions enabled in any given model state. With offline test generation, the main idea is that the model is analyzed *globally* and a test suite is derived that provides a traversal of the model.

The offline case is a special case of a more general form of testing where the tester has a *strategy* selecting the action to be executed next or what result is to be expected from the system under test. In addition to the model state, a tester also has

```csharp
using System;
using NModel.Conformance;
using NModel.Terms;

namespace BagImplTestHarness
{
    public class Stepper : IStepper
    {

        BagImpl bag = new BagImpl.BagImpl();

        public Action DoAction(Action a)
        {
            switch (a.Name)
            {
                case ("Add"):
                    bag.Add((string)a[0]);
                    return null;
                case ("Delete"):
                    bag.Delete((string)a[0]);
                    return null;
                case ("Lookup_Start"):
                    int c = bag.Lookup((string)a[0]);
                    return Action.Create("Lookup_Finish", c);
                case ("Count_Start"):
                    return Action.Create("Count_Finish", bag.Count);
                default :
                    throw new Exception("Unexpected action " + a);
            }
        }

        public void Reset()
        {
            bag = new BagImpl();
        }
    }
}
```

Figure 12.4. Bag stepper.

```
using System;
using System.Collections.Generic;
using NModel.Terms;
using NModel.Execution;
using NModel;

namespace NModel.Conformance
{
    public interface IStrategy
    {
        Set<Symbol> ActionSymbols { get; }
        IState CurrentState { get; }
        bool IsInAcceptingState { get; }
        void Reset();
        bool IsActionEnabled(Action action, out string reason);
        Action SelectAction(Set<Symbol> actionSymbols);
        void DoAction(Action action);
    }
}
```

Figure 12.5. The IStrategy interface.

a tester state. For example, the tester may have a counter of how many individual test steps (transitions) have been made in total to be able to distinguish between different occurrences of the same model state. In the offline case the value of the counter is enough for the tester to know what action to select or to expect next, namely if the counter is n then the next action is the nth action in the test suite (assuming the test suite contains a single sequence of actions).

With on-the-fly testing, the selection of actions is dynamic and happens during testing; there is no precomputed test suite and the full state machine does not need to be known in advance. The tester state needs to be rich enough to record information needed to select the next action. In particular, the tester state must have a reference to the current model state in order to know what actions are enabled. An action that is not enabled in the model must not be selected by the tester, because conformance to the model would be violated.

A way to realize a particular on-the-fly tester is to implement a custom strategy. The ct tool can be provided with a custom strategy using the strategy option. A strategy is implemented by providing the IStrategy interface shown in Figure 12.5 that is assumed to provide the following functionality:

- The ActionSymbols property gets the set of all possible action symbols in the model.
- The CurrentState property gets the current model state.

- The `IsInAcceptingState` property returns true if the current model state is an accepting state. A test run is allowed to finish only in an accepting state.
- The `Reset` action restores the model to its initial state. After reset `CurrentState` is the initial state of the model. This does not mean that the full tester state is restored to the initial state. Typically, the strategy keeps history of prior test runs that affects what action is selected next.
- The `IsActionEnabled` method returns true if the given action is enabled in the current model state. It returns false otherwise, and outputs a reason why the action is not enabled.
- The `SelectAction` method returns an action that is enabled in the current model state and whose action symbol is in the given set of action symbols. The given set of action symbols may be a proper subset of `ActionSymbols`. The method returns `null` if no action can be selected.
- The `DoAction` method executes the given action in the model so that `CurrentState` gets the target state of this transition. A precondition of this method is that the given action is enabled in the current state. If the action is not enabled, the behavior of the model program is unpredictable.

The strategy is constructed for a given model program and holds a reference to it. The strategy stores the current state of the model and it knows, by using the model program, which actions are currently enabled, that is, which actions are enabled in the current state. The strategy can use additional state to record history, for example, previously taken actions, in order to implement a particular algorithm for selecting the next action to be executed.

12.3.1 Default strategy

A default or basic strategy for a given model program is provided by the `Strategy` class. The basic strategy has no additional tester state, it implements a so-called *memoryless* action selection strategy; a call to `SelectAction` computes, in the current state, the set of all enabled actions with the given action symbols and returns a *randomly* chosen action from among those, or null if the set is empty.

We can use the conformance tester `ct` to run the restricted bag model program against the bag stepper. As it happens, the very first test fails with a trace consisting of a single action `Lookup_Start(null)` with a failure reason that `null` cannot be a key in the dictionary that is used to implement the bag. We can fix that bug easily by counting `null` values separately and not trying to insert `null` or to look it up in the dictionary. For now let us assume that the set of parameters is restricted to `""` and `"b"`; that is, we change the definition of `E` in Figure 12.3 to

```
readonly static Set<string> E = new Set<string>("","b");
```

After a couple of executions of ct we get another failure trace:

```
TestResult(2, Verdict("Failure"),
            "Action 'Count_Finish(1)' not enabled in the model
Unexpected return value of finish action, expected: Count_Finish(2)
Unexpected finish action",
    Trace(
        Count_Start(),
        Count_Finish(0),
        Delete(""),
        Add(""),
        Add("b"),
        Add(""),
        Delete("b"),
        Delete("b"),
        Count_Start(),
        Count_Finish(1)
    )
)
```

Here the error is that the last call to Count returns 1 instead of 2. Note that there must be two empty strings in the table at this point. By inspecting the implementation we can see that when an element is deleted, a case is missing for the situation when the count of the element that is deleted becomes 0. If this happens then the deletion should also remove the element from the table. It is left as an exercise to the reader to correct the two errors in the implementation and rerun ct.

12.4 Coverage-directed strategies

Coverage is a measure of how much testing has been done. Testing achieves better coverage by exercising the implementation more thoroughly. A custom strategy can be designed to achieve good coverage according to a measure chosen by the designer.

The basic strategy provides random walks of a given number of steps, restarting from the initial state each time. Purely random selection of actions may be wasteful, and often one can do better. The basic idea is to keep a history of previously taken steps. Here we look at how to implement a customized strategy for a given model program that keeps track of a set of abstract coverage points. The algorithm that we are presenting here should be seen as an example of how to implement your own testing strategies, using the IStrategy and the ModelProgram interfaces as extension points of the modeling library.

12.4.1 Coverage points

There are many ways to measure coverage. Coverage points provide a uniform way to handle different coverage measures. A *coverage point* is a part or property of a program used to measure coverage, by counting how many times it is executed, visited, or otherwise exercised. A state, an action, or a branch in the code could be a coverage point.

Let us a consider a fixed explorable model program. Suppose that given a state *s* and an action *a*, one can calculate a collection of *coverage points* that are visited (covered) in the model program if *a* is executed from state *s*. In general, the same coverage point can be visited multiple times but the order in which the coverage points are visited is irrelevant; thus, the collection is intuitively a bag. A coverage point is represented by a term. The type of a function that, given a state and an action, computes a bag of coverage points is called a CoverageFunction and is defined in the NModel.Conformance namespace as follows.[1]

```
delegate Bag<Term> CoverageFunction(IState s, Action a);
```

Coverage points can reflect *structural coverage* as well as *behavioral coverage* of the model program. Here are some concrete examples of some common notions of coverage. The first two are examples of structural coverage of the model program, whereas the remaining three are examples of behavioral coverage because they are independent of the structure of the model program.

Vocabulary coverage. The simplest example of a coverage function is one that returns a bag containing just the action symbol. In other words, it is ignored from which state the action is explored and what arguments the action takes.

```
Bag<Term> GetVocabularyCoverage(IState s, Action a)
{ return new Bag<Term>(a.FunctionSymbol.AsTerm); }
```

Annotation coverage. Suppose you want to cover different cases or code branches inside one action method. You can annotate the model program with explicit coverage points using the Execute.AddCoveragePoint method in order to record what case has been taken. The following example shows how to annotate the bag model in Figure 12.2 with two coverage points that distinguish between the two cases when an element that is to be deleted occurs in the bag or does not occur in the bag.

```
[Action]
static void Delete(string element)
{
```

---

[1] A method type such as CoverageFunction is called a *delegate* in .NET.

```
if (content.Contains(element))
{
  Execute.AddCoveragePoint("in the bag")
  content = content.Remove(element);
}
else
  Execute.AddCoveragePoint("not in the bag")
}
```

You can define a method `GetCoveragePoints` in your custom strategy as follows. (A concrete example of a custom strategy definition is shown in the next section.) It is assumed here that the strategy has a field called `model` that references a given model program. The reserved name for getting all the coverage points that are covered by executing an annotated action from a given state is `"CoveragePoints"`.

```
Bag<Term> GetCoveragePoints(IState s, Action a)
{
  Bag<Term> cps;
  model.GetTargetState(s, a, "CoveragePoints", out cps);
  return cps;
}
```

Note that the target state of the transition is irrelevant in this context; only the bag of all the coverage points that were covered is relevant and is returned.

Action coverage. If you only care about covering the different actions, independent of the start state, then you can use the following coverage function. If the actions take no arguments then this coverage function is equivalent to the first one above.

```
Bag<Term> GetActionCoverage(IState s, Action a)
{ return new Bag<Term>(a); }
```

State coverage. A widely used notion of behavioral coverage is to visit all the different states of the state machine. You can implement a state coverage function as follows. It is useful to map states to their hash codes here, rather than keeping around full states as coverage points.

```
Bag<Term> GetStateCoverage(IState s, Action a)
{
  int stateHash = model.GetTargetState(s, a).GetHashCode();
  return new Bag<Term>(new Literal(stateHash));
}
```

Transition coverage. Another widely used notion of behavioral coverage is to visit all the different transitions of the state machine. You can implement a transition coverage function as follows. It is useful to map states to their hash codes here, rather than keeping around full states.

```
Bag<Term> GetTransitionCoverage(IState s, Action a)
{
    return new Bag<Term>(Term.Create("Cp",
                          new Literal(s.GetHashCode()),a));
}
```

Notice that it is not necessary to compute the actual target state of the transition, because it is uniquely determined by the source state and the action, and would therefore not affect the coverage.

12.4.2 Action selection

Our custom strategy derives from the basic strategy. It takes a given model program `model` and a given coverage function `getCoverage`.

```
partial class CustomStrategy : Strategy
{
    CoverageFunction GetCoverage;

    public CustomStrategy(ModelProgram model,
                          CoverageFunction getCoverage) : base(model)
    {
        this.CctCoverage = getCoverage;
    }
}
```

The custom strategy uses a history variable `coveragePoints`, which also happens to be a bag, that keeps count of the total number of occurrences of all the coverage points seen so far. Initially the bag is empty.

```
partial class CustomStrategy
{
    Bag<Term> coveragePoints = Bag<Term>.EmptyBag;
}
```

The main purpose of the custom strategy is to provide a particular implementation of the method `SelectAction`. The idea is that an action is selected in such a way that its *reward* is maximized. The `GetReward` function is defined below. If there are several actions with the same reward, then one of the actions is chosen randomly. The GetEnabledActions method is defined in the basic strategy; it enumerates all the actions with the given action symbols that are enabled in the current state.

```
partial class CustomStrategy
{
  public override Action SelectAction(Set<Symbol> actionSymbols)
  {
    double bestRewardSoFar = 0;
    Set<Action> bestActionsSoFar = Set<Action>.EmptySet;
    foreach (Action a in GetEnabledActions(actionSymbols))
    {
      double reward = GetReward(a);
      if (reward == bestRewardSoFar)
        bestActionsSoFar = bestActionsSoFar.Add(a);
      else if (reward > bestRewardSoFar)
      {
        bestRewardSoFar = reward;
        bestActionsSoFar = new Set<Action>(a);
      }
    }
    return (bestActionsSoFar.IsEmpty ? null
                                : bestActionsSoFar.Choose());
  }
}
```

The idea behind the reward function is that it maps each enabled action in the current state to a numeric real value that characterizes how "rewarding" it would be to explore that action. Suppose that we wish to reward those actions more that either cover new coverage points or cover more coverage points. We can calculate a reward value as follow:

```
partial class CustomStrategy
{
  double GetReward(Action a)
  {
    double reward = 0;
    Bag<Term> cps = GetCoverage(CurrentState, a);
    foreach (Term cp in cps)
    {
      int newC = cps.CountItem(cp);
      int oldC = coveragePoints.CountItem(cp);
```

```
            reward += ((double)newC / (double)(newC + oldC));
        }
        return reward;
    }
}
```

Notice the special case when GetCoverage always returns a bag with a single coverage point p, for example, if GetVocabularyCoverage is being used as the GetCoverage function. The reward will in this case be $1/(1+m)$, where m is the number of times that p has been visited before.

Finally, we need to override the method DoAction that records that a given action is taken, because it needs to update the state variable coveragePoints by including all the new coverage points and by increasing the counts of all the previously covered coverage points.

```
partial class CustomStrategy
{
    public override void DoAction(Action a)
    {
        coveragePoints = coveragePoints.Union(GetCoverage(CurrentState, a));
        base.DoAction(a);
    }
}
```

In order to illustrate the effect of using GetVocabularyCoverage, let us add the statement

```
Console.WriteLine("reward: " + bestRewardSoFar + " actions: "
                  + bestActionsSoFar);
```

right before the return statement of the SelectAction method. We also need to provide a creator method for the custom strategy. Assume also that the custom strategy has been compiled into an assembly CustomStrategy.dll and uses the namespace CustomStrategy. Consider the following settings for ct defined in a settings file named args.txt.

```
# references
/r:BagModel.dll /r:BagImpl.dll /r:CustomStrategy.dll
# factory method of the model
BagModel.Factory.CreateScenario
# factory method of the strategy
/strategy:CustomStrategy.CustomStrategy.CreateStrategy
```

```
# factory method of the stepper
/iut:BagImpl.Stepper.Create
# number of steps and runs
/runs:1 /steps:20
```

We can now execute ct @args.txt in a directory that contains the referenced libraries and get the following output:

```
reward: 1 actions: Set(Count_Start(), Add("b"), Lookup_Start("b"),
  Lookup_Start(""), Add(""), Delete(""), Delete("b"))
reward: 1 actions: Set(Count_Start(), Add("b"), Add(""), Delete(""),
                    Delete("b"))
reward: 1 actions: Set(Count_Start(), Delete(""), Delete("b"))
reward: 1 actions: Set(Delete(""), Delete("b"))
reward: 0.5 actions: Set(Count_Start(), Add("b"),
  Lookup_Start("b"), Lookup_Start(""), Add(""), Delete(""), Delete("b"))
reward: 0.5 actions: Set(Count_Start(), Add("b"), Add(""), Delete(""),
                    Delete("b"))
reward: 0.5 actions: Set(Count_Start(), Add("b"), Add(""))
TestResult(0, Verdict("Failure"),
"Action 'Count_Finish(-1)' not enabled in the model
Unexpected return value of finish action, expected: Count_Finish(0)
Unexpected finish action",
    Trace(
        Lookup_Start("b"),
        Lookup_Finish(0),
        Add("b"),
        Count_Start(),
        Count_Finish(1),
        Delete("b"),
        Lookup_Start(""),
        Lookup_Finish(0),
        Delete("b"),
        Count_Start(),
        Count_Finish(-1)
    )
)
```

What is interesting to note here is the effect that the coverage function and the reward functions have on the action selection process. Notice that all action symbols are used k times before any of them is used $k + 1$ times.

12.5   Advanced on-the-fly settings

The command-line utility ct is used throughout the book to illustrate how to run conformance tests against an implementation under test. The utility can be configured in several different ways, depending on the testing needs and requirements. In this section we take a closer look at the main configuration options, some aspects of the internal architecture, and some of the various extension points of the tool that can be used to implement more advanced testing heuristics.

The modeling library can be used as a building block of a custom tool with more advanced features than ct. In particular, the ConformanceTester class that is used by ct has additional extension points that are not exposed through the settings for ct, but can be accessed programmatically. The ct utility is implemented by the static method RunWithCommandLineArguments of the ConformanceTester class in the NModel.Conformance namespace. This method creates an instance of the ConformanceTester class for a given stepper and strategy, configures its settings, and invokes its Run method.

In the rest of this section we look at the following topics related to on-the-fly testing. Most of the topics are illustrated by using various settings of ct.

- Specifying the model programs.
- Test execution and termination.
- The role of different kinds of actions.
- More on strategies.
  - Using sampling.
  - Using action weights to match operational profiles.
  - Using state groupings to prune the search space.

12.5.1   Specifying the model programs

The main input to a model based on-the-fly testing algorithm is a model. In our case a model is given by one or more model programs. A model program can be provided either through a fully qualified name of a factory method, as a finite state machines (FSM) (by using the fsm option of ct) or in the form of an offline test suite (using the testSuite option). An FSM or an offline test suite is converted into an equivalent model program. If several model programs are given, say m_1, m_2, and m_3, then they are composed into a single model program $m = m_1 * m_2 * m_3$.

Composing several model programs together can be used for different purposes, that has been illustrated on several occasions in previous chapters, and is discussed in more detail in Chapter 14. It is always possible to provide a factory method that creates a composed model program and one can provide that factory method as the single model program. Sometimes it is more convenient and flexible to keep the model programs separate and provide them as separate model arguments to ct. One common case is when one of the model programs represents the model of the expected behavior, whereas the other model programs are various scenarios.

Probes. In some applications of model-based testing, it is useful to be able to check that some abstract view of the state of the IUT is consistent with the corresponding view of the model state. The actions that provide or check that view are sometimes called *probes* (or *observers*). The main property of a probe is that it does not change the state, that is, that the resulting state transition is a self-loop.

Let us consider a concrete example using the bag model. First, we add a new feature called Probe to the bag model that contains a new action symbol CheckView. The purpose of a CheckView action is to serve as a probe. An action CheckView(v) that is enabled in a state s provides an abstract view of s by showing that the set of elements in the bag is v. The view is clearly an abstraction of the actual state because the multiplicity of the individual elements is omitted.

```
namespace BagModel
{
  [Feature]
  static class Probe
  {
    static Set<Set<string>> E()
    { return new Set<Set<string>>(Contract.content.Keys); }
    [Action]
    static void CheckView([Domain("E")]Set<string> elems) { }
    static bool CheckViewEnabled(Set<string> elems)
    { return elems.Equals(Contract.content.Keys); }
  }
}
```

Test harness. When new actions, such as CheckView, are added to the model program, the test harness may need some adaptation. In this case the bag implementation stepper needs to be modified to deal with CheckView actions. This can be done as follows. An exception is thrown if the view of the model state is not consistent with the view of the implementation state. Note that the first (and only) argument of a CheckView action is a term that represents a set of strings. In order to convert that term into a value, the term is interpreted as a compound value that is then cast to a set of strings.

```
switch (a.FunctionSymbol.Name)
{
  case ("CheckView") :
    Set<string> modelView =
      (Set<string>)CompoundValue.InterpretTerm(a.Arguments[0]);
    Set<string> implView = new Set<string>(bag.table.Keys);
    if (!modelView.Equals(implView))
      throw new Exception("Inconsistent views of state: model:" +
                          modelView + " iut:" + implView);
    return null;
  case ...
}
```

Scenarios. Probes are usually checked more frequently than other actions. For the bag model, we can express this using an FSM scenario called `ProbeScenario`. It requires that each `Add` action and each `Delete` action must be followed by a `CheckView` action. In the same scenario we also disable all lookup and count actions.

```
FSM(0,AcceptingStates(0),
    Transitions(t(0,Add(),1),t(0,Delete(),1),t(1,CheckView(),0)),
    Vocabulary("Lookup_Start","Count_Start"))
```

The following additional FSM scenario called `AddDeleteScenario` requires that all `Add` actions happen before all `Delete` actions:

```
FSM(0,AcceptingStates(0,1),
    Transitions(t(0,Add(),0),t(0,Delete(),1),t(1,Delete(),1)))
```

In general, it may be useful to have a whole collection of FSM scenarios stored in separate files and experiment with various combinations of them using the `fsm` option of `ct`, without having to create factory methods for all of the combinations.

Running `ct`. Let us add another factory method `CreateModelWithProbe` to the `Factory` class in `BagModel` that constrains the bag model by including the `ElementRestriction` and the `Probe` features.

```
public static ModelProgram CreateModelWithProbe()
{
  return new LibraryModelProgram(typeof(Contract).Assembly,
      "BagModel", new Set<string>("ElementRestriction","Probe"));
}
```

Figure 12.6 shows a partially explored part of the state machine of `CreateModelWithProbe` composed with `ProbeScenario` and `AddDeleteScenario`, using `mpv`.

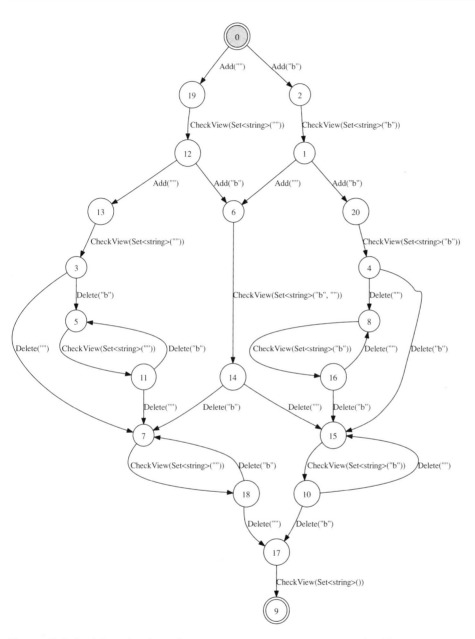

Figure 12.6. Partial exploration of `CreateModelWithProbe` composed with `ProbeScenario` and `AddDeleteScenario`.

Probes typically increase the possibility of finding errors earlier. We can see how ct discovers the bug in the faulty bag implementation much sooner than before, by using CreateModelWithProbe composed with ProbeScenario and AddDeleteScenario

```
TestResult(1, Verdict("Failure"),
    "Inconsistent views of state: model:Set() iut:Set(\"b\")",
    Trace(
        Add("b"),
        CheckView(Set<string>("b")),
        Delete("b"),
        CheckView(Set<string>())
    )
)
```

12.5.2 Test execution and termination

The two primary options of ct that directly control the size of a generated test suite are runs and steps. The value of runs is the desired number of *test runs*. Each test run starts from the initial state of the model program. Both the IUT and the strategy are reset between test runs. Recall that resetting the strategy resets the underlying model program. This is an outline of the top-level loop:

```
int k = 0;
while (k < runs)
{
   if (!TestResultNotifier(RunTest(k))) return;
   strategy.Reset();
   stepper.Reset();
   k += 1;
}
```

The test result notifier is a delegate that can be set in the conformance tester. This delegate controls when the conformance tester should terminate. In ct this delegate is set to a function that outputs the test result and returns false, if the test run failed and the continueOnFailure option of ct is turned off, and returns true otherwise. Each test result is written either to the console or to a log file if one is provided by the logfile option of ct.

Test execution algorithm. An outline of the algorithm that executes a single test run is shown in Figure 12.7. Each individual test run starts from the initial state and attempts to produce a run of at least as many actions as specified by

```
TestResult RunTest(int k)
{
  Sequence<Action> trace = Sequence<Action>.EmptySequence;
  Action o = null;  // optional output from the stepper

  while (trace.Count < steps ||
        (!strategy.IsInAcceptingState && trace.Count < maxSteps))
  {
    if (o != null)
    {
      trace = trace.AddLast(o);
      string reason = "";
      if (strategy.IsActionEnabled(o, out reason)) //check conformance
        { strategy.DoAction(o); o = null; }
      else
        return new TestResult(k, Verdict.Failure, reason, trace);
    }
    else
    {
      Action a = strategy.SelectAction(testerActionSymbols);
      if (a == null)
        if (strategy.IsInAcceptingState)
          return new TestResult(k, Verdict.Success, "", trace);
        else
          return new TestResult(k, Verdict.Failure,
                                "Did not finish in accepting state", trace);
      else
      {
        strategy.DoAction(a);
        trace = trace.AddLast(a);
        if (!internalActionSymbols.Contains(a.FunctionSymbol))
        {
          try
            o = InvokeStepper(a);
          catch (Exception e)
            return new TestResult(k, Verdict.Failure, e.Message, trace);
        }
      }
    }
  }
}
```

Figure 12.7. Outline of the algorithm executing a single test run.

steps. When that lower limit is reached, the algorithm tries to reach an accepting state without exceeding an upper limit `maxSteps` on the number of actions. The `InvokeStepper` method uses a worker thread to invoke the stepper to do the given action in the implementation. This thread calls the `DoAction` method in the stepper (see Figure 12.4, for example). If the invocation does not return within a time limit given by the `timeout` option of `ct`, then the test run fails.

12.5.3   Classification of actions

Actions are generally divided into *controllable* and *observable* ones. The option `observableAction` of `ct` is used to declare that an action symbol is observable. Moreover, controllable actions can be classified as being *internal*, using the `internalAction` option of `ct`. Furthermore, controllable actions can also be marked as being *cleanup* actions, using the `cleanupAction` option of `ct`.

Controllable and observable actions. In a closed system it is generally assumed that all actions are controlled by the tester; that is, all action symbols are assumed to be *controllable*. Controllable action symbols are also called *tester action symbols*. A *tester action* or a *controllable action* is an action that has a controllable action symbol. An exception to this general rule are finish action symbols that are typically classified as being *observable* because they are returned by the stepper. An action with an observable action symbol is called an *observable* action. The general treatment of observable actions is deferred to Chapter 16.

In the case of the bag example the action symbols `Lookup_Finish` and `Count_Finish` are observable because the corresponding actions are returned by the stepper. Notice, however, that even if the finish actions are considered as controllable actions, the algorithm in Figure 12.7 will work in exactly the same way, because the strategy cannot be in a state where `SelecAction` is called and a finish action is enabled, unless the stepper is faulty and returns `null` when a finish action should be returned.

Internal actions. Tester actions are generally divided into two categories: the actions that are related to an operation that the IUT must perform, and the actions that are not related to any such operation. The latter case arises when the action is used for making internal choices in the model or scenario. Such actions are called *internal*. An internal action is not executed in the stepper, which can be seen in the algorithm in Figure 12.7. A typical case where internal actions arise are in selecting a test case in a test suite. Suppose, for example, that you have the following two test cases for the bag example. The first test case is to add one `"b"` and then delete one "b". The second test case is to add two "b"'s and then delete two "b"'s. This is an FSM that represents these two test cases:

```
FSM(0,AcceptingStates(S(1,2),S(2,4)),
    Transitions(t(0,Test(1),S(1,0)), t(S(1,0),Add("b"),S(1,1)),
                                      t(S(1,1),Delete("b"),S(1,2)),
                t(0,Test(2),S(2,0)), t(S(2,0),Add("b"),S(2,1)),
                                      t(S(2,1),Add("b"),S(2,2)),
                                      t(S(2,2),Delete("b"),S(2,3)),
                                      t(S(2,3),Delete("b"),S(2,4))))
```

In this case Test is an internal action symbol. The purpose of the Test(k) action is to select the test case that performs k add operations followed by k delete operations. The action Test(k) is itself not related to any operation that the IUT must perform.

Cleanup actions. Another classification of tester actions that is commonly used in on-the-fly testing is to mark certain actions as *cleanup* actions. The purpose of a cleanup action is to help to drive the model program into an accepting state to finish off a test run. After the desired number of steps has been reached in a test run, but the strategy is not yet in an accepting state, then only cleanup actions are enabled. This part of the test execution algorithm has been omitted in Figure 12.7. In the bag example, Delete should be marked as a cleanup action symbol, but not Add.

12.5.4 More on strategies

Implementing a particular strategy is the most flexible way of creating a customized on-the-fly testing algorithm.

Sampling. The technique that was illustrated in Section 12.4 uses a particular sampling algorithm. There are many different ways to implement similar algorithms that may, for example, keep more tester state and use other criteria besides rewards to select actions. One may, for example, assign penalties to certain actions or action paths in order to avoid failures that have already been discovered. This is useful if on-the-fly testing is used as a stress testing tool that may run millions of test runs. In that case it is desirable not to run into the same error over and over again.

Using action weights to match operational profiles. Another technique that can be implemented with a custom strategy is the use of *decrementing action weights*. The idea is the following. Let us for simplicity assume that all actions are without parameters, the idea can be generalized for actions with parameters, or it can be applied to action symbols only by ignoring the parameters. Imagine that there is a weight associated with each action that is initially some positive number. When an action is selected the corresponding weight is decremented by one. If, in a given state, the enabled actions are $a_1, \ldots, a_k$ with weights $w_1, \ldots, w_k$, then an action a_i is not selected if $w_i = 0$, a_i is selected with probability $w_i/(w_1 + \cdots + w_k)$, otherwise. A useful analogy is with a box of colored marbles. Each action corresponds to a particular color and selecting an action corresponds to removing one randomly chosen marble from the box. This continues until the box is empty. This is a powerful and computationally cheap technique to produce test runs where weights are chosen in a way that matches a certain operational profile.

Using groupings for pruning. A further technique that is a powerful way to deal with complex state is to use state or transition *groupings*. Suppose that each model state is mapped to an abstract value called a *group label* that characterizes some interesting properties of that state. The grouping function can, for example, be a coverage function. The grouping function may also be predicate abstraction in which case the group label is a sequence of Boolean values, or it may be a function that takes a sequence to a set. The idea is to dynamically keep track of all group labels encountered during test execution; an action that leads to a new group is prioritized over an action that does not. Here the driving factor is coverage of new groups, and the search space is pruned accordingly. The same idea can be applied to transitions.

12.6 Exercises

1. Correct the faulty bag implementation and rerun `ct` on it.
2. The custom strategy shown in Section 12.4 chooses an action with maximum reward. Implement another `SelectAction` method that chooses an action with probability that is *proportional* to the reward.
3. Implement a strategy for decrementing action weights discussed in Section 12.5.4. In order to assign initial weights to actions, use state properties.
4. Implement a strategy that records for each transition (s_1, a, s_2) an abstract transition $(g(s_1), g(a), g(s_2))$, where g is a grouping function; use `GetHashCode` for g. If in a given state, there are enabled actions that transition to states in new groups, select one of those actions randomly, otherwise choose any action randomly.
*5. A state s is *partially explored* if there exists an unexplored action that is enabled in s. A state s is *interesting* either if it is *partially explored* or if there exists an explored path from s to a partially explored state. Implement a strategy that gives priority to actions that lead to interesting states.

13 Further Reading

There are many existing formal methods that support modeling and analysis with complex state, including Alloy (Jackson, 2006), ASMs (Gurevich, 1995; Börger and Stärk, 2003), B (Abrial, 1996), Promela (Holzmann, 2004), TLA (Lamport, 2002), Unity (Chandy and Misra, 1988), VDM (Fitzgerald and Larsen, 1998), and Z (Woodcock and Loomes, 1989; Spivey, 1992; Davies and Woodcock, 1996; Jacky, 1997). Case studies in these methods demonstrate many ways to use sets, bags, sequences, maps, and other data types similar to the ones in the modeling library.

AsmL (abstract state machine language) (Gurevich et al., 2005) includes high-level data structures like sets and maps and builds on the theory of partial updates (Gurevich and Tillmann, 2005) that allows pointwise changes to such data structures that may, moreover, be nested. AsmL was first supported in the model-based testing tool AsmL-T (Barnett et al., 2003) and is also supported in the Spec Explorer tool (SpecExplorer, 2006). Spec Explorer also supports an extension of the Spec# language (Barnett et al., 2005) with high-level data structures such as sets and maps.

The pruning techniques discussed in Section 11.2 are mostly based on work that was done in Spec Explorer (Veanes et al., in press). The use of composition in this context is based on Veanes et al. (2007a). The state grouping technique discussed in Section 11.2.5 is introduced in Grieskamp et al. (2002). The algorithm is also explained in Börger and Stärk (2003, Section 3.2). The technique can be extended to multiple groupings (Campbell and Veanes, 2005) that can be used to define groupings per feature in a model program with multiple features. State grouping is related to abstraction in model checking (Clarke et al., 1999).

Strategies for fully controlled systems is a special case of strategies for reactive systems. In Yannakakis (2004) such strategies are classified as *preset* strategies as opposed to *adaptive* strategies where (possibly nondeterministic) outputs of the IUT may affect the strategy. (See also Chapter 17 in this connection.) The custom strategy defined in Section 12.4.2 originates from Veanes et al. (2006).

The various notions of coverage mentioned in Section 12.4 are related to correspodning classical notions of coverage in the context of black-box testing

(Beizer, 1995). Besides the use of composition, techniques discussed in Section 12.5 originate from Spec Explorer (Veanes et al., in press). The test execution algorithm described in Section 12.5.2 is a special case of the algorithm described in Chapter 16. (See also Chapter 17 in this connection.)

The book by Utting and Legeard (2006) describes several other model-based testing tools, both commercial and noncommercial.

Part IV

Advanced Topics

14 Compositional Modeling

We have seen many different uses of composition in the previous chapters. In this chapter we are going to take a closer look at the use of composition as a general modeling technique to break down larger models into smaller models.

We are going to look at an example that illustrates how this technique can be applied to real-life complex application-level network protocols. Such protocols are abundant. Modern software architectures rely heavily on the fact that two parties that need to communicate, for example a client and a server, or two servers, do so by using a well-defined (application-level network) protocol.

We then discuss some of the main properties of model program composition and provide a summary of the various uses of model program composition.

14.1 Modeling protocol features

A real-life protocol can be intrinsically complex. There are several reasons for this. A protocol typically has multiple layers and depends on or uses other protocols. In a good protocol design, internal details of the underlying protocols should not leak out and the layering principle should be maintained. Another reason is that a protocol typically includes many different *features* within a single layer. Intuitively, a feature is a part or an aspect of the overall functionality of the protocol. Features interact and together define the protocol as a whole.

An important property of protocols is that enough information is present in messages, usually in message headers, so that it is possible to maintain a consistent view of the state of the protocol on both sides of the protocol users.

In the protocol model in this chapter, the actions of the model program represent the messages of the protocol. A run of the model program represents a session where client and server exchange messages, as shown in Figure 14.18. The steps we follow in the *feature-oriented modeling* of a protocol are the following:

223

1. First, the *action vocabulary* is identified. Typically the action vocabulary corresponds to the set of possible value combinations of particular fields in the message header. Consider for example two fields, one that identifies whether a message is a `Request` or a `Response`, and another field that identifies a particular operation that is being performed, say a `Read` or a `Write`. The actions symbols could then be `ReadRequest`, `ReadResponse`, `WriteRequest`, `WriteResponse`.

2. Second, a mapping is defined from concrete messages "on the wire" to abstract actions in the model program. This mapping may omit all fields of a message that are not used in any of the features. For example, fields that represent layout constraints on the message structure may be omitted.

3. Third, a separate model program is written for each feature. The state variables of the feature model programs should be disjoint, so that independent analysis of the feature model programs is possible.

4. Finally, some or all of the feature model programs, say $M_1, M_2, \ldots, M_k$, can be composed into a model program $M_1 \times M_2 \times \cdots \times M_k$ to validate feature interactions or to be used as the contract during conformance testing.

14.2 Motivating example: a client/server protocol

We are considering a sample client/server protocol that supports various operations on shared resources across different machines. Here we are considering a fixed client and a fixed server. The sample protocol model is called *SP* here. There are two kinds of messages, *requests* and *responses*. All requests are initiated by the client and all responses are sent by the server. The feature model programs shown here are realistic approximations of the corresponding features described in the document. We have omitted certain details that are not relevant for explaining the ideas. The full protocol contains over 300 pages of natural language specification, and the complete model program would all in all comprise between 20 and 30 feature model programs. The following features are considered here:

- *Credits* feature is a variation of the *sliding window* algorithm (Section 14.2.1, below) that enables the client and the server to maintain a consistent view of which message IDs are used.
- *Cancellation* feature enables prior requests from the client to be cancelled later by the client.
- *Commands* feature ensures that response messages from the server match with respect to the particular commands being requested by the client.
- *Setup* feature is a handshake between the client and the server that activates the protocol.

Only a subset of the information that is present in the concrete messages of the protocol is relevant for modeling these protocol features. Therefore, concrete messages of the protocol are mapped to the abstract actions of the model program as follows. Each message has a particular *command* field that indicates the operation requested by the client or responded by the server. For this protocol it is natural to map the kind of the message, that is, whether it is a request or a response message, together with the command field of the message to one action symbol. This is because there are only a couple of dozen commands in total and different features are very naturally related to different groups of commands. Without loss of generality, we suppose that the commands are Setup, Work, and Cancel. The corresponding action symbols are as follows:

- ReqSetup and ReqWork are action symbols that represent requests from the client to execute the commands Setup and Work, respectively. A *setup* (*work*) *request* is an action ReqSetup(m,c) (ReqWork(m,c)), where m is a message ID and c is a number of requested credits.
- ResSetup and ResWork are action symbols that represent responses from the server to commands Setup and Work, respectively. A *setup* (*work*) *response* is an action ResSetup(m,c,s) (ResWork(m,c,s)), where m is a message ID, c is a number of granted credits, and s is a status value.
- Cancel is used as an action symbol that represents a request from the client to cancel a previous operation; that is, the command is Cancel. A *cancel request* has the form Cancel(m), where m is a message ID. There is no response to a cancel request.

Each action symbol has a number of parameters that corresponds to the number of relevant fields in the messages. As said, not all of the fields of messages are relevant. If we were to consider more features of the protocol, the number of parameters of the action symbols would be bigger but the remaining arguments would be ignored in the model programs of the above features.

14.2.1 Credits feature

The protocol is designed to prevent the client from overwhelming the server with too many requests. The client can only use certain message identifiers to communicate with the server. Each identifier can only be used once. The identifiers that the client can use can be seen as a pool of numbers. The client can ask for additional credits in the requests that it sends to the server in order to expand the pool. The server may grant credits in its responses to the client. The number of credits granted by the server determines how the pool grows or shrinks as time progresses. There is quite a lot of implementation freedom in the way that the server can grant credits and in the way that the client can ask for new credits or use the available message IDs.

This is an example of a *sliding window* protocol. Here the pool of identifiers is the "window" whose contents change or "slide" as time progresses. However, the pool is not necessarily a consecutive interval of numbers because the client does not have to pick the numbers from the pool in any particular order.

This feature is defined uniformly for all of the commands that are communicated between the server and the client, except for `Cancel`.

State variables

The model program of the credits feature is shown in Figure 14.1. The model program has three state variables: `window` is the set of all message IDs that the client may use to send new requests to the server, `requests` is a map containing all the outstanding credit requests with message IDs as keys, and `maxId` is the largest ID that has been granted by the server. In the initial state of the model program the only possible message ID is 0, the maximum ID is also 0, and there are no pending requests.

Actions

The action vocabulary of the credits model program consists of the action symbols `ReqSetup`, `ReqWork`, `ResSetup`, and `ResWork`. The action symbol `Cancel` is not in the vocabulary.

In order to use features and composition most effectively, we treat the relation between actions and methods more freely here than in previous examples. The actions (`ResSetup` etc.) which were defined at the beginning of Section 14.2 are distinct from the methods (`Res` etc.) in the code in Figure 14.1; they have different names and different parameters. It is the actions that appear in the traces (Figure 14.18 etc.), not the methods.

Each action is associated with its method (`ResSetup` with `Res` etc.) by labeling the method with an `Action` attribute whose argument indicates the action names and parameters, following the rules given in Appendix A. Two or more actions may use the same update rule (that is why actions and methods have different names here). For example, the setup response and the work response actions `ResSetup` and `ResWork` both use the update rule `Res`. Furthermore, these actions have three parameters but the update rule only has two. An underscore _ in the attribute indicates that the action's third parameter is not used by this update rule. These same two actions are associated with a different update rule (also named `Res`) in the cancellation model program (Figure 14.7). In that rule, it is the action's second parameter which is not used.

In the product model program which is formed by composition, the actions of the separate model programs are combined. When a combined action executes, all of its update rules execute and all of its parameters are used. It is the actions (the

```
namespace SP
{
  [Feature]
  class Credits
  {
    static Set<int> window = new Set<int>(0);
    static int maxId = 0;
    static Map<int,int> requests = Map<int,int>.EmptyMap;

    [Action("ReqSetup(m,c)")]
    [Action("ReqWork(m,c)")]
    static void Req(int m, int c)
    {
      requests = requests.Add(m, c);
      window = window.Remove(m);
    }

    [Requirement("Section ...: Message IDs must not be repeated")]
    static bool ReqEnabled(int m){return window.Contains(m);}

    [Requirement("Section ...: Requested credits must be > 0.")]
    static bool ReqEnabled(int m, int c){return c > 0;}

    [Action("ResSetup(m,c,_)")]
    [Action("ResWork(m,c,_)")]
    public static void Res(int m, int c)
    {
      for (int i = 1; i <= c; i++) window = window.Add(maxId + i);
      requests = requests.RemoveKey(m);
      maxId = maxId + c;
    }

    [Requirement("Section ...: Must be a pending credit request")]
    static bool ResEnabled(int m){return requests.ContainsKey(m);}

    [Requirement("Section ...: Must not grant more credits than requested")]
    static bool ResEnabled(int m, int c){return requests[m] >= c;}

    [AcceptingStateCondition]
    static bool IsAcceptingState() { return requests.IsEmpty; }

    [StateInvariant("Section ...: Client must have enough credits")]
    static bool ClientHasEnoughCredits()
    {
      if (requests.Count == 0) return window.Count > 0;
      else return true;
    }
  }
}
```

Figure 14.1. Credits feature model program.

terms) that are considered when combining actions, not the methods (the C# code). Section 14.3 (below) explains in detail how actions are combined.

The action ReqSetup (m, c), where m is a message ID and c a requested number of credits, has an update rule, given by the method Req, that records in the state variable requests that m has an outstanding credit request for c credits, and removes m from the window. The guard of this update rule is defined by the conjunction of the two *predicates* (Boolean methods) named ReqEnabled (recall that an action method is enabled only when all of its enabling conditions are true). The first predicate requires m to appear in the window, and the second one requires c to be positive.

A Requirement attribute associated with each of the predicates provides a connection between the model program and the corresponding section or paragraph in the natural language document, and motivates the split of the enabling condition into two predicates, rather than just one predicate.

The action ResSetup $(m, c, \_)$, where m is a message ID and c is a granted number of credits, has an update rule given by the action method Res. It adds to the window the set of new IDs $\{maxId + 1, \ldots, maxId + c\}$, which is empty if c is zero, records that the new maximum ID is $maxId + c$ and removes m from the pending requests map. This action is enabled if m is an outstanding request, and the granted credits do not exceed the requested credits.

Accepting states

It is useful to identify those states where no requests are pending. From the clients point of view, these are states where the server is stable; that is, the server is not processing a request. All accepting traces of the credits model program have to end in an accepting state.

State invariants

An important property of the credits algorithm is that the client must not starve. In other words, it should never be the case that the client runs out of credits and cannot send further requests. This does not mean that the server always has to grant at least one credit to the client in every response. It may be that the client has pending requests that will eventually grant the client more credits. Thus, the state invariant is that if there are no pending requests then the window must be nonempty.

Exploration

A natural question that arises here is whether the model program in Figure 14.1 has any *unsafe* states, that is, states reachable from the initial state that violate the state invariant. If this is the case then the model program should be amended.

To explore the credits model program, we use a finite state machine (FSM) model program that restricts the credits model program to a finite set of states (see

```
FSM(0, AcceptingStates(0),
    Transitions(t(0,ReqSetup(0,0),0), t(0,ReqSetup(0,1),0),
                t(0,ResSetup(0,0),0), t(0,ResSetup(0,1),0)),
    Vocabulary("ReqWork", "ResWork"))
```

Figure 14.2. A parameter restriction scenario for the credits model.

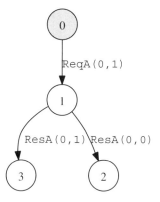

Figure 14.3. Composition of the model programs in Figures 14.1 and 14.2. State 2 violates the state invariant in Figure 14.1.

Figure 14.2). The FSM disables all Work actions and provides concrete parameter domains for message IDs and credits in the Setup actions. We can compose the credits model program with the FSM. The resulting finite state machine is shown in Figure 14.3. We can see that state 2 is unsafe, because the update rule of the action ResSetup(0,0,_) from state 1 removes all pending requests and adds no credits, so the client cannot send further requests.

We need to strengthen the enabling condition of the response action so that if there are no pending requests and the window is empty, then the granted number of credits must be at least one. We do so by adding the additional enabling condition to the credits model.

```
[Requirement("Section ...: Client must have enough credits")]
static bool ResEnabled1(int m, int c)
{
    return requests.Count > 1 || window.Count > 0 || c > 0;
}
```

Notice that if the window is empty and no credits are granted then there must be at least two requests pending when this enabling condition is checked, because the response action update rule will remove one of the requests.

```
FSM(0, AcceptingStates(0),
    Transitions(t(0,ReqSetup(0,2),0),t(0,ReqSetup(1,2),0),
        t(0,ResSetup(0,0),0),t(0,ResSetup(0,1),0),t(0,ResSetup(0,2),0),
        t(0,ResSetup(1,0),0),t(0,ResSetup(1,1),0),t(0,ResSetup(1,2),0)),
    Vocabulary("ReqWork", "ResWork"))
```

Figure 14.4. Another scenario,CreditsScenario2, for the Credits model program. Message IDs are 0 and 1. Requests ask for two credits. Responses grant up to two credits.

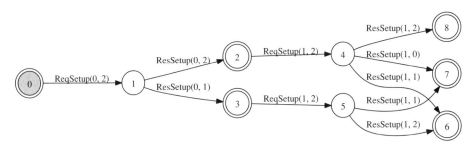

Figure 14.5. Composition of the scenario in Figure 14.4 with the amended credits model program.

Let us consider another scenario that allows two message IDs to be used and assumes that the client always requests two credits, whereas the server grants at most two credits (see Figure 14.4). The full exploration of the composition of this scenario with the amended credits model program is shown in Figure 14.5.

14.2.2 Message parameters

It is useful to identify those parameter domains of actions that have finite domains that can be derived from the model program state. These domains can be used to make the model program explorable. Recall that for a model program to be explorable, all action parameters must have finite domains. Looking at the credits model program for example, we can see that all responses from the server must have message identifiers present in the requests map. Also, all granted credits from the server must be between zero and the maximum credit requested by the client. We add these derived parameter domains as another feature model program to SP (see Figure 14.6).

Notice that this feature has no state variables of its own. It is a *dependent feature* of the credits feature model program. We could also have annotated the credits feature model program in Figure 14.1 directly, but it is useful to keep the dependent feature separate for readability and for later use in compositions. In some cases the dependent feature is not needed and can be omitted.

```
namespace SP
{
  [Feature]
  class MessageParameters
  {
    [Action("ResSetup(m,c,_)")]
    [Action("ResWork(m,c,_)")]
    static void Res([Domain("M")]int m, [Domain("C")]int c){}
    static Set<int> M() { return Credits.requests.Keys; }
    static Set<int> C()
    {
      if (Credits.requests.Values.IsEmpty)
        return Set<int>.EmptySet;
      else{
        int maxCredits = Credits.requests.Values.Minimum();
        Set<int> res = Set<int>.EmptySet;
        for (int c = 0; c <= maxCredits; c++) res = res.Add(c);
        return res;
      }
    }

    [Action("ReqSetup(m,_)")]
    [Action("ReqWork(m,_)")]
    static void Req([Domain("ReqM")]int m){}
    static Set<int> ReqM() { return Credits.window; }

    [Action]
    static void Cancel([Domain("CancelM")]int m) { }
    static Set<int> CancelM() { return Credits.requests.Keys; }
  }
}
```

Figure 14.6. Message parameters.

14.2.3 Cancellation feature

The cancellation feature of the protocol enables the client to cancel requests that have been sent to the server. In order to cancel a previously sent request with message ID k, the client sends a Cancel request to the server that identifies the request to be cancelled by including the ID k in the message. A Cancel request is a "meta" request in the sense that it triggers no response of its own, it has no separate ID besides k, and it is not considered as part of the credits feature; that is, a `Cancel` request cannot be used by the client to get more credits. The model program of the cancellation feature is shown in Figure 14.7.

State variables

The cancellation model program has one state variable `mode` whose value is a map of pending request IDs that records for each entry whether it has been sent or cancelled by the client. Initially no request has been either sent or cancelled, so the value of `mode` is the empty map.

Actions

The action vocabulary of the cancellation model program contains all of the action symbols listed above. The credits field is ignored in all actions.

The update rule of a `Setup` or a `Work` request updates the mode of that request ID to indicate that the request has been sent to the server. The enabling condition is that a request with the same ID is not pending.

A `Cancel` request is enabled for all requests. This is needed to avoid race conditions between the client and the server. A `Cancel` request must have no effect on the behavior of the server unless the request being cancelled has actually been sent to the server and is not yet cancelled or completed.

The update rule of a response action removes the pending request. A response action has a status field as the third argument. The value of the status field indicates whether the requested operation was cancelled or completed by the server. If the status of a response is `Cancelled`, it must be the case that cancellation of the corresponding request was sent by the client. Notice that the client may try to cancel a request but the cancellation arrives too late to the server who has already completed the request. Therefore, the status of a response to a request that has been cancelled by the client may be either `Cancelled` or `Completed`.

Exploration

Let us look at a particular scenario of the cancellation model program. First note that the model program behaves uniformly for all message IDs and there are no interactions or dependencies between actions with distinct message IDs. It is therefore enough to fix a single message ID, say 2. A convenient way to do so is to use the FSM scenario shown in Figure 14.8. Notice that the scenario disables all the work actions by including them in the vocabulary of the FSM. The composition of the scenario in Figure 14.8 with the cancellation model program is shown in Figure 14.9.

For visual inspection and validation it is important to choose a small set of parameters. For example, if we add another message ID 3 into the scenario in Figure 14.8, that is, we consider the FSM in Figure 14.10 and compose it with

```
namespace SP
{
  enum Mode { Sent, CancelRequested }
  enum Status { Cancelled, Completed }

  [Feature]
  class Cancellation
  {
    static Map<int, Mode> mode = Map<int, Mode>.EmptyMap;

    [Action("ReqSetup(m,_)")]
    [Action("ReqWork(m,_)")]
    static void Req(int m) { mode = mode.Add(m, Mode.Sent); }
    static bool ReqEnabled(int m) { return !mode.ContainsKey(m); }

    [Action]
    static void Cancel(int m)
    {
      if (mode.ContainsKey(m) && mode[m] == Mode.Sent)
        mode = mode.Override(m, Mode.CancelRequested);
    }

    [Action("ResSetup(m,_,s)")]
    [Action("ResWork(m,_,s)")]
    public static void Res(int m, Status s)
    {
      mode = mode.RemoveKey(m);
    }
    public static bool ResEnabled(int m, Status s)
    {
      return mode.ContainsKey(m) &&
        (s != Status.Cancelled || mode[m] == Mode.CancelRequested);
    }

    [AcceptingStateCondition]
    static bool IsAcceptingState() { return mode.IsEmpty; }
  }
}
```

Figure 14.7. Cancellation feature model program.

```
FSM(0, AcceptingStates(0),
    Transitions(t(0,Cancel(2),0), t(0,ReqSetup(2),0), t(0,ResSetup(2),0)),
    Vocabulary("ResWork", "ReqWork"))
```

Figure 14.8. A scnenario used to restrict the cancellation model program.

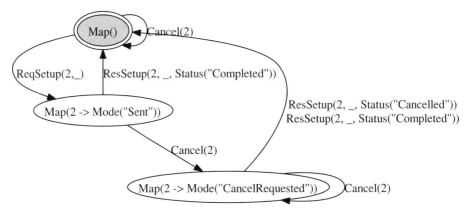

Figure 14.9. Composition of the cancellation model program in Figure 14.7 with the scenario in Figure 14.8. The labels on the states show the value of `mode`.

```
FSM(0, AcceptingStates(0),
    Transitions(t(0,Cancel(2),0), t(0,ReqSetup(2),0), t(0,ResSetup(2),0),
                t(0,Cancel(3),0), t(0,ReqSetup(3),0), t(0,ResSetup(3),0)),
    Vocabulary("ResWork", "ReqWork"))
```

Figure 14.10. Another scnenario used to restrict the cancellation model program.

the cancellation model program, then the complexity increases quadratically in the number of states (is proportional to the square of the number of states) as is shown in Figure 14.11, because the modes of distinct message IDs are independent.

14.2.4 Commands feature

The third protocol feature that we consider specifies that if a request and a response message have the same message identifiers then the command fields must also be the same (see Figure 14.12). The action vocabulary of this model program includes all the action symbols besides `Cancel`.

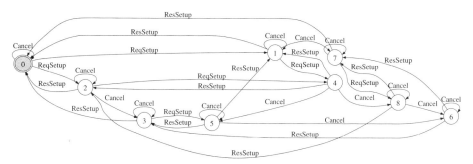

Figure 14.11. Composition of the cancellation model program in Figure 14.7 with the scenario in Figure 14.10. Labels on transitions are abbreviated by action symbols.

State variables
The model program uses an enumeration CMD of commands. Each element x of CMD is used to relate an x request with an x response. The state variable cmd maps message IDs to commands.

Actions
Each action has a separate update rule. When the client issues a request with command X and message ID m, the update rule records that using the cmd variable. The request is enabled only if the request is not pending already. When the server responds with a message ID m, then the command in that response must be cmd[m]. Notice that both the credits and the status fields are ignored in this model program.

Exploration
The model program is rather straigthforward in this case. It is still useful to visualize a scenario of this model program. We use the FSM in Figure 14.13. The composition of this FSM with the commands model program is shown in Figure 14.14.

14.2.5 Setup feature

The fourth and final feature of the protocol that we model here is the initial setup phase of the protocol. Before the protocol is initialized, the client must issue a setup request to the server and the server has to respond that the setup is completed. Once the protocol has been initialized the setup command can no longer be issued. We can model this feature as an FSM shown in Figure 14.15.

Note that all fields besides the status field in the setup response are ignored in this model program. The setup model program does not include Cancel in the vocabulary.

```
namespace SP
{
  enum CMD { Setup, Work }
  [Feature]
  public class Commands
  {
    static Map<int, CMD> cmd = Map<int, CMD>.EmptyMap;

    [Action("ReqSetup(m,_)")]
    static void ReqSetup(int m) {cmd = cmd.Add(m, CMD.Setup);}
    static bool ReqSetupEnabled(int m) {return !cmd.ContainsKey(m);}

    [Action("ResSetup(m,_,_)")]
    static void ResSetup(int m) {cmd = cmd.RemoveKey(m);}
    static bool ResSetupEnabled(int m)
    {
      return cmd.ContainsKey(m) && cmd[m] == CMD.Setup;
    }

    [Action("ReqWork(m,_)")]
    static void ReqWork(int m) {cmd = cmd.Add(m, CMD.Work);}
    static bool ReqWorkEnabled(int m) {return !cmd.ContainsKey(m);}

    [Action("ResWork(m,_,_)")]
    static void ResWork(int m) {cmd = cmd.RemoveKey(m);}
    static bool ResWorkEnabled(int m)
    {
      return cmd.ContainsKey(m) && cmd[m] == CMD.Work;
    }

    [AcceptingStateCondition]
    static bool IsAcceptingState() { return cmd.IsEmpty; }
  }
}
```

Figure 14.12. Commands feature model program.

```
FSM(0, AcceptingStates(0),
    Transitions(t(0,ReqSetup(3),0), t(0,ReqWork(4),0),
                t(0,ResSetup(3),0), t(0,ResWork(4),0)))
```

Figure 14.13. A scnenario used to restrict the commands model program.

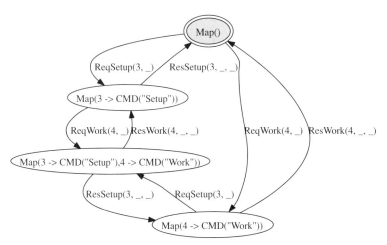

Figure 14.14. Composition of the commands model program in Figure 14.12 with the FSM in Figure 14.13. Labels on states show the value of cmd.

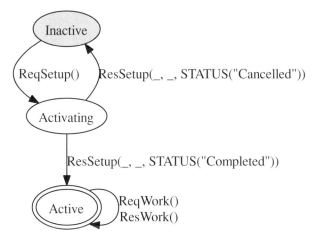

```
FSM("Inactive", AcceptingStates("Active"),
    Transitions(t("Inactive",ReqSetup(),"Activating"),
                t("Activating",ResSetup(_,_,STATUS("Cancelled")),"Inactive"),
                t("Activating",ResSetup(_,_,STATUS("Completed")),"Active"),
                t("Active",ReqWork(),"Active"),
                t("Active",ResWork(),"Active")))
```

Figure 14.15. Setup model program.

14.2.6 Composing the features

Let us now consider a composition of all of the features. We also need some scenarios to restrict the parameter domains, so that the composed model program becomes explorable. We consider two scenarios shown in Figure 14.16.

The scenario CreditScenario describes a client who always uses the minimum available request ID and asks for two credits when sending a request. The scenario also limits the number of requests to three. In addition, the scenario describes a "generous" server who always grants the maximum number credits to the client. Note that this scenario model program is a dependent feature of the credits model program and can therefore not be explored independently of it.

The second scenario, called CancelScenario, describes a client that cancels only the last request that was sent, and only if there is more than one request pending. This scenario is also a dependent feature of the sample protocol model because it references the state of the cancellation model program.

Full exploration of the sample protocol model with all the features composed with the scenarios in Figure 14.16 is shown in Figure 14.17. Notice how the features interact by synchronizing on actions whose symbols are shared. The allowed action traces of the composed model program belong to the intersection of the traces of the individual model programs.

A valid trace of actions is illustrated in Figure 14.18. In this trace all requests were completed, even though request 1 was cancelled by the client. The status field in the response actions comes from the cancellation model program, whereas the allowed message IDs come from the credits model program. The fact that setup has to precede work is due to the setup model program. In state 2 the window of the credits model program is the set $\{3, 4, 5, 6\}$ and all the map-valued state variables are empty maps. If we would remove the restriction that the server always grants the maximum number of credits, we would obtain a state transition graph that represents all the valid server behaviors for the given client behaviors. The state graph would have 24 states and 62 transitions. The final state of every valid trace would have a credits window equal to one of the sets $\{3\}$, $\{3, 4\}$, $\{3, 4, 5\}$, or $\{3, 4, 5, 6\}$, depending on the actual number credits granted by the server in the responses.

For visual validation of the behavior it is useful to restrict the size of the explored state space to a small portion of the full state space. However, if the client is being controlled by the tester and the server is observed only by the tester, it is important not to restrict the behavior of the server in order to use the composition as a test oracle. Restricting the observable behavior in the composition may lead to false negatives during testing. Testing with observable actions is the topic of Chapter 16.

```
namespace SP
{
    [Feature]
    public static class CreditScenario
    {
        static readonly Set<int> C = new Set<int>(2);
        static Set<int> M()
        {
            if (Credits.window.IsEmpty)
                return Set<int>.EmptySet;
            else
                return new Set<int>(Credits.window.Minimum());
        }

        [Action("ReqSetup(m,c)")]
        [Action("ReqWork(m,c)")]
        static void Req([Domain("M")]int m, [Domain("C")]int c) { }
        static bool ReqEnabled(int m) { return m < 3; }

        [Action("ResSetup(m,c,_)")]
        [Action("ResWork(m,c,_)")]
        static void Res(int m, int c){}
        static bool ResEnabled(int m, int c)
        {
            return Credits.requests.ContainsKey(m) &&
                    Credits.requests[m] == c;
        }
    }
    [Feature]
    public static class CancelScenario
    {
        static Set<int> M()
        {
            if (Cancellation.mode.Keys.Count < 2)
                return Set<int>.EmptySet;
            else
                return new Set<int>(Cancellation.mode.Keys.Minimum());
        }

        [Action]
        static void Cancel([Domain("M")]int m) { }
        static bool CancelEnabled(int m)
        {
            return Cancellation.mode[m] == Mode.Sent;
        }
    }
}
```

Figure 14.16. Two scenarios for the composition with the protocol features.

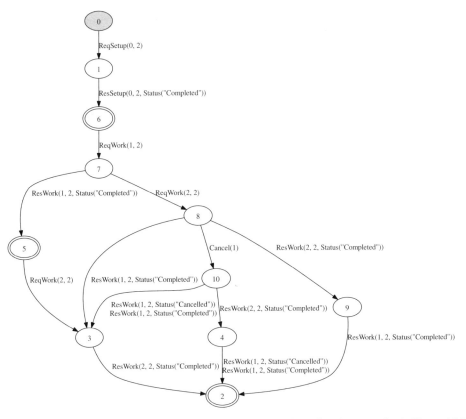

Figure 14.17. Full exploration of the sample protocol model including the scenarios in Figure 14.16.

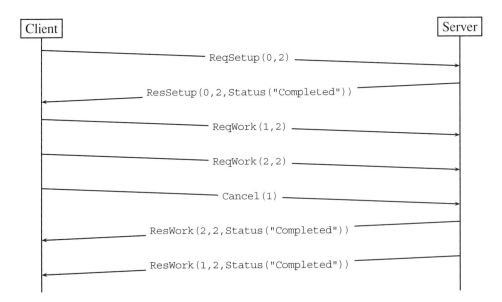

Figure 14.18. A valid trace of actions in Figure 14.17.

14.3 Properties of model program composition

Recall from Section 7.3 that, under composition, model programs synchronize steps for shared actions and interleave actions not found in their common action vocabulary. We now describe in greater detail how actions are combined, taking into account both action symbols and arguments, including the placeholder _ (underscore). Recall that it is the actions (the terms) that are considered when combining actions, not the action methods (the C# code).

It is sometimes easier to reason about properties of composition when the action vocabularies of the composed model programs are the same. In order to do so we use a simple transformation. The effect of interleaving for nonshared actions is achieved by treating actions not in the vocabulary as *self-loops*. We transform a model program M with respect to a set of action symbols $a_1, \ldots, a_k$ into a new model program called a *loop extension of M for* $a_1, \ldots, a_k$, as follows. For each action symbol a_i not in the action vocabulary of M, add a trivial guarded update rule for a_i whose enabling condition is *true*, and whose update rule produces no state updates, that is, every action whose symbol is a_i produces a self-loop in all states of M. In reality, this transformation is not done explicitly but is built into the product operation of model programs.

For example, consider the setup model program in Figure 14.15. The loop extension of the setup model program for Cancel, say SetupC, has the additional transitions

```
t("Inactive", Cancel(), "Inactive")
t("Activating", Cancel(), "Activating")
t("Active", Cancel(), "Active")
```

The *arity* of an action (symbol) is the number of arguments or parameters that it takes. When describing a model program it is often convenient to omit trailing parameters of an action that are not referenced by its guarded update rule. For example, in the sample protocol model, the arity of a cancel action is one, the arity of a request action is two, and the arity of a response action is three. Given an action symbol f with arity k we often use the abbreviated form $f(t_1, \ldots, t_i)$ for some i, $0 \leq i \leq k$, to stand for the term $f(t_1, \ldots, t_i, \_, \ldots, \_)$ with $k - i$ trailing underscores called *placeholders*.[1] For example, Cancel() stands for Cancel(_). An *instance* of an action with placeholders is a replacement of some (or none) of the placeholders with concrete values. A *trace with placeholders* is a sequence of actions with placeholders and an *instance* of a trace with placeholders is an instantiation of some of the placeholders in it. We often say *trace* to mean a trace that may contain

---

[1] Formally, each occurrence of a placeholder represents a fresh logic variable. A term without logic variables is called *ground*.

placeholders. We say that an action or a trace is *concrete* when it has no placeholders. If a trace of a model program has placeholders, then any instance of it is a trace of that model program as well, because a placeholder indicates that the corresponding argument has no behavioral significance with respect to this model program.

For example,

```
ReqSetup(),ResSetup(_,_,STATUS("Completed")),ReqWork()
```

is a trace of the setup model program, whereas

```
ReqSetup(),ResSetup(),ReqWork()
```

is not, because the following instance of it is not a trace of the setup model program.

```
ReqSetup(),ResSetup(_,_,Status("Cancelled")),ReqWork()
```

Two traces *match* if they have a common instance. Notice that two traces that have no placeholders match if and only if they are equal. For example, the trace

```
ReqSetup(1,2),ResSetup(1,_,Status("Completed")),ReqWork(_,3)
```

is an instance[2] of the trace

```
ReqSetup(1),ResSetup(_,_,Status("Completed")),ReqWork()
```

as well as the trace

```
ReqSetup(_,2),ResSetup(1),ReqWork(_,3)
```

Notice that none of the above traces are concrete.

14.3.1 Trace intersection

A desired property of $M_1 \times M_2$ is that the set of all traces of $M_1 \times M_2$ is the *intersection* of the set of all traces of the loop extension of M_1 for A_2, say M_1', and the set of traces of the loop extension of M_2 for A_1, say M_2'. A reason why this property is important is that it makes it possible to do compositional reasoning over the traces in the following sense. If all traces of M_1' satisfy a property p and all traces of M_2' satisfy a property q, then all traces of $M_1 \times M_2$ satisfy both properties p and q. A sufficient condition for the trace intersection property to be true is if M_1 and M_2 don't share any state variables.

Let M_1 be the setup model program in Figure 14.15 and let M_2 be the cancellation model program in Figure 14.7. First, let us see how the model program $M_1 \times M_2$ is constructed. The state variables of $M_1 \times M_2$ is the union of the state variables of M_1 and M_2. Let us call the state variable of M_1 setupMode that may take one of the three

---

[2] It is in fact the *most general common instance* of both traces; i.e., any other instance of both traces is also an instance of the most general common instance.

values "Inactive", "Activating", or "Active". Initially the value of setupMode is "Inactive". The guarded update rule for ResSetup in $M = M_1 \times M_2$ can be given as

```
[Action("ResSetup(m,_,s)")]
public static void ResSetup(int m, Status s)
{
  mode = mode.RemoveKey(m);
  if (s == Status.Cancelled)
    setupMode = "Inactive";
  else
    setupMode = "Active";
}
public static bool ResSetupEnabled(int m, Status s)
{
  return
    setupMode == "Activating" &&
    mode.ContainsKey(m) &&
    (s != Status.Cancelled || mode[m] == Mode.CancelRequested);
}
```

The guarded update rule for ResWork in $M_1 \times M_2$ can be given as

```
[Action("ResWork(m,_,s)")]
public static void ResWork(int m, Status s)
{
  mode = mode.RemoveKey(m);
}
public static bool ResWorkEnabled(int m, Status s)
{
  return
    setupMode == "Active" &&
    mode.ContainsKey(m) &&
    (s != Status.Cancelled || mode[m] == Mode.CancelRequested);
}
```

In $M_1 \times M_2$ the guarded update rule of Cancel is the same as in M_2, because in M_1 Cancel is a self-loop. The following is a trace of $M_1 \times M_2$:

```
ReqSetup(3)
ResSetup(3,_,STATUS("Completed"))
ReqWork(7)
Cancel(7)
ResWork(7,_,STATUS("Completed"))
```

It is clearly also a trace of M_2. It is also a trace of setupC because it is an instance of the trace

```
ReqSetup()
ResSetup(_,_,STATUS("Completed"))
ReqWork()
Cancel()
ResWork()
```

14.3.2 Crosscutting

It is often easier to write separate model programs for different features and to use the product construction to create the product rather than creating the product directly. When creating the product directly, one has to take into account all the possible combinations of the state variables from the different features. Moreover, the full model program can be developed incrementally by adding more feature model programs without having to change the existing ones.

Another advantage of creating separate model programs is that it helps to separate crosscutting concerns by using distinct state variables and in this way simplifies compositional reasoning. Imagine, for example, a model program with a single feature that includes all the features of SP. When doing so, it is natural to introduce a *single* state variable that maps request IDs to compound "request info" values. A request info describes the relevant information about a pending request in a given state, namely the command associated with it, the mode of the request, and the number of requested credits. Separate analysis of the features now requires fairly sophisticated analysis techniques because the state information about the different features is stored in a shared state variable.

14.3.3 Trace inclusion

For scenario control, it is sometimes useful to refer to the state variables of a feature of a model program in order to write a scenario for it. In other words, there is a given model program M with a feature F_1 that is the contract and there is a dependent feature F_2 of M that may read the state variables of F_1 but it may not change the values of those variables. A property that is preserved in this case is that the set of traces of $M[F_1]$ is a *superset* of the set of traces of $M[F_1, F_2]$. Such use of features is usually safe because no new traces can arise.

Two typical uses of dependent features for scenario control are state-dependent parameter generation and enabling condition strengthening. Both uses were illustrated earlier in this chapter with the CreditScenario scenario in Figure 14.16.

14.4 Modeling techniques using composition and features

Composition and features can be used for many different purposes. This has been illustrated with numerous examples in the book. In this section we provide a brief summary of the techniques according to the following topics:

- Feature-oriented modeling
- Scenario control
- Parameter generation
- Property checking
- State refinement

14.4.1 Feature-oriented modeling

This was the main topic of this chapter. The idea is that a large system is divided into separate features. There is one model program per feature. The composition of all the feature model programs is the model program of the whole system. It helps to separate concerns and helps to keep the individual feature model programs managable size. When the features use disjoint state variables it is a matter of style whether to introduce separate model programs (with distinct namespaces) or to use a single model program (with a single namespace) and with multiple *Feature* classes.

14.4.2 Scenario control

The most common style of scenario contol is to write an FSM model program that describes a particular pattern of actions. Such a pattern is usually a regular expression (see also Exercise 4 in this connection). For testing, there is often a *startup* phase consisting of a particular sequence of actions that drive the system under test to a particular state, followed by an *exploration* phase that allows most of the actions to be explored exhaustively, followed by a *finalization* phase that is again a particular sequence of actions that causes the system under test to be cleaned up so that a new test run can be started.

For scenario control one can also use dependent features of model programs for state-dependent enabling condition strengthening.

14.4.3 Parameter generation

A typical use of FSM model programs is to restrict parameter domains of actions of the contract model program so that the composition of the contract model program and the FSM scenario is explorable.

For parameter generation one can also use dependent features of model programs if parameter selection is most conveniently done by reading the state of the contract model program.

14.4.4 Property checking

One can write a model program to describe a temporal property that describes a "bad" behavior of the contract. For example, a certain pattern of actions leads to a state where a safety condition in the property model program is violated. Composition of the contract model program with the property model program can be explored for safety analysis (as we demonstrated in Chapter 7, Section 7.5).

One can also write a state-dependent condition in a separate feature that reads state variables of *multiple* features and defines a global safety condition spanning those features. It is asssumed here that the feature model programs use distinct state variables, so the safety condition is not specific to any single feature model program.

14.4.5 State refinement

One can use composition to abstract details of subbehaviors. The idea is the following. Suppose you have a model program A that includes two actions StartB() and FinishB(). There is another model program B that describes the behavior of B. The only action symbols that A and B have in common are StartB() and FinishB(). When A is explored in isolation, then StartB() leads to a state "B-Is-Working" where the only enabled action is FinishB(). The only action that is initially enabled in B is StartB() and the last action of B is FinishB(). A composition of A and B provides a refinement of the state "B-Is-Working" where all the behavior of B is included.

14.5 Exercises

1. Finish the model program M for $M_1 \times M_2$ that was started in Section 14.3.1 for all actions. Use mpv to convince yourself that the traces of M are the same as the traces of $M_1 \times M_2$.
2. Extend the previous exercise to include also the credits model program and the commands model program.
3. Write a model program M with two features F_1 and F_2 such that F_1 and F_2 share state variables and use the same actions A and B, and the set of traces of M is *not* an intersection of the set of traces of M restricted to F_1 and the set of traces of M restricted to F_2. Use mpv to check the result.
4. Write a utility that given a regular expression over actions (possibly including placeholders) generates the corresponding FSM.

15 Modeling Objects

In the previous chapters we showed how the state variables of a model program can be expressed as the fields of classes declared in a given C# namespace. Up to this point in our presentation such fields have all been global, that is, declared with the C# `static` keyword. In this chapter, we show how model programs can be written to use instance-based fields as state variables. This is sometimes called an *object-oriented* style of modeling.

We will also show how instances of C# classes ("objects") be thought of as abstract identifiers. Abstract values like object IDs may be considered to be an equivalence class when exploring the model. Ignoring states that are structurally identical to a previous state except for their choice of object IDs can make exploration more efficient.

There is nothing fundamental about the object-oriented style of modeling; equivalent behavior can also be expressed using the structure-based style presented in Chapter 10. The motivation for objects is primarily convenience. Many programmers are familiar with the object-oriented style, and writing a model in this style can sometimes improve its readability.

15.1 Instance variables as field maps

Structures like maps can be used to encode state that occurs "per-instance." For example, we could use maps to model a payroll system:

```
namespace Payroll1
{
  class Employee : CompoundValue
  {
    public readonly int id;
    public Employee(int id) { this.id = id; }
  }
```

```
static class Contract
{
    static Map<Employee, int> salary = Map<Employee, int>.EmptyMap;
    // ...
}
}
```

In this example each employee has a salary. There is a state variable called `salary` that maps `Employee` values to integers that represent an employee's pay rate. The value `Employee(1)` might be associated with the salary `200`. The salary field is an example of a *field map*, or table that relates an object identifier to an associated data value. A field map is a way of encoding in a single state variable elements of state that occur on a per-instance basis. Note that the `salary` field itself is global (`static` in C#).

Introducing an identifier class like `Employee` is a modeling idiom that allows us to build up arbitrary object graphs, with independently updated fields. For example, we use a field map to treat salary as a separate element of state. The type `Employee` provides keys for the `salary` field map. The `Employee` class contains only fields that establish identity. Other kinds of data are excluded.

The field map idiom is especially useful when we want to encode *object graphs* with possibly circular references. For example, an employee might have a "backup contact" who handles work in the employee's absence. Backup contacts might introduce circular references in the object graph. (A has B as backup contact and vice versa.)

Note that it wouldn't be possible to add a "backup contact" field to a compound value type like the `Employee` class. You may recall from Section 10.3 that compound values like `Employee` are immutable types with structural equality. Circular references among fields of such types are not possible.

Since the idiom of independently updated per-instance fields occurs frequently, object-oriented languages like C# provide built-in support for instance fields. The NModel framework supports instance fields with a special class that implements field maps in the background. This class is called `LabeledInstance<T>`. You must use this class (or a subclass) to program with objects in NModel. Here is an example:

```
namespace Payroll2
{
    class Employee : LabeledInstance<Employee>
    {
        int salary;
```

```
        public override void Initialize() { this.salary = 0; }
        // ...
    }
}
```

Model program `Payroll1` and `Payroll2` behave similarly. In the case of object-oriented `Payroll2`, the NModel framework will create the field map for `salary` automatically. The field map will record the associated value of each reachable instance of class `Employee`. An object is *reachable* if it occurs within a global state variable, or if it occurs within an instance field of a reachable object. Reachability will be discussed in more detail in Section 15.2.

When inherited by type `T` the `LabeledInstance<T>` class provides the following features:

- An implicit field map for instance fields of `T`, as explained above.
- A serialized *term label* for each instance of `T`. For example, the first instance of class `Employee` may appear as the term `Employee(1)` inside of an action argument. The role of the term label in composition is discussed in Section 15.3. The role of the term label in test harnessing is discussed in Section 15.4.
- A parameter generator for type `T` named `new`. You can use the attribute `[Domain ("new")]` on an action parameter whenever a new object should appear. This is covered in Section 15.2.
- A static factory method called `Create`. This factory method is used instead of C# operator `new` in contexts where a instance of `T` needs to be created within a method. This is an advanced feature; most model programs will use the parameter generator `[Domain("new")]` as a way to introduce new objects instead of the `Create` factory method.
- A virtual method `Initialize`. The model program should override this method for type `T` and reset all instance fields to their initial state.

In the following sections we present some topics that relate to the use of `LabeledInstance<T>` for object-oriented modeling.

15.2 Creating instances

Whenever you model objects, you have to deal with the issue of instantiation. How do instances come into existence? How are they deleted?

For example, we might extend our employee example as follows with actions that add and remove employees from the system. Here we program in an object-oriented style, but without using `LabeledInstance`, managing the IDs and the field map explicitly in our code.

```
namespace Payroll1
{
  class Employee : CompoundValue
  {
      public readonly int id;
      public Employee(int id) { this.id = id; }
  }

  static class Contract
  {
      static int nextId = 1;
      static Set<Employee> allEmployees = Set<Employee>.EmptySet;
      static Map<Employee, int> salary = Map<Employee, int>.EmptyMap;

      static Set<Employee> NextEmployee()
      {
         return new Set<Employee>(new Employee(nextId));
      }

      [Action]
      static void CreateEmployee([Domain("NextEmployee")] Employee emp)
      {
          nextId = nextId + 1;
          allEmployees = allEmployees.Add(emp);
          salary = salary.Add(emp, 0);    // default salary
      }

      [Action]
      static void DeleteEmployee([Domain("allEmployees")] Employee emp)
      {
          allEmployees = allEmployees.Remove(emp);
          salary = salary.RemoveKey(emp);
      }

      [Action]
      static void SetSalary([Domain("allEmployees")] Employee emp, int x)
      {
          salary = salary.Override(emp, x);
      }
  }
}
```

This example shows the basics of maintaining a field map. There is an action CreateEmployee that instantiates new objects. The action DeleteEmployee removes a previously created employee from the state. The SetSalary action changes the salary of a given employee (Override is a method on Map).

```
Trace 1                             Trace 2


CreateEmployee(Employee(1))         CreateEmployee(Employee(1))
SetSalary(Employee(1), 200)         CreateEmployee(Employee(2))
CreateEmployee(Employee(2))         DeleteEmployee(Employee(1))
SetSalary(Employee(2), 400)         SetSalary(Employee(2), 400)
DeleteEmployee(Employee(1))
```

Trace 1 and Trace 2 produce the same end state. In this state the values of the state variables are

```
nextId       = 3
allEmployees = Set<Employee>(Employee(2))
salary       = Map<Employee, int>(Employee(2), 400)
```

This example shows that you can model instances using only the features introduced in the previous chapters.

Now, let's show this same example using C# instance fields. This is an example of how to do object-oriented programming in NModel.

```
namespace Payroll2
{
  class Employee : LabeledInstance<Employee>
  {
    static Set<Employee> allEmployees = Set<Employee>.EmptySet;
    int salary;

    [Action]
    static void CreateEmployee([Domain("new")] Employee emp)
    { allEmployees = allEmployees.Add(emp); }

    [Action]
    [Domain("allEmployees")]
    void DeleteEmployee()
    { allEmployees = allEmployees.Remove(this); }

    [Action]
    [Domain("allEmployees")]
```

```
    void SetSalary(int x)
    { this.salary = x; }

    public override void Initialize()
    { this.salary = 0; }
  }
}
```

If you compare this version to the previous example, you will notice that we have introduced a C# instance field for salary. Also, instance methods have replaced some of the static methods for the actions.

The method of instance creation differs as well. The Domain attribute that supplies parameter values for the CreateEmployee is given the string "new" as its argument. The NModel framework provides a parameter generator function for each class that inherits LabeledInstance<T>.

Both versions of this example have exactly the same possible traces. For example, Payroll1 and Payroll2 may both have the trace:

```
CreateEmployee(Employee(1))
SetSalary(Employee(1), 200)
CreateEmployee(Employee(2))
SetSalary(Employee(2), 400)
DeleteEmployee(Employee(1))
```

If you were to inspect the state, you would see that the modeling tool maintains a field map for you for the salary field. It also maintains state for the next object ID to be allocated.

The keys of a field map created for an instance field contain all reachable instances of the class. At the end of the sample trace shown above, there is just one reachable object, Employee(2). An action like DeleteEmployee(Employee(1)) can eliminate an element in the salary field map because when Employee(1) is removed from the allEmployees field, it becomes unreachable.

Note that actions of the model program may be instance methods. In this case the this parameter becomes the first parameter of the action. Appendix A.1.3 describes in more detail how the parameters of C# methods correspond to the parameters of actions of the model program.

Also, the action vocabulary of a model program consists of distinct symbols. Overloading is not supported for action names. Action names should be chosen so that they are easy to understand and unambiguous. For example, we used CreateEmployee rather than the shorter name Create that would more conflict with action names associated with other data types.

15.3 Object IDs and composition

Whether a model program is written in an object-oriented style is not visible during composition. All kinds of model programs can be composed. In this section we explain how this works.

When a class T inherits the LabeledInstance<T> base class, it gets a built-in term label for instances of T. By default, the term label uses the name of class T as the function symbol of the term and an integer value as the term's argument. For example, in the model program Payroll2, instances of the Employee class have labels like Employee(1), Employee(2), etc.[1]

When objects of type T appear as arguments to actions, the term label of the object is used. Using terms in action arguments provides an insulating layer of syntax. This allows us to compose arbitrary model programs, regardless of whether they are written in an object-oriented style, or with compound value types or as finite state machines.[2]

For example, suppose we have the following scenario described as a finite state machine:

```
FSM(0, AcceptingStates(2), Transitions(
            t(0, CreateEmployee(Employee(1)), 1),
            t(1, CreateEmployee(Employee(2)), 2),
            t(2, SetSalary(_, 0), 2),
            t(2, SetSalary(_, 200), 2)),
        Vocabulary("CreateEmployee", "SetSalary", "DeleteEmployee"))
```

This scenario FSM allows two employees to be created. It then permits any number of SetSalary actions, using either 0 or 200 as the salary argument. It explicitly disallows any DeleteEmployee actions. Figure 15.1 shows this graphically.

This FSM may be composed with model program Payroll2. Figure 15.2 shows the result of the composition.

Notice that the FSM did not define objects or .NET types. It was only necessary that the FSM and the Payroll2 model program agree on the term vocabulary (Employee(1), Employee(2), etc.). When the model program Payroll2 sees a term like Employee(1) it knows to interpret this term as an instance of the Employee class within its context.

---

[1] The NModel framework allows you to choose a symbol other than the type name by means of the [Sort] attribute. For example, we could have annotated class Employee with [Sort("Emp")] if we wanted labels in the form Emp(1), Emp(2), etc.

[2] It is even possible to program your own type of ModelProgram using a derived class. As long as you choose the same vocabulary for the actions and data elements, composition with any of the other ModelProgram types is possible.

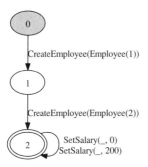

Figure 15.1. Payroll scenario FSM.

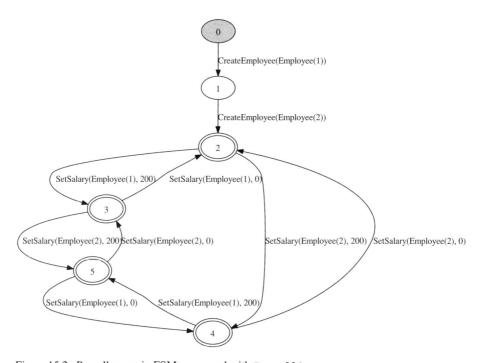

Figure 15.2. Payroll scenario FSM composed with `Payroll2`.

15.4 Harnessing considerations for objects

The term label described in the previous section is also used for harnessing. In other words, whether the model program has been expressed using an object-oriented style or not, the harnessing approach will be the same. This is shown in Figure 15.3.

```
namespace PayrollImpl
{
  class XyzEmployee
  {
    int salary = 0;
    bool active = true;

    public void SetSalary(int x) { this.salary = x; }
    public void Delete() { this.active = false; }
    static public XyzEmployee Create() { return new XyzEmployee(); }
  }

  class Stepper : IStepper
  {
    static Dictionary<IComparable, XyzEmployee> employees =
              new Dictionary<IComparable, XyzEmployee>();

    public CompoundTerm DoAction(CompoundTerm action)
    {
      switch (action.Name)
      {
        case "CreateEmployee":
          XyzEmployee emp = XyzEmployee.Create();
          employees.Add(action[0], emp);
          return null;

        case "DeleteEmployee":
          XyzEmployee emp2 = employees[action[0]];
          emp2.Delete();
          return null;

        case "SetSalary":
          XyzEmployee emp3 = employees[action[0]];
          int value = (int) action[1];
          emp3.SetSalary(value);
          return null;

        default:
          throw new Exception("Unknown action");
      }
    }

    public void Reset() { employees.Clear(); }
  }
}
```

Figure 15.3. Implementation and harness for Payroll2.

The most important part of the harnessing is the dictionary maintained by the harness. This dictionary keeps track of the correspondence between implementation objects and term labels of the model program.

15.5   Abstract values and isomorphic states

It is sometimes useful to think of certain values as being abstract. An *abstract value* in this sense is a value whose only operation is equality. For example, in the `Payroll1` model program of this chapter we might consider values of the `Employee` type to be abstract.

When enumerating the possible states of a model program, it is often useful to exclude states that are structurally identical to a previously seen state except for their choice of term labels for abstract values. We call any two such states *isomorphic states*. The concept of *isomorphism* comes from mathematics and refers to a structure-preserving transformation.

Let's look at an example. If you were to examine the states of Figure 15.2, you would see that state 3 is the following:

```
nextId      = 3
allEmployees = Set<Employee>(Employee(1), Employee(2))
salary      = Map<Employee, int>(Employee(1), 200, Employee(2), 0)
```

State 4 is:

```
nextId      = 3
allEmployees = Set<Employee>(Employee(1), Employee(2))
salary      = Map<Employee, int>(Employee(1), 0, Employee(2), 200)
```

You probably noticed that states 3 and 4 are similar. Both contain one employee with salary 0 and another employee with salary 200. If you were to transform state 4 by renaming `Employee(1)` to `Employee(2)` and vice versa, then you would end up with state 3. If `Employee` values are abstract, then states 3 and 4 are isomorphic states. In other words, two states are isomorphic if there exists a substitution of abstract values that makes them equal.

In NModel we can mark the values of a data type as abstract by annotating the type declaration with an attribute:

```
namespace Payroll1
{
   [Abstract]
   class Employee : CompoundValue
   {
```

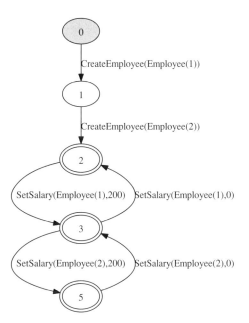

Figure 15.4. Scenario FSM composed with `Payroll1`, with isomorphism reduction.

```
        public readonly int id;
        public Employee (int id) { this.id = id; }
    }
}
```

Figure 15.4 shows the result of eliminating isomorphic states while exploring the composition of `Payroll1` and the FSM scenario of Figure 15.1. This graph was produced by using the `/ExcludeIsomorphicStates` and `/CollapseExcludedIsomor-phicStates` options to the `mpv` tool.

You may annotate `enum` types with the `[Abstract]` attribute as well as classes.

The term labels produced for any subtype `T` of `LabeledInstance<T>` are considered to be abstract. In other words, if you run the exploration tool in a mode that prunes away isomorphic states, states that differ only in the choice of object ID will be eliminated. For example, substituting `Payroll2` (with instance fields) for `Payroll1` (with the compound value type `Employee` marked as abstract) would produce the same exploration graphs.

15.6 Exercises

1. Rewrite the revision control system described in Section 10.4 in a style that uses `CompoundValues` for `File` and `User` data types. Maintain the field maps explictly.

What effect will marking `File` and `User` with the `[Abstract]` attribute have? How is this different from the original model?

2. Rewrite the revision control system described in Section 10.4 in an object-oriented style that uses `LabeledInstance<T>`.

3. How many different ways are there to color the edges of a triangle using two colors? Assume that each side of the triangle is initially uncolored and assume also that colors and triangle edges are abstract values. Check your answer by writing a model program and using the isomorphism reduction feature of `mpv`.

16 Reactive Systems

This chapter discusses testing of reactive systems. Reactive systems take inputs as well as provide outputs in the form of spontaneous reactions. The behavior of a reactive system, especially when distributed or multithreaded, can be nondeterministic. Therefore, the main difference compared to testing of closed systems is that some of the outputs of the implementation under test (IUT) may be outside the control of the tester; that is, the tester cannot predict what the exact output will be during testing. There may be multiple possible outputs and the subsequent tester inputs may depend on those outputs.

Many software systems are reactive, for example many application-level network protocols and multithreaded APIs are reactive. Such systems may produce spontaneous outputs like asynchronous events. Factors such as thread scheduling are not entirely under the control of the tester but may affect the observable behavior. In these cases, a test suite generated offline may be infeasible, since all of the observable behaviors would have to be encoded a priori as a decision tree, and the size of such a decision tree can be very large.

The main topic of this chapter is *on-the-fly* testing of reactive systems. The presentation of most of the material builds on on-the-fly testing of closed systems that was the topic of Chapter 12. In reactive systems, the action vocabulary is divided into *controllable* and *observable* action symbols. This terminology is tailored to match the point of view of the tester. Actions whose symbol is controllable are under the control of the tester and actions whose symbol is observable are under the control of the IUT.

16.1 Observable actions

The action vocabulary of every model program can be split into two sets of action symbols, controllable ones and observable ones. Whether an action symbol is controllable or observable often depends on what part of the system is being tested and what part of its behavior is being controlled. Therefore, this distinction is mostly relevant in the context of generating and executing tests. For ct the option that is used to declare an action symbol observable is `observable` (or `o` for short).

A typical example of an observable action is a response from the server in a client/server protocol model, assuming that the server is being tested for conformance and the behavior of the client is being controlled by the tester. Consider, for example, the model program SP in Chapter 14 and suppose that you want to test that a server conforms to SP. In this case all the responses from the server are observable actions; that is, the actions whose symbol is either `ResSetup` or `ResWork`.

16.1.1 Conformance relation

Given is a model program *MP* and an implementation under test *IUT*, and the question under consideration is whether *IUT conforms* to *MP*. What does that mean? There are two ways to answer this question. The first one is *declarative*; the explanation is in terms of action traces. The second one is *operational*; the explanation is in terms of executing actions in *MP* and *IUT*.

Declarative view. The intuition behind this view is what constitutes a *failure* or a witness of a conformance violation. *MP* and *IUT do not conform* if there exists a trace of actions that is allowed in both *MP* and *IUT*, and after executing that trace in *MP* and *IUT*, either there is a controllable action that is allowed in *MP* but not allowed in *IUT*, or there is an observable action that is allowed in *IUT*, but not allowed in *MP*. In other words, after a sequence of actions which both *MP* and *IUT* agree upon, either there is a controllable action that causes the *IUT* to throw an exception, or there is an observable action output by the *IUT* that causes an enabling condition violation in *MP*.

Operational view. The intuition behind this view is how to implement a conformance tester that detects failures in the above sense. Let S_{MP} stand for the current state of the *MP* and let S_{IUT} stand for the current state of the *IUT*. Say *MP* and *IUT* *conform from S_{MP} and S_{IUT}* if the following two conditions hold:

- If there is a controllable action a that is allowed in S_{MP}, then a must be allowed in S_{IUT}, and *MP* and *IUT* must conform from the states after executing a.
- If there is an observable action a that is allowed in S_{IUT}, then a must be allowed in S_{MP}, and *MP* and *IUT* must conform from the states after executing a.

MP and *IUT conform*, if they conform from the initial states.

Example. Consider the model program SP from Chapter 14 and a server implementation that may sometimes grant too few credits to the client. In Section 16.3 a mock implementation of the server is illustrated that has such a bug. Consider the trace in

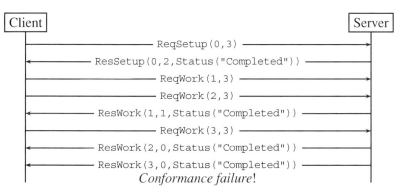

Figure 16.1. A trace of actions illustrating a conformance failure in SP. Observable actions are sent from the server to the client.

Figure 16.1. After the first seven actions, the value of `window` in SP is the empty set and the only request that is still pending is 3. The implementation then outputs the response `ResWork(3,0,Status("Completed"))`. This causes a conformance failure, because this action is not enabled in SP[Credits] (the model program SP with the `Credits` feature included).

16.2 Nondeterminism

Nondeterminism means here that there may be multiple possible observable actions enabled in a given model program state. Although the main emphasis of this chapter is on reactive systems, nondeterministic behavior arises also because of reasons other than reactive behavior.

A common reason for nondeterminism is that the model program is written at a much higher abstraction level than the system that is being modeled. This typically means that there may be many possible IUT states corresponding to a single model program state and therefore the exact behavior of the IUT is not known in a given model program state. Usually the model program needs to be more abstract because it is a *contract* and there may be multiple possible implementations that conform to that contract.

The implementation that is being modeled may also exhibit random behavior. This will also cause nondeterminism in the model program. The difference compared to nondeterminism due to abstraction is that the model program may be more or less at the same abstraction level as the IUT.

In general, reactive behavior leads to spontaneous reactions from the IUT that need to be queued as observable actions by the conformance tester. This leads to asynchronous stepping that is the topic of Section 16.3. There is an important special case of nondeterminism, discussed next, that does not require asynchronous

```
namespace BagModel
{
  [Feature]
  static class Draw
  {
    static Bag<string> B { get { return Contract.content; } }
    static bool drawing = false;

    [Action]
    static void Draw_Start() { drawing = true; }
    static bool Draw_StartEnabled() { return !drawing && !B.IsEmpty; }

    [Action]
    static void Draw_Finish([Domain("B")]string e)
    { drawing = false; Contract.content = B.Remove(e); }
    static bool Draw_FinishEnabled(string e)
    { return drawing && B.Contains(e); }

    [Action("Add"), Action("Delete")]
    [Action("Lookup_Start"), Action("Lookup_Finish")]
    [Action("Count_Start"), Action("Count_Finish")]
    static void Other() { }
    static bool OtherEnabled() { return !drawing; }
  }
}
```

Figure 16.2. A dependent Draw feature for BagModel in Figure 12.2.

stepping. In other words, queueing of obsevable actions is not needed. In this case, nondeterminism is resolved immediately when it occurs. Synchronous stepping, as discussed in Section 12.2.3, is then an adequate solution to harness the IUT for testing.

Shallow nondeterminism. In some cases, nondeterminism arises only because of multiple possible outputs to some inputs. In particular, all states of the model program are such that either all enabled actions in a state are controllable or all enabled actions in a state are observable. Say a state is *active* in the first case and *passive* in the second case. Moreover, a transition from a passive state leads to an active state.

To illustrate this case on a concrete example, recall the bag example from Chapter 12. Suppose that a dependent feature called Draw is added to the bag model program that allows elements to be chosen and removed (drawn) from the bag (see Figure 16.2).

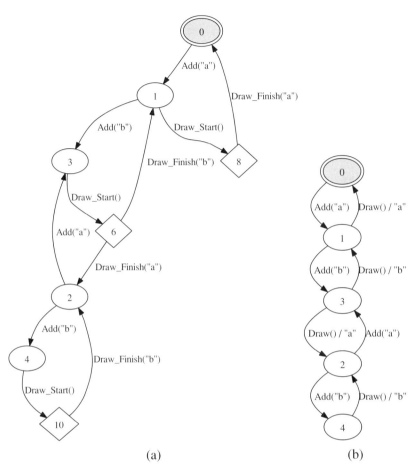

Figure 16.3. Partial exploration of BagModel [Draw]. In (b) passive states are hidden.

The model program has two new actions Draw_Start() and Draw_Finish(e), where the first action represents a request to draw and the second action represents a particular element e that was drawn. This action is nondeterministic because any element in the bag might be drawn (any element from the domain B might be chosen). The state variable drawing is used to disable all actions besides Draw_Finish until the draw operation has been completed.

A partial exploration of BagModel [Draw] with mpv is illustrated in Figure 16.3. All passive states are shown as diamonds in Figure 16.3(a). (The mpv tool can generate a partial exploration interactively, as described in Chapter 6, Section 6.2.3.) The nondeterminism is indicated by the two Draw_Finish transitions exiting from state 6 in Figure 16.3(a) and the two Draw transitions exiting from state 3 in Figure 16.3(b).

16.3 Asynchronous stepping

Recall that testing requires a test harness called a *stepper* (Sections 8.3 and 12.2.3). In order to test a reactive IUT, the IUT has to support the *asynchronous stepper* interface IAsyncStepper that is declared in the NModel.Conformance namespace. The interface derives from the IStepper interface (see Section 12.2.3) and has one additional method called SetObserver. The SetObserver method is invoked initially by the conformance tester to set a callback function that enters observable actions into an *observation queue*. The observation queue is monitored by the conformance tester during test execution, as explained in Section 16.5.

```
namespace NModel.Conformance
{
    public delegate void ObserverDelegate(Action action);

    public interface IAsyncStepper : IStepper
    {
        void SetObserver(ObserverDelegate observer);
    }
}
```

When implementing an (asynchronous) stepper, the basic stepping functionality has not changed. The difference is that the stepper can now, in addition, implement a mechanism that directs asynchronous or spontaneous events produced by the IUT to the conformance tester. In other words, the job of the stepper is to map those events to observable actions that the model program understands and invoke the observer. By invoking the observer, the observable actions are entered into the observation queue to be processed by the conformance tester.

Consider the SP protocol from Chapter 14. Figure 16.4 shows a mock implementation of an SP server. The server has a method Request that starts processing of requests, and an event ResponseEvent that is raised with feedback about finished requests to subscribers of the event. The server also has a Boolean property IsBusy that returns true if the server is not idle. To process a request, the server simply starts a worker thread that, after a short random delay, produces a response where the number of granted credits is a random number not more than the requested number of credits. This server is faulty, because it may grant no credits to the client even when the client has no pending requests and no more unused message ids.

An asynchronous stepper for the server is shown in Figure 16.5. A call to SetObserver with an observer delegate subscribes a response handler (responder) to the response event of the server. The responder maps concrete responses from the server to observable actions and invokes the observer delegate that will enqueue

```
namespace SPImpl
{
  public enum Status { Cancelled, Completed }
  public delegate void ResponseEventDelegate(string cmd, int id,
                                        int credits, Status s);
  public class Server
  {
    Random rnd = new Random();
    int activeRequests = 0;
    public event ResponseEventDelegate ResponseEvent;

    public bool IsBusy { get { return activeRequests > 0; } }

    public void Request(string cmd, int id, int credits)
    {
      activeRequests += 1;
      new Thread(Req).Start(new IComparable[] {cmd, id, credits });
    }

    void Req(object data)
    {
      IComparable[] args = (IComparable[])data;
      Thread.Sleep(rnd.Next(100));
      if (ResponseEvent != null)
        ResponseEvent((string)args[0], (int)args[1],
                      rnd.Next((int)args[2]), Status.Completed);
      activeRequests -= 1;
    }
  }
}
```

Figure 16.4. Mock implementation of an SP server.

them in the observation queue of the conformance tester. The only controllable actions that the stepper recognizes are setup and work actions. The stepper maps a request action to actual request data and calls the server to process the request.

16.4 Partial explorability

Recall that a model program is explorable if all the parameters of all the actions have finite domains in all states. This condition is needed in order to explore the state space of a model program and to visualize it using mpv for example. The

```
namespace SPImpl
{
  public class Stepper : IAsyncStepper
  {
    ObserverDelegate Respond;
    Server server = new Server();

    public void SetObserver(ObserverDelegate obs)
    {
      Respond = obs;
      server.ResponseEvent += new ResponseEventDelegate(Responder);
    }

    void Responder(string cmd, int id, int credits, Status status)
    {
      Action response = Action.Create("Res" + cmd, id, credits, status);
      Respond(response);
    }

    public Action DoAction(Action a)
    {
      switch (a.Name)
      {
        case ("ReqSetup"):
          server.Request("Setup", (int)a[0], (int)a[1]);
          return null;
        case ("ReqWork"):
          server.Request("Work", (int)a[0], (int)a[1]);
          return null;
        default: throw new Exception("Unknown action: " + a);
      }
    }

    public void Reset()
    { if (server.IsBusy) throw new Exception("Server is busy"); }

    public static IAsyncStepper Make() { return new Stepper(); }
  }
}
```

Figure 16.5. Asynchronous stepper of an SP server.

condition can be relaxed when the model program is used for on-the-fly testing with observable actions.

Given a set of action symbols A, a model program is *explorable for* A if the parameters of all the actions in A have finite domains in all states. For on-the-fly testing with observable actions, the model program does not need to be explorable for observable actions. The reason is that the arguments for the observable actions are provided by the stepper. Recall that the fundamental property of model program exploration is that it is *lazy*. During on-the-fly testing, an observable action is executed in the model program only when it has occurred in the implementation, at which point all the parameters have been provided.

Consider the model program SP[Credits,Commands,Setup] with the three included features from Chapter 14. Notice that Cancel is not in the action vocabulary of that model progam. Let us add another feature to SP that restricts the parameters of all the request actions so that each request asks for 3 credits and the requests use ids from the window of allowed message ids.

```
namespace SP
{
  [Feature]
  public static class ReqParams
  {
    readonly static Set<int> C = new Set<int>(3);
    readonly static Set<int> M() { return Credits.window; }

    [Action("ReqSetup(m,c)")]
    [Action("ReqWork(m,c)")]
    static void Req([Domain("M")]int m, [Domain("C")]int c){ }
  }
}
```

The model program SP[Credits,Commands,SetupModel,ReqParams] is explorable for controllable actions but not for observable actions. Nevertheless, it is possible to run ct with the following options, where SP.OTFTest.Make is a factory method for this model program.

```
/r:SPImpl.dll /r:SP.dll SP.OTFTest.Make /iut:SPImpl.Stepper.Make
/o:ResWork /o:ResSetup
```

The following is a sample output that shows a conformance failure similar to the one shown in Figure 16.1. Notice that the reason in the failure has been extracted from the requirement attribute of the ResEnabled1 condition in Section 14.2.1 that refers to the part of the natural language document that specifies the condition that clients must not starve.

```
TestResult(7, Verdict("Failure"),
  "Action 'ResWork(1, 0, Status(\"Completed\"))' not enabled in the model
  Section ...: Client must have enough credits",
    Trace(
      ReqSetup(0, 3),
      ResSetup(0, 1, Status("Completed")),
      ReqWork(1, 3),
      ResWork(1, 0, Status("Completed"))
    )
  )
```

16.5   Adaptive on-the-fly testing

Recall the test execution algorithm from Section 12.5.2. The top-level loop of the adaptive version of the algorithm remains the same. The algorithm RunTest that executes a single test run is extended here to handle the presence of observable actions. The outline of the algorithm is shown in Figure 16.6 and follows very closely the actual implementation in NModel. The extensions, that are emphasized in Figure 16.6, affect only a few places in the code.

In the conformance tester a Boolean variable isAsync indicates if the operation mode is asynchronous. There is an additional variable called obs that is an observation queue or a queue of observable actions. The observation queue is of type TimedQueue<Action> that is defined in the NModel.Algorithms namespace. When a conformance tester is created for a given asynchronous stepper, the stepper is called with SetObserver(obs.Enqueue) to initialize the observer in the stepper with the method that enqueues actions into the observation queue.

When the observation queue is nonempty, the next observation is dequeued from it and conformance to the model program is validated by using the strategy. If the observation queue is empty, a controllable (tester) action is selected using the strategy. If no tester action is enabled in the current state of the strategy, the conformance tester waits for an observable action to arrive within a time limit of obsTimeout milliseconds.

16.5.1   Wait and time-out actions

When the conformance tester is executed in the asynchronous mode, it uses two auxiliary actions. The *wait* action is an internal action that is used when there are no

```
TestResult RunTest(int k)
{
  Sequence<Action> trace = Sequence<Action>.EmptySequence;
  Action o = null;
  while (trace.Count < steps ||
         (!strategy.IsInAcceptingState && trace.Count < maxSteps))
  {
    if (isAsync && o == null && !obs.IsEmpty) o = obs.Dequeue();
    if (o != null)
    {
      trace = trace.AddLast(o);
      string reason = "";
      if (strategy.IsActionEnabled(o, out reason))
      { strategy.DoAction(o); o = null; }
      else return new TestResult(k,Verdict.Failure,reason,trace);
    }
    else
    {
      Action a = strategy.SelectAction(testerActionSymbols);
      if (a == null)
      {
        if (isAsync)
        {
          Action w = strategy.SelectAction(new Set<Symbol>(waitAction));
          int obsTimeout = (w == null ? 0 : (int)w[0]);
          if (w != null){ trace = trace.Add(w); strategy.DoAction(w);}
          if (!obs.TryDequeue(obsTimeout, out o))
            if (strategy.IsInAcceptingState)
              return new TestResult(k,Verdict.Success,"",trace);
            else
              else o = timeoutAction;
        }
        else
        {
          if (strategy.IsInAcceptingState)
          return new TestResult(k,Verdict.Success,"",trace);
          else
            return new TestResult(k, Verdict.Failure,
                        "Did not finish in accepting state", trace);
        }}
      else
      {
        strategy.DoAction(a);
        trace = trace.AddLast(a);
        if (!internalActionSymbols.Contains(a.FunctionSymbol))
        {
          try
          { o = InvokeStepper(a); }
          catch (Exception e)
          { return new TestResult(k,Verdict.Failure,e.Message,trace); }
        }}}}
  if (strategy.IsInAcceptingState)
    return new TestResult(k,Verdict.Success,"",trace);
  else
    return new TestResult(k,Verdict.Failure,
                    "Did not finish in accepting state", trace);
}
```

Figure 16.6. Extension of the algorithm in Figure 12.7 with observable actions.

tester actions enabled and when the observation queue is empty. The default name of a wait action is `"Wait"`, which can be customized using the `waitAction` option of `ct`. A wait action takes one integer argument that specifies the amount of time in milliseconds, called an *observation time-out*. The conformance tester uses the observation time-out to wait for an observable action to arrive.

The simplest way to define a state independent wait action is to use a finite state machine (FSM) model program and to compose it with the main model program. The following FSM, say `Wait20`, specifies a 20-ms observation time-out:

```
FSM(0,AcceptingStates(0),Transitions(t(0,Wait(20),0)))
```

The *time-out* action is an observable action without arguments. It happens if the observation queue is empty after executing a wait action. This results in a conformance failure, unless the time-out action is enabled in the model program. The default name of the time-out action is `"Timeout"`, which can be customized using the `timeoutAction` option of `ct`.

To see the effect of the wait and time-out actions, execute `ct` with the above arguments and add the option `/fsm:Wait20` in order to compose the main model program with `Wait20`. The following is a possible output from this execution:

```
TestResult(0, Verdict("Failure"),
           "Action symbol 'Timeout' not enabled in the model",
      Trace(
          ReqSetup(0, 3),
          Wait(20),
          Time-Out()
      )
)
Reset failed.
```

The specified observation timeout is too small. After the first test case fails, reset also fails because the implementation is still busy. (See the defintion of `Reset` in Figure 16.5.)

16.5.2 Adaptive strategies

Recall the discussion on strategies from Chapter 12. All the techiques discussed there apply in the presence of observable actions as well. For example, execution of `ct` in the previous section used the default strategy that selects controllable actions randomly.

With observable actions one can do more. Note that each time an observable action is consumed in the algorithm in Figure 16.6 the strategy is told to execute that action. When executing an action, the strategy may record history. The selection of actions is always performed on controllable actions, because the strategy is really the *tester* strategy. By knowing that certain actions are observable, the strategy can *learn* from the behavior of the IUT and use that knowledge to improve its selection of controllable actions. The following two situations are particularly interesting.

IUT is determinisitic. A typical situation is that the behavior of the IUT is known to be *deterministic*. This means that if an observable action happens in a certain state, then the same observable action will happen again when that same state is visited. Assume that the model program is written in such a way that its states correspond to the states of the IUT so that there are no "hidden" states. The model program may still allow multiple choices, because it is not known *what* the particular implementation is, only that it is deterministic. Suppose also that all states of the model program are either passive or active.

The strategy can record in a map P for each reached passive state the observable action that occurred in that state. Say that a state is *partially explored* if it is active and there exists an unexplored controllable action that is enabled in that state. Suppose that the goal of the strategy is to maximize transition coverage. When computing what controllable action to select, a possible algorithm could be to select an action that has not been explored or to select an action that takes the strategy closer to a partially explored state. Such an algorithm should be incremental. In this calculation, P is used to determine what transitions take place from passive states.

Suppose, for example, that the bag implementation in Figure 12.1 is extended so that it implements the draw operation deterministically by picking the lexicographically least element from the bag. This would imply that, during test execution, each time state 6 is visited in Figure 16.3, the observable action is Draw_Finish("a").

IUT is random. Another situation is that the behavior of the IUT is random. In this case the notion of partially explored states can be applied to all states, including passive states. If the probabilities of the different observable actions are known, the strategy can select a controllable action that is either unexplored or leads, with high probability, closer to a partially explored state.

Suppose, for example, that the bag implementation in Figure 12.1 is extended so that it implements the draw operation in such a way that each element in the bag is equally likely to be drawn. This would imply that, during test execution, each time state 6 is visited in Figure 16.3(a), both Draw_Finish("a") and Draw_Finish("b") are equally likely to occur. If state 6 is visited multiple times, it is very unlikely that the same element is chosen each time. In fact, it follows under the given assumptions that the probability that both "a" and "b" where chosen at least once at some point grows exponentially in the number of times that state 6 is visited.

16.5.3 Passive testing

An important special case of adaptive on-the-fly testing occurs when *all* the actions are observable. In that case the role of the strategy reduces to checking conformance without ever needing to select tester actions. *Passive testing* can be used, for example, to validate existing logs of events of a concurrent system. In that case each log represents a sequence of events produced by a single agent. Multiple per-agent event logs can be merged into a single log, for example by using the multiplexing technique discussed below.

16.6 Partially ordered runs

This section discusses the problem of producing a sequence of events of a reactive system, such that the sequence respects an underlying *partial order* of those events.

If the IUT is sequential, such as a single-threaded program, events can be enqueued in the order they are observed by the stepper. This is, for example, the case with the bag example above. If the IUT is concurrent, such as a multithreaded program or a distributed system, the problem is that the chronological order in which the events are observed by the stepper and enqueued into the observation queue may differ from the chronological order in which they actually happened, due to buffering and communication delays. This may render the testing process incorrect.

Dependencies between agents, where agents are either threads or processes, usually impose a partial order on the events. For example, send events happen before corresponding receive events in communicating systems. In multithreaded programs, a partial order of events is defined by access to shared resources. An example of a shared resource is a lock.

Suppose that each shared resource R is associated with a *usage count* uc_R that is initially 0. View R as a unary function symbol, and assume that each access (e.g. read or write) to R generates a *resource usage* event $R(uc_R)$ and causes the usage count uc_R to be incremented by one.

Now suppose that there are multiple agents and each agent A generates a sequence of events $(e_1^A, e_2^A, \ldots)$. Say that an event e_i^A *happens immediately before* an event e_j^B, if one of the following two conditions holds:

1. A and B are the same agent and $j = i + 1$.
2. A and B are distinct agents, e_i^A is a resource usage event $R(k)$, and e_j^B is a resource usage event $R(k + 1)$ for some shared resource R.

Figure 16.7 illustrates events of a concurrent system with two agents A_1 and A_2. The sequence of events of an agent is shown as labeled dots along the corresponding horizontal line. An arrow from event x to event y indicates that x happens immediately before y.

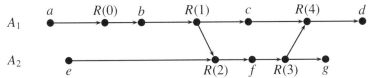

Figure 16.7. Example of a partial order of events of two agents A_1 and A_2.

An event x *happens before* an event z if either x happens immediately before z or if there is an event y such that x happens before y and y happens before z. The happens-before relation is a strict partial order of events. Two events x and y are *incomparable* with respect to the happens-before order if neither x happens before y nor y happens before x.

For example, c happens before d in Figure 16.7. The order is clearly partial; for example, c and e are incomparable, even though both c and e happen before d.

A sequence of events is a *linearization* of a given happens-before order of events if for all events x and y such that x occurs before y in the sequence, either x happens before y or x and y are incomparable.

For example,

$$(a, R(0), b, R(1), c, e, R(2), f, R(3), g, R(4), d)$$

is a linearization of the partial order of events depicted in Figure 16.7.

16.6.1 Multiplexing

Multiplexing is a technique that produces a single sequence of events generated by multiple agents that is a linearization of the happens-before relation. It relies on additional assumptions about the IUT. In particular, this technique assumes an instrumentation of the IUT in such a way that all shared resource usage events are observed.

The multiplexing algorithm (or multiplexer) works as follows. It consumes events from multiple incoming event queues, one queue per agent, and outputs the events in an order that is consistent with the happens-before relation. It is assumed that all events from an agent are enqueued into the event queue of that agent in the same order the events occur in that agent. For each shared resource R the multiplexer records the *expected* usage count k_R that is initially 0. An event E is dequeued from some event queue, if

1. E is not a resource usage event, or
2. E is a resource usage event $R(k)$ for some shared resource R, and $k = k_R$. In this case, k_R is incremenetd by one.

The stepper consumes the events produced by the multiplexer, filters out the resource usage events, and maps all the other events into observable actions that are enqueued into the observation queue of the conformance tester.

Consider the example with two agents A_1 and A_2 depicted in Figure 16.7. A possible sequence of events that are entered into the observation queue is

$$(a, e, b, c, f, g, d)$$

An asynchronous stepper can use a multiplexer to enqueue events into the observation queue of the conformance tester. For example, in the stepper of the SP server shown in Figure 16.5, if the different requests to the server always start different threads that may share resources and the server supports per-thread response handlers, then multiplexing of the thread-based events could be integrated into the responder.

16.7 Exercises

1. Consider the revision control system model program in Chapter 10. What actions are controllable and what actions are observable? Motivate.
2. Extend the sample SP server and stepper to handle cancellation and run ct to experiment with it.
3. Define an FSM that accepts the closure Timeout()* and compose it with the model program SP[Credits,Commands,Setup] and Wait20 as defined in Section 16.5.1. What kind of test results do you expect when you run ct on this?
4. Write a adaptive strategy that tries to cover partially explored states as discussed in Section 16.5.2 assuming that the IUT is determinisitic.
5. Implement the multiplexing algorithm discussed in Section 16.6.1.
6*. Implement a passive tester (as discussed in Section 16.5.3) that multiplexes events from multiple log files.

17 Further Reading

There is a lot of research that has been done in the areas discussed in this part of the book. We mention some works that are related to the topics under discussion, and from which further related work can be found. The selection is far from exhaustive. The discussion follows the structure of this part of the book.

Compositional modeling. Protocol design and the layering principle mentioned in Section 14.1 are discussed in-depth in Comer (2000). The notion of features and the topic of feature interaction have been focused on telecommunication software. There is a series of books (see, e.g., Reiff-Marganiec and Ryan, 2005) that discuss approaches to alleviate the problem in that context. The sample protocol SP used in Section 14.2, although abstract, is related to real-life application-level network protocols such as the ones discussed in Hertel (2003).

Properties of model program composition that are discussed in Section 14.3 are analyzed formally in Veanes et al. (2007a), where composition, as treated in this book, is called parallel composition. The composition of model programs is effectively a program transformation that is most interesting when it is formally grounded in an existing semantics and has useful algebraic properties. The semantics of executing an action in a state with a rich background is founded on *abstract state machines* or ASMs (Gurevich, 1995; Blass and Gurevich, 2000). Determining the action traces that are produced and the properties of traces that are preserved when model programs are composed is founded on the view of model programs as *labeled transition systems* or LTSs (Keller, 1976; Lynch and Tuttle, 1987). The composition of model programs is also related to product of classical automata (Hopcroft and Ullman, 1979). When considering *interaction* of model programs that require synchronization or communication on elements other than actions, composition of model programs may be too limited. A more general notion of composition can be based on the theory interactive ASMs (Blass and Gurevich, 2006).

The topic of Section 14.3.2 is related to the notion of cross-cutting of concerns in aspect-oriented programming (Elrad et al., 2001; Douence et al., 2004).

An approach of using scenario style modeling with model programs written in AsmL (see, e.g., Gurevich et al., 2005) was elaborated in Grieskamp et al. (2004). In order to address a practical demand of Spec Explorer (SpecExplorer, 2006) users, a limited support for scenario-oriented modeling was added to the Spec Explorer tool through *scenario actions*. In Spec Explorer, the user can write models either in AsmL (Gurevich et al., 2005) or in Spec# (Barnett et al., 2005). The need for a general notion of composition, in order to handle other forms of scenario control and parameter generation, has been discussed in several sources (Campbell et al., 2005a; Veanes et al., 2005, 2007a). In this context, *action machines* have been proposed to compose partial behavioral descriptions as a variation of symbolic-labeled transition systems (Grieskamp et al., 2006).

The use of scenarios in the form of *live sequence charts* is discussed as a way both to model and to program reactive systems with the Play-Engine (Harel and Marelly, 2003).

The idea of property checking using model program composition (see Section 14.4.4) is related to the automata theoretic approach to model checking where an automaton corresponding to the negation of the property to be checked is composed with the model (Clarke et al., 1999; Holzmann, 2004).

Modeling objects. The formal treatment of objects is based on the notion of reserve elements from the ASM theory (Gurevich, 1995). In particular, creation of a new object corresponds to importing of a reserve element. The support for modeling with objects was already supported in the AsmL-T tool (Barnett et al., 2003) that is the predecessor of Spec Explorer. Support for dynamic object graphs was also present in the Agedis tools (Hartman and Nagin, 2004).

The state isomorphism problem discussed in Section 15.5 arises when unordered data structures and objects are combined and is as hard as graph isomorphism (Ullmann, 1976; McKay, 1981). The problem occurs very frequently. Already the standard Spec Explorer example known as the chat system uses objects as well as sets and maps; see Utting and Legeard (2006, Section 6.5) for a detailed exposition of this example. The state isomorphism problem was not solved in Spec Explorer.

If objects are not used, then state isomorphism reduces to state equality that can be checked in linear time. This is possible because the internal representation of all data structures can then be canonicalized. The same argument is true if objects are used but all data structures are ordered. Then state isomorphism reduces to heap canonicalization in the context of model checking and can be implemented in linear time (Iosif, 2004; Musuvathi and Dill, 2005). *Bogor* (Robby et al., 2006) is a customizable software model checking engine that uses the method of Iosif (2004) to perform heap canonicalization based on an ordering of object ids. *Korat* (Boyapati et al., 2002) is a tool for automated test generation based on Java specifications. It also uses the concept of heap isomorphism. *Symstra* (Xie et al., 2005) uses a technique that linearizes heaps into integer sequences to reduce checking heap isomorphism to just comparing the integer sequence equality. A survey of symmetry reductions in temporal logic model checking is given in Miller et al. (2006). The general state isomorphism problem and more related work is discussed in Veanes et al. (2007b).

Reactive systems. The idea of on-the-fly testing was pioneered in the context of labeled transition systems using the *IOCO* theory (Tretmans and Belinfante, 1999; Brinksma and Tretmans, 2001; van der Bijl et al., 2004) and has been implemented in tools such as TorX (Tretmans and Brinksma, 2003) and TGV (Jard and Jéron, 2005). IOCO theory is a formal testing theory based on LTSs with input actions and output actions, where input actions correspond to controllable actions and output actions correspond to observable action as discussed in Section 16.1. The IOCO theory is closely related to refinement of interface automata (de Alfaro and Henzinger, 2001; de Alfaro, 2004) that is based on the notion of alternating refinement (Alur et al., 1998). Refinement of interface automata supports the view of testing as a game between a tester and the IUT and is used as the basis for the conformance relation implemented in the Spec Explorer tool (Veanes et al., 2005). The idea of using reinforcement learning during on-the-fly (or online) testing is discussed in Veanes et al. (2006). The relation between IOCO and refinement of interface automata is briefly discussed in Veanes et al. (2005). The declarative view of the conformance relation in Section 16.1.1 when the IUT accepts all inputs is closely related to IOCO, whereas the operational view discussed in the same section is closely related to refinement of interface automata. The use of games for testing is pioneered in Alur et al. (1995). A recent overview of using games in testing is given in Yannakakis (2004). The main emphasis of Chapter 16 is on on-the-fly testing, offline test generation for nondeterministic systems, and related work is discussed in Nachmanson et al. (2004) and Blass et al. (2005). The view of testing as a game is also related to Markov decision processeses (Puterman, 1994; Filar and Vrieze, 1996). On-the-fly testing of real-time embedded systems using model checking theory has been implemented in the Uppaal-Tron tool (Larsen et al., 2005).

The multiplexing technique discussed in Section 16.6.1 is based on Campbell et al. (2005b). The inadequacy of using fully sequential time as a way to understand the runs of a distributed system was first discussed in Lamport (1978). The view presented in Campbell et al. (2005b) is consistent with Lamport's formulation of partially ordered distributed runs. Other work related to multiplexing is discussed in Campbell et al. (2005b).

Part V

Appendices

A Modeling Library Reference

A model program created from C# source consists of actions and variables defined by the types declared in a single namespace. The namespace name is the model program name. For example:

```
namespace MyModelProgram
{
    static class Contract
    {
        static bool MyStateVariable1 = true;

        [Action]
        static void Reset() { /* ... */ }
    }

    class Client : LabeledInstance<Client>
    {
        bool isEntered = false;
        // ...
    }
}
```

The model program named `MyModelProgram` has two state variables, `MyState-Variable1` and `isEntered`, as well as one action named `Reset`. The `isEntered` state variable can be seen as a field map of `Client` object IDs to Boolean values, since it has a value for each instance of the class.

The tools require you to provide a factory method as a command-line argument. The factory method should be a static public method with return type `ModelProgram`. For example,

```
namespace MyModelProgram
{
    public static class Factory
    {
        public static ModelProgram Create()
        {
            return new LibraryModelProgram(typeof(Factory).Assembly,
                                           "MyModelProgram");
        }
    }
}
```

The `Create` method in this example instantiates a `ModelProgram` object from the definitions for the `MyModelProgram` namespace found in the current assembly.

The rest of this appendix describes the attributes and classes provided by the modeling library. The attributes label types, members, and parameters in model program source files. The classes define structural and collection data types for model programs. As described in Section 10.2, a model program must use these classes (instead of the usual .NET collection types) in order to work with the tools.

The final section of this appendix describes how to construct and access the terms used to represent actions, particularly when writing test harnesses.

A.1 Attributes

A.1.1 Features

Classes defined within a model program may be labeled as belonging to named feature sets using the `[Feature]` attribute. A feature is a cluster of related state variables and actions. Only classes may have the `[Feature]` attribute. More than one `[Feature]` attribute may be used on a given class.

Feature attributes may appear in either of two forms: `[Feature]` and `[Feature ("name")]`. If no name is given, then the class name is used as the feature name.

The modeling tools provide a way to selectively load all classes tagged with a given feature name. A typical use of features is to strengthen enabling conditions of the model for scenario control. Another use might be to model slices of functionality in a way that does not require explicit composition of separate model programs.

The following example shows a case of an enabling condition based on the state of other model elements. Note that feature interaction may occur if state defined within one feature is referenced outside of that feature.

```
namespace MyModelProgram
{
    [Feature]
    static class CreditsRestriction
    {
        static int nMsg = 0;

        static bool ResetEnabled()
        {
            return (nMsg < 10 && Contract.MyStateVariable1);
        }

        [Action]
        static void Reset()
        {
            nMsg += 1;
        }
    }
}
```

The factory method to instantiate this feature is the following:

```
namespace MyModelProgram
{
    public static class Factory
    {
        public static ModelProgram Create()
        {
            return new LibraryModelProgram(typeof(Factory).Assembly,
                        "MyModelProgram",
                        new Set<string>("CreditsRestriction"));
        }
    }
}
```

The features to be loaded are included as a Set-valued argument to the constructor. All classes in the given assembly and namespace that contain a matching feature attribute will be loaded as part of the model.

A.1.2 State variables

The state vocabulary of a model program consists of all fields declared within the model program's namespace. Both instance and static fields are included. Public and nonpublic fields are included. Fields inherited from base classes (even those outside of the model namespace) are included.

Sometimes it is useful to exclude a field from state. This might arise for debugging or other purposes, including the implementation of the modeling tool itself. The `[ExcludeFromState]` attribute can be used to annotate fields that should not be part of state. This attribute may only be applied to fields.

Fields excluded from the set of state variables must have no behavior affect on the model, or unpredictable results will occur.

```
namespace MyModelProgram
{
    static class Operations
    {
        [ExcludeFromState]
        static int debugCount = 0;

        // ...
    }
}
```

A.1.3 Actions

The action vocabulary of the model is given by the `[Action]` attribute. The `[Action]` attribute applies only to methods.

There are three forms:

```
[Action]
[Action("label")]
[Action(Start="label", Finish="label")]
```

where `label` is a string in the form

```
label       :== action-name [ "(" [ arg { "," arg }* ] ")" ]
action-name :== id
arg :== "this" | "result" | "_" | id
id :== ( letterOrDigit | '@') { letterOrDigit | '_' }*  // lexical
letterOrDigit :== ... as defined by Char.IsLetterOrDigit method in .NET
```

The simple form of the `[Action]` attribute indicates that a default action label should be used.

- If the target method has no outputs (i.e., it has a void return value and does not have any byref or out parameters), then a single action with the same name and arguments as the target method is produced. For example,

```
[Action] static void Foo(int x) { /* ... */ }
```

produces an action label in the form Foo(x). The action is atomic.
- If the method has outputs, then the default vocabulary is a start action (whose arguments are the inputs) and a finish action (whose arguments are the outputs). In that case, the default action names are methodName_Start and methodName_Finish, respectively. For example,

```
[Action]
static bool Foo(int x, byref string s, out int val) { /* ... */ }
```

produces in start action label with the input parameters

```
Foo_Start(x, s)
```

and a finish action label whose arguments are the outputs with result first and the remaining out or byref arguments in the order they appear in the target method.

```
Foo_Finish(result, s, val)
```

Note that that byref argument s appears in both input and output labels.

If a name (without parentheses) is given in the action attribute, then the same default behavior occurs as above, except that the user-provided action name is used instead of the method name. For example,

```
[Action("Bar")]
static bool Foo(int x, byref string s, out int val) { /* ... */ }
```

produces labels Bar_Start(x, s) and Bar_Finish(result, s, val).

The symbol this is used for the implicit first argument of an instance method. By default, the parameter this appears as the first input action parameter for an action whose target method is instance-based.

The symbol result is used to denote the return value of the method. By default, the parameter result appears as the first output action parameter.

The extended forms of the [Action] attribute give the user control over the action names, order of parameters, and the possibility of adding placeholder parameters. The idea is that in cases when you need to give more detail, you can use a form of the [Action] attribute that lets you define the action vocabulary more explicitly.

"Don't care" parameters. Sometimes (especially when composition is involved, but also for certain test harnessing requirements) you want to include a placeholder parameter in an action's signature. In this case, you would indicate the placeholder with an underscore, _, in the signature.

```
[Action("Foo(_, x)")] static void
MyFoo(int x) { _ }
```

The action label takes two parameters, but the first parameter is ignored.

Reordering of arguments. Overriding the default action label lets you specify a different order of arguments for the action label than is provided by the method being attributed. For example,

```
[Action("Foo(y, x)")]
static void MyFoo(int x, int y) { /* ... */ }
```

In this example the order of x and y are swapped. Note that all of the input parameters of the method must be mentioned in the action label. No output parameter may be mentioned in the input action label.

Similarly, the order of outputs may be customized:

```
[Action(Start="Foo_Start(x, s)",
        Finish="Foo_Finish(s, result)")]
static bool Foo(int x, byref string s, out int val) { /* ... */ }
```

In this example the order of result and s are swapped in the label for the output action. It is possible to omit some output parameters of the target method from the output action label if desired. Also, input parameters may appear in the output label.

"Split" actions. Sometimes (especially in describing scenarios) it is necessary to say that a method that produces no outputs should be split into start and finish actions. In this case the start and finish actions can be given explicitly.

```
[Action(Start="Foo_Start(x)", Finish="Foo_Finish()")]
static void Foo(int x) { /* ... */ }
```

Multiple attributes per method. More than one action attribute may appear for a given method. This is interpreted as separate actions that share a common update rule.

```
[Action("Foo(_, x)")]
[Action("Bar(x)")]
static void MyFoo(int x) { /* ... */ }
```

The example above defines two actions with differing signatures that share a common enabling condition and update. In the example, the MyFoo method is the implementation of the Foo action and the Bar action. (This case arises when modeling feature slices.)

Multiple methods per action. The same action attribute (with user-provided label) may appear in front of methods split across features. This is interpreted as defining a single action whose preconditions and updates are composed. (This case arises when modeling feature slices.)

```
[Feature("Feature1")]
static class C1
{
    [Action("Foo(y, x)")]
    static void MyFoo(int x, int y) { /* ... */ }
}

[Feature("Feature2")]
static class C2
{
    [Action("Foo(_, z)")]
    static void MyBar(int z) { /* ... */ }
}
```

In this example, a single action with two parameters is defined. The enabling condition of action Foo is the conjunction of the enabling conditions given in the body of MyFoo and MyBar. The update of action Foo is the state change produced by invoking MyFoo and MyBar in any order (the model must be written such that order of update of partial action methods does not matter).

A.1.4   Enabling conditions

Actions are enabled by Boolean-valued methods called *enabling conditions*, *preconditions*, or *guards*.

By convention, the enabling conditions of an action method have the same name as the action method plus Enabled, possibly followed by one or more decimal digits. For example,

```
static void FooEnabled() { return mode == Mode.Start; }
static void FooEnabled(int x) { return x > 0; }
static void FooEnabled2(int x) { return x < 100; }
```

```
[Action]
static void Foo(int x)
{
    mode = Mode.Running;
}
```

In this example, the methods `FooEnabled()`, `FooEnabled(int)`, and `FooEn-abled2(int)` are enabling conditions of action `Foo`.

Note that an action method may have more than one enabling condition by overloading. An enabling condition method may have fewer arguments than (but no more than) its associated action method. The type of each parameter of enabling condition method must match the type of the corresponding parameter in the action method.

A static enabling condition method may be used for an instance-based action method. If the static enabling condition method takes parameters, the first parameter must represent the `this` parameter:

```
class Bar
{
    static void FooEnabled(Bar obj)
    {
        return obj != null && obj.mode == Mode.Start;
    }

    static void FooEnabled(Bar obj, int x)
    {
        return x > 0;
    }

    [Action]
    void Foo(int x)
    {
        this.mode = Mode.Running;
    }
}
```

A.1.5 Parameter domains

Model programs may be given finite domains for exploration. This is done using the [Domain] attribute applied to method parameters. The form of the domain attribute is

```
[Domain("name")]
```

where *name* is a string naming a method, property, or field in the containing class. An example of its use is

```
[Action]
static void Foo([Domain("SomeInts")] int x)
{
    /* ... */
}

static readonly Set<int> SomeInts = new Set<int>(1, 2, 3, 4);
```

If a method name is given as the domain name and the action method is static, then the domain method must also be static. For an instance-based action method, domain methods may be either static or instance-based. Domain methods must take no parameters. Their return type must be a Set<T>, where T is the type of the parameter being attributed.

Only types with finite domains have default domains. This includes System. Boolean and all enum types.

The domain attribute may be applied to instance methods to give the possible values of the implicit this parameter of the instance method.

A.1.6   Accepting state conditions

Runs of a model program may terminate only in an accepting state. The predicates that determine whether a given state is an accepting state are given by the [AcceptingStateCondition] attribute. The target of this attribute may be a method, field, or property.

An example of the use of this attribute is

```
namespace MyModelProgram
{
    static class Contract
    {
        static Set<int> pendingRequests = Set<int>.EmptySet;

        [AcceptingStateCondition]
        static bool NoPendingRequests()
        {
            return pendingRequests.IsEmpty;
        }
    }
}
```

If the target of an [AcceptingStateCondition] attribute is a method, it is possible for the method to be a static method or an instance method. In the case of an instance method, the state is accepting if the condition holds for all reachable instances of the class. The return type must be System.Boolean.

A.1.7   State invariants

It is possible to indicate conditions called state invariants that must hold in every state. The failure of any state invariant indicates a modeling error.

The [StateInvariant] attribute indicates that the target method, field, or property must hold in every state.

An example of the use of this attribute is

```
namespace MyModelProgram
{
    static class Contract
    {
        static Set<int> pendingRequests = Set<int>.EmptySet;
        static int nPendingRequests = 0;

        [StateInvariant]
        static bool IsConsisitent()
        {
            return pendingRequests.Count == nPendingRequests;
        }
    }
}
```

If the target of an [StateInvariant] attribute is a method, it is possible for the method to be a static method or an instance method. In the case of an instance method, the state invariant is said to hold if the return value is true for all reachable instances of the class. The return type must be System.Boolean.

A.1.8   State filters

A state filter is a Boolean condition that indicates that a state, although valid, should be excluded from exploration. The [StateFilter] attribute indicates that its target method, property, or field is a state filter. A value of true indicates that the state will be included; false means exclusion from exploration.

```
namespace MyModelProgram
{
    static class Contract
```

```
    {
        static Set<int> pendingRequests = Set<int>.EmptySet;

        [StateFilter]
        static bool LimitNumberOfRequests()
        {
            return pendingRequests.Count < 4;
        }
    }
}
```

State filters are often used in conjuction with a [Feature] attribute so that they may selectively applied.

A.1.9   State properties

The [StateProperty] attribute indicates additional information that may be used by the exploration algorithm when deciding which states to explore. It may be applied to a method, property, or field. Properties are named. If a name is not given in the attribute, the property name defaults to the target name.

```
namespace MyModelProgram
{
    static class Contract
    {
        static Set<int> pendingRequests = Set<int>.EmptySet;

        [StateProperty("NumberOfRequests")]
        static int RequestCount()
        {
            return pendingRequests.Count;
        }
    }
}
```

A.1.10 Requirements

It is sometimes useful to document the link between the elements of a model program and a natural language requirements document. We use an attribute in the form [Requirement("*string*")] for this purpose. The string *string* provides traceability back to an external requirement source.

Requirement strings are printed in error contexts such as conformance failures and state invariant violations. They can also be used to check for coverage of requirements.

The [Requirement] attribute may be applied to any .NET attributable element. More than one [Requirement] attribute may be provided for an entity.

```
static class Bar
{
    [Requirement("XYZ spec 3.2.4: Foo parameter must be nonnegative")]
    static void FooEnabled(int x)
    {
        return x > 0;
    }

    [Action]
    static void Foo(int x)   { /* ... */ }
}
```

A.2 Data types

A.2.1 Compound value

CompoundValue
Base class for data records with structural equality.

Syntax

public abstract class CompoundValue : AbstractValue, IComparable

Methods

CompareTo(Object)
  Term order. Comparison is based on type and recursively on fields.

ContainsObjectIds()
  Determines if this value has an object id (i.e., is of type LabeledInstance) or has a subvalue that has an object id (e.g., a set of instances).

Equality(CompoundValue, CompoundValue)
  Term equality.

FieldValues()
  Returns an enumeration of all (readonly) field values of this compound value in a fixed order.

GreaterThan(CompoundValue, CompoundValue)
   Term greater than.

GreaterThanOrEqual(CompoundValue, CompoundValue)
   Term greater than or equal.

Inequality(CompoundValue, CompoundValue)
   Inequality of terms.

LessThan(CompoundValue, CompoundValue)
   Term less than.

LessThanOrEqual(CompoundValue, CompoundValue)
   Term less than or equal.

Properties

AsTerm
   Returns the term representation of this value.

Sort
   Returns the sort (abstract type) of this value.

Remarks

A CompoundValue is similar to a .NET struct, but unlike a struct subtypes of CompoundValue may implement tree structures. By construction, such values may be recursive but must have no cycles. (From the point of view of mathematical logic, values of this type can be thought of as a term whose function symbol is the type and whose arguments are the field values.)

CompoundValues are commonly used in modeling abstract state. They should be used instead of mutable classes whenever practical because they can reduce the amount of analysis required when comparing if two program states are equal. They also tend to promote a clear style, since they are read-only data structures. Aliased updates can thus be avoided.

Invariant: All field values (returned by the FieldValues method) must have a fixed order and contain elements of type IComparable that satisfy the predicate IsAbstractValue(Object). All fields of subtypes of this class must be readonly. This invariant holds for subtypes of CompoundValue such as the collection types desribed below. The type parameter T for the collection types must support interface IComparable.

A.2.2   Set

Set<T>
An unordered collection of distinct values. This type is immutable and uses structural equality. Add/remove operations return a new set.

Syntax

```
public sealed class Set<T> : CollectionValue<T>
```

Constructors

Set<T>()

Constructs an empty set of type T. The static field Set<T>.EmptySet should be used instead of this constructor.

Set<T>(IEnumerable<T>)

Constructs a set containing all enumerated elements.

Set<T>(T[])

Constructs a set from the elements given in the argument list.

Methods

The following entries describe some of the methods of this type. Many more are described in the library documentation.

Add(T)

Returns a set with all of the elements of the current set, plus the value given as an argument.

BigIntersect(Set<Set<T>>)

(Static method.) Distributed intersection. Returns the set that is the intersection of all the sets contained in the argument value; that is, the result contains the elements that are shared among all of the sets.

BigUnion(Set<Set<T>>)

(Static method.) Distributed set union. Returns a set containing all of the elements of each set contained in the argument value.

Choose()

Selects an arbitrary value from the current set using internal choice.

Contains(T)

Tests whether the given element is found in the set.

Difference(Set<T>)

Set difference. Same as operator -.

Exists(Predicate<T>)

Existential quantification. Returns true if the predicate holds for at least one element of the current set.

ExistsOne(Predicate<T>)

Unique quantification. Returns true if the predicate holds for exactly one element of the set, false otherwise.

Forall(Predicate<T>)
: Universal quantification. Returns `true` if the predicate holds for all elements of the set and `false` otherwise.

Intersect(Set<T>)
: Set intersection. Same as operator *. This is the set of all elements shared by the current set and the set given as the argument.

IsProperSubsetOf(Set<T>)
: Proper superset relation.

IsProperSupersetOf(Set<T>)
: Proper subset relation.

IsSubsetOf(Set<T>)
: Subset relation.

IsSupersetOf(Set<T>)
: Superset relation.

Maximum()
: Returns the greatest value in the set under the term ordering defined by Compare-Values(Object, Object).

Minimum()
: Returns the least value in the set under the term ordering defined by Compare-Values(Object, Object).

Reduce<S>(Reducer<T, S>, S)
: Iteratively applies a reducing function to map a set into a single summarized value.

Remove(T)
: Returns a set containing every element of this set except the value given as a parameter. If value is not in this set, then returns this set.

Union(Set<T>)
: Same as operator + (set union).

etc. . . .

Many more methods are described in the library documentation.

Properties
The following entries describe some of the properties of this type. Several more are described in the library documentation.

Count
: Returns the number of elements in the set (also known as the cardinality of the set).

IsEmpty
> Returns `true` if the set has no elements. Returns `false` otherwise.

etc. ...

Fields
EmptySet
> (Static.) The empty set of sort T.

Remarks
Set is an immutable type. Add/remove operations return a new set. Comparison for equality uses `Object.Equals`.

Formally, this data type denotes a pair (elementType, untyped set of values), where the element type is given by the type parameter T. As a consequence, sets are equal only if they are of the same sort (element type) and contain the same elements. For example, `Set<int>.EmptySet != Set<string>.EmptySet`.

A.2.3   Map

Map<T,S>

A finite mapping of keys to values. This type is immutable and uses structural equality. Add/remove operations return a new map.

Syntax
```
public sealed class Map<T, S> : CollectionValue<Pair<T, S>>
```

Constructors
The following entries describe some of the constructors of this type. Several more are described in the library documentation.

Map<T,S>()
> Default constructor. The static field `Map<T,S>.EmptyMap` is preferred and should be used instead of this constructor.

Map<T,S>(T,S)
> Creates a map from the key and value given as arguments.

Map<T,S>(IEnumerable<Pair<T,S>>)
> Creates a map from pairs of keys and values.

Map<T,S>(Pair<T,S>[])
> Creates a map with a `params` array of key/value pairs.

etc. ...

Methods

The following entries describe some of the methods of this type. Many more are described in the library documentation.

`Add(T, S)`

Produces a map that contains all the key/value pairs of the current map, plus the given key/value pair.

`Add(Pair<T,S>)`

Produces a map that contains all the key/value pairs of the current map, plus the given key/value pair.

`Contains(Pair<T,S>)`

Tests whether the given key/value pair is found in the current map. See `ContainsKey(T)` instead if you want to check if a given key is in the map.

`ContainsKey(T)`

Returns `true` if the map contains the given key, `false` otherwise.

`Difference(Map<T,S>)`

Map difference. Returns all of the key/value pairs in the current map that are not found in the map given as the argument. If the two maps share keys, the corresponding values must be the same, or an exception is thrown. This is the same as C# infix operator `-`.

`Override(T, S)`

Map override. Returns a map with the same key/value pairs as the current map, plus the key/value pair given by the arguments. If the key exists in the current map, the value of this key in the result will be the value of the second argument to this method.

`Override(Map<T, S>)`

Map override. Returns the map that contains all key/value pairs of the map `s` given as the argument and those key/value pairs of the current map for which there is no corresponding key in `s`. In other words, this operation combines the current map and `s` in a way that gives priority to `s`.

`Override(Pair<T, S>)`

Map override. Returns the map that contains all key/value pairs of the current map along with key/value pair `d` given as the argument, except that if the key of `d` is in the current map, the value of `d` will replace (i.e., override) the corresponding value from the current map in the result.

`Remove(Pair<T, S>)`

Returns a map with the same key/value pairs as the current map, except for the key/value pair given as the argument. If the key is present in the current map but is associated with a different value, then an exception is thrown.

`RemoveKey(T)`
> Returns a map with the same key/value pairs as the current map, except for the key/value pair whose key is given as the argument.

`RestrictKeys(IEnumerable<T>)`
> Returns a map consisting of the elements in the current map whose key is *not* in the collection given as an argument.

`RestrictValues(IEnumerable<S>)`
> Returns a map consisting of the elements in the current map whose value is *not* in values.

etc. . . . .

Many more methods are described in the library documentation.

Properties
The following entries describe some of the properties of this type. Several more are described in the library documentation.

`Count`
> The number of key/value pairs contained in the map.

`EmptyMap`
> The empty map of sort `<T, S>`.

`IsEmpty`
> Returns `true` if the map has no elements. Returns `false` otherwise.

`Keys`
> The set of keys in the map (i.e., the domain of the map).

`Values`
> The set of values in the map (i.e., the range of the map).

etc. . . . .

Remarks
Maps associate keys with values. Maps are similar to the .NET `Dictionary` objects but are immutable and use structural equality. Add/remove operations return new maps.

A.2.4 Sequence

`Sequence<T>`
An ordered collection of (possibly repeating) values. This type is immutable and uses structural equality. Add/remove operations return a new sequence.

Syntax

```
public sealed class Sequence<T> : CollectionValue<T>
```

Constructors

`Sequence<T>()`

Constructs an empty sequence. The static field `Sequence<T>.EmptySequence` is preferred instead of this constructor.

`Sequence<T>(IEnumerable<T>)`

Constructs a sequence from the elements in a collection.

`Sequence<T>(T[])`

Constructs a sequence from `params` arguments.

Methods

The following entries describe some of the methods of this type. Many more are described in the library documentation.

`AddFirst(T)`

Returns a sequence whose `Head` is the element given as the argument and whose `Tail` equals the current sequence.

`AddLast(T)`

Returns a sequence whose `Front` equals the current sequence and whose `Last` is the element given as the argument.

`BigConcatenate(IEnumerable<Sequence<T>>)`

(Static method.) Distributed concatenation. Returns the sequence formed by concatenating each sequence from a collection of sequences in turn. Returns the empty sequence if the collection given as the argument is empty.

`Concatentate(Sequence<T>)`

Sequence concatenation. Returns the sequence consisting of the elements of the current sequence followed by the elements of the sequence given as the argument. This is the same as the C# infix operator `+`.

`Contains(T)`

Tests whether the given element is found in the sequence.

`IndexOf(T)`

Returns the zero-based index of the first occurrence of the given element in the sequence, or `-1` if it doesn't occur.

`IsPrefixOf(Sequence<T>)`

Returns `true` if the elements of the current sequence are the first elements of the sequence given as the argument, and `false` otherwise.

LastIndexOf(T)

Returns the zero-based index of the last occurrence of the given object in the sequence, or -1 if it doesn't occur.

Remove(T)

Returns a sequence that is identical to the current sequence but without the first occurrence of the element given as the argument.

Reverse()

Returns a sequence whose elements are the same as the current sequence but in reverse order.

Unzip<T2>(Sequence<Pair<T, T2>>)

(Static method.) Returns a pair of sequences whose elements are drawn from a sequence of pairs.

Zip<T2>Sequence<T>, Sequence<T2>

(Static method.) Returns a sequence of pairs of elements from the sequences given as arguments.

etc. . . .

Many more methods are described in the library documentation.

Properties

The following entries describe some of the methods of this type. Several more are described in the library documentation.

Count

Gets the number of elements contained in the sequence.

Front

Returns the subsequence of the current sequence where the last element is removed.

Head

Returns the first element of the sequence. Throws an exception if the sequence is empty.

IsEmpty

Returns true if the sequence has no elements. Returns false otherwise.

Item(int)

Gets the element at the specified index. This is the C# indexer operator. Note: This is a linear-time lookup provided for convenience when sequences have only a few elements or when accessing elements near the beginning or end of a larger sequence. The data type ValueArray<T> is better suited to large numbers of elements that require frequent random access but infrequent addition or removal of elements. The data type `Sequence<T>` is better suited to frequent addition or deletion and recursive subdivision via `Head` and `Tail` operations.

`Last`

Returns the last element of the current sequence.

`Tail`

Returns the subsequence of the current sequence where the first element is removed. Throws an exception if the sequence is empty.

etc. . . .

Several more properties are described in the library documentation.

Fields

`EmptySequence`

The empty sequence of sort `T`.

Remarks

Sequences contain indexable elements. Sequences are similar to ArrayLists, but unlike ArrayLists, they are immutable. Sequences are implemented as doubly linked lists (concatenation to the beginning or end is constant time). Lookup is linear time; if possible, callers should use `foreach(T val in sequence)` . . . instead of `for(int i = 0; i < sequence.Count; i += 1)` . . . `sequence[i]` . . .

A.2.5   Value array

ValueArray<T>

Immutable type that provides structural equality for arrays.

Syntax

`public sealed class ValueArray<T> : CollectionValue<T>`

Constructors

`ValueArray<T>(T[])`

Methods

The library documentation describes the methods of this type. They are similar to the methods for the other NModel collection types.

Properties

The following entries describe some of the methods of this type. Several more are described in the library documentation.

`Count`
   Returns the number of elements in the value array.

`IsEmpty`
   Returns `true` if the value array has no elements. Returns `false` otherwise.

`Item(int)`

`Length`

etc. . . .

A.2.6   Bag

`Bag<T>`
An unordered collection of possibly repeating elements. This is also known as a multiset. The type is immutable; add/remove methods return a new bag.

Syntax
```
public sealed class Bag<T> : CollectionValue<T>
```

Constructors
`Bag<T>()`
   Constructs an empty bag. The static field `Bag<T>.EmptyBag` is preferred instead of using this form of the constructor.

`Bag<T>(IEnumerable<T>)`
   Constructs a bag with elements taken from a collection. The `Count` of the resulting bag will be the same as the number of values in the collection given as the argument.

`Bag<T>(T[])`
   Constructs a bag with elements given as `params` arguments. The `Count` of the bag will be the same as the number of arguments to the constructor.

`Bag<T>(IEnumerable<Pair<T, int>>)`
   Constructs a bag with elements and their corresponding multiplicities given as a pair enumeration.

`Bag<T>(Pair<T, int>[])`
   Constructs a bag with `params` arguments that are pairs of elements and their corresponding multiplicities.

Methods
The following entries describe some of the methods of this type. Many more are described in the library documentation.

`Add(T)`

Creates a bag that is the same as this bag except that the multiplicity of the value given as the argument is one larger.

`CountItem(T)`

Returns the number of times the value given as the argument appears in this bag. This number is called the item's multiplicity.

`Difference(Bag<T>)`

Creates a bag where the multiplicity of each element is the difference of the multiplicities in the current bag and the bag `s` given as the argument; that is, it returns a bag where all the elements of `s` have been removed from this bag. This is the same as the C# infix operator `-`.

`Intersection(Bag<T>)`

Bag intersection. Returns the bag containing the elements that are shared by the current bag and the bag given as the argument. The multiplicities of the result are pairwise minimums of those of the arguments. This is the same as the C# infix operator `*`.

`Remove(T)`

Creates a bag with the same elements as the current bag, except that the multiplicity of the element `x` given as the argument is decremented by one. This operation returns the current bag if the multiplicity of `x` is zero.

`RemoveAll(T)`

Creates a bag with the same elements as this bag, except that all occurrences of the element given as the argument are omitted.

`Union(Bag<T>)`

Creates a bag where the multiplicities of each element are the sum of the multiplicities of the elements of the current bag and the bag given as the argument.

etc. . . . .

Many more methods are described in the library documentation.

Properties

The following entries describe some of the properties of this type. Several more are described in the library documentation.

`Count`

Returns the number of elements in the bag. This is sum of all multiplicities of the unique elements in this bag.

`CountUnique`

Returns the number of unique elements in this bag. (Note: This is less than the number of elements given by `Count` if some elements appear more than once in the bag.)

IsEmpty
> Returns `true` if the bag has no elements. Returns `false` otherwise.

Keys
> Returns a set of all elements with multiplicity greater than zero.

etc. ...

Several more properties are described in the library documentation.

Fields

EmptyBag
> (Static field.) The bag of type T that contains no elements.

Remarks

For any value x, the multiplicity of x is the number of times x occurs in the bag, or zero if x is not in the bag.

The data type is immutable; add/remove operations return a new bag.

Equality is structural. Two bags are equal if they contain the same elements with the same multiplicities. Order does not affect equality.

A.2.7   Pair

`Pair<T,S>`
Binary tuples with structural equality.

Syntax

```
public struct Pair<T, S> : IAbstractValue, IComparable
```

Constructors

Pair<T, S>(T, S)
> Initializes a new instance of a pair with the given arguments.

Methods

Equality(Pair<T, S>, Pair<T, S>)
> Deep structural equality on Pairs

etc. ...

Properties

First
> The first value.

Second
  The second value.

etc. . . .

A.2.8   Triple

`Triple<T,S,R>`
Triples with structural equality.

Syntax
`public struct Triple<T, S, R> : IAbstractValue, IComparable`

Constructors
`Triple<T, S, R>(T, S, R)`
  Initializes a new instance of a triple with the given arguments.

Methods
`Equality(Triple<T, S, R>, Triple<T, S, R>)`
  Structural equality.

etc. . . .

Properties
`First`
  The first value.

`Second`
  The second value.

`Third`
  The third value.

etc. . . .

A.2.9   Labeled instance

`LabeledInstance<T>`
Base class for types with instance fields as state variables. Each type `T` that includes
instance fields that act as state variables of a model program must inherit the base
class `LabeledInstance<T>`.

Syntax
`public class LabeledInstance<T> : LabeledInstance`

Constructors

`LabeledInstance<T>()`

Each subtype `T` of `LabeledInstance<T>` must provide a public default constructor. This constructor may not change state.

Methods

`CompareTo(Object)`

`ContainsObjectIds()`

Returns `true`.

`Create()`

(Static method.) Factory method that allocates a new object. This factory must be used in the model instead of the public constructor. Most models will create instances via the `[Domain("new")]` attribute applied to an action argument instead of this factory method. The `Create` method may only be invoked within the context of an action method.

`GetSort()`

The sort (abstract type) of `T`. Sorts are used to match types across model programs.

`Initialize()`

Each subtype `T` of `LabeledInstance<T>` must override the `Initialize` method. This method resets all of the instance fields of the current object to their initial values.

Properties

`AsTerm`

Returns the term representation of this value.

`Label`

`Sort`

Returns the sort (abstract type) of this value.

Remarks

You must use a type `T` that is a subtype of `LabeledInstance<T>` to program with objects in NModel. See Chapter 15.

A.3 Action terms

This section explains how to construct and access the terms used to represent actions.

The `Action` data type is derived from the underlying data type `CompoundTerm` that is derived from `Term`. It represents an immutable type whose values are actions.

The main methods used to create and access actions are the following. The same methods can also be used for the `CompoundTerm` type but are most relevant when manipulating actions.

`Create(string, params IComparable[])`

Static method that creates an action with the given string name and an array of .NET values. Values that are not terms are converted into terms.

For example, `Action.Create("A", 5, new Set<string>("c", "b"))` creates the action `A(5,Set<string>("c","b"))`.

`Parse(string)`

Static method that parses the given string into an action.

For example, `Action.Parse("A(5,Set<string>(\"c\",\"b\"))` creates the action `A(5,Set<string>("c","b"))`.

`Name`

Returns the name of (the function symbol of) the action.

For example, given an action a as above, `a.Name` is the string `"A"`.

`this[int]`

An action has an *indexer* that, for each valid argument position k of an action a, takes the kth subterm of a and returns the underlying .NET value as an `IComparable`. If the kth subterm of a does not have a valid, context independent, interpretation as a .NET value, then the returned value is the term itself.

For example, given a as above, `(int)a[0]` is the integer 5, `(Set<string>)a[1]` is the string set containing the strings `"c"` and `"b"`, `a[2]` throws an `InvalidOperationException`.

As another example, let a be the action `Foo(bar(3),"baz")`, then `(Term)a[0]` is the term `bar(3)` and `(string)a[1]` is the string `"baz"`.

B Command Reference

This appendix describes the command-line options for the visualization and analysis tool mpv (model program viewer), the test generator tool otg (offline test generator), and the test runner tool ct (conformance tester).

B.1 Model program viewer, mpv

B.1.1 Usage

```
mpv [/reference:<string>]* [/initialTransitions:<int>]*
[/transitionLabels:{None|ActionSymbol|Action}]*
[/nodeLabelsVisible[+|-]]* [/initialStateColor:<string>]*
[/hoverColor:<string>]* [/selectionColor:<string>]*
[/deadStateColor:<string>]* [/deadStatesVisible[+|-]]*
[/unsafeStateColor:<string>]* [/maxTransitions:<int>]*
[/loopsVisible[+|-]]* [/mergeLabels[+|-]]*
[/acceptingStatesMarked[+|-]]*
[/stateShape:{Box|Circle|Diamond|Ellipse|Octagon|Plaintext}]*
[/direction:{TopToBottom|LeftToRight|RightToLeft|BottomToTop}]*
[/combineActions[+|-]]* [/livenessCheckIsOn[+|-]]*
[/safetyCheckIsOn[+|-]]* [/testSuite:<string>]* [/fsm:<string>]*
[/startTestAction:<string>]* [/group:<string>]* <model>* @<file>
```

B.1.2 Examples

```
mpv @mpv_args.txt
mpv /fsm:M1.txt /fsm:M2.txt
mpv /testSuite:ContractTest.txt
mpv /r:NewsReaderUI.dll NewsReader.Factory.Create
mpv /r:Controller.dll Reactive.Factory.Create /safetyCheckIsOn+
```

B.1.3   Options

`/?, /help`
Displays usage information and exits.

`[/reference:<string>]*`
Referenced assemblies. (Short form: /r)

`[/initialTransitions:<int>]*`
Number of transitions that are explored initially up to maxTransitions. Negative
value implies no bound. Default value: '-1'.

`[/transitionLabels:None|ActionSymbol|Action]*`
Determines what is shown as a transition label. Default value: 'Action'.

`[/nodeLabelsVisible[+|-]]*`
Visibility of node labels. Default value: '+'.

`[/initialStateColor:<string>]*`
Background color of the initial state. Default value: 'LightGray'.

`[/hoverColor:<string>]*`
Line and action label color to use when edges or nodes are hovered over. Default
value: 'Lime'.

`[/selectionColor:<string>]*`
Background color to use when a node is selected. Default value: 'Blue'.

`[/deadStateColor:<string>]*`
Background color of dead states. Dead states are states from which no accepting
state is reachable. Default value: 'Yellow'.

`[/deadStatesVisible[+|-]]*`
Visibility of dead states. Default value: '+'.

`[/unsafeStateColor:<string>]*`
Background color of states that violate a safety condition (state invariant). Default
value: 'Red'.

`[/maxTransitions:<int>]*`
Maximum number of transitions to draw in the graph. Default value: '100'.

`[/loopsVisible[+|-]]*`
Visibility of transitions whose start and end states are the same. Default value:
'+'.

`[/mergeLabels[+|-]]*`
Multiple transitions between same start and end states are shown as one transition
with a merged label. Default value: '+'.

`[/acceptingStatesMarked[+|-]]*`
Mark accepting states with a bold outline. Default value: '+'.

`[/stateShape:Box|Circle|Diamond|Ellipse|Octagon|Plaintext]*`
State shape. Default value: 'Ellipse'.

`[/direction:TopToBottom|LeftToRight|RightToLeft|BottomToTop]*`
Direction of graph layout. Default value: 'TopToBottom'.

`[/combineActions[+|-]]*`
Whether to view matching start and finish actions by a single label. Default value: '-'.

`[/livenessCheckIsOn[+|-]]*`
Mark states from which no accepting state is reachable in the current view. Default value: '-'.

`[/safetyCheckIsOn[+|-]]*`
Mark states that violate a safety condition (state invariant). Default value: '-'.

`/testSuite:<string>]*`
File name of a file containing a sequence of actions sequences (test cases) to be viewed.

`[/fsm:<string>]*`
File name of a file containing the term representation `fsm.ToTerm()` of an `fsm` (object of type FSM). Multiple FSMs are composed into a product.

`[/group:<string>]*`
Name of a state property to use as the abstraction function for grouping, as described in Section 11.2.5.

`[/startTestAction:<string>]*`
Name of start action of a test case. This value is used only if a `testSuite` is provided. Default value: 'Test'.

`<model>*`
Fully qualified names of factory methods returning an object that is an instance of `ModelProgram`. Multiple model programs are composed into a product.

`@<file>`
Read response file for more options.

B.2 Offline test generator, otg

B.2.1 Usage

```
otg [/reference:<string>]* [/file:<string>]* [/append[+|-]]*
[/fsm:<string>]* <model>* @<file>
```

B.2.2 Examples

```
otg @otg_args.txt
otg /r:ClientServer.dll ClientServer.Factory.Create /fsm:Scenario.txt
otg /r:ClientServer.dll ClientServer.Factory.Create /file:Test.txt
```

B.2.3 Options

`/?, /help`
Displays usage information and exits.

`[/reference:<string>]*`
Referenced assemblies. (Short form: `/r`)

`[/file:<string>]*`
File where test suite is saved. The console is used if no file is provided. (Short form: `/f`)

`[/append[+|-]]*`
If false, the file is overwritten; otherwise the generated test suite is appended at the end of the file. Default value: "-" (Short form: `/a`).

`[/fsm:<string>]*`
File name of a file containing the term representation `fsm.ToTerm()` of an `fsm` (object of type FSM). Multiple FSMs are composed into a product.

`<model>*`
Fully qualified names of factory methods returning an object that is an instance of `ModelProgram`. Multiple models are composed into a product.

`@<file>`
Read response file for more options.

B.3   **Conformance tester,** ct

B.3.1   Usage

```
ct /iut:<string> [/modelStepper:<string>] /reference:<string>+
[/coverage:<string>]* [/steps:<int>]* [/maxSteps:<int>]*
[/runs:<int>]* [/observableAction:<string>]*
[/cleanupAction:<string>]* [/internalAction:<string>]*
[/waitAction:<string>]* [/timeoutAction:<string>]* [/timeout:<int>]*
[/continueOnFailure[+|-]]* [/logfile:<string>]* [/randomSeed:<int>]*
[/overwriteLog[+|-]]* [/testSuite:<string>]* [/fsm:<string>]*
[/startTestAction:<string>]* <model>* @<file>
```

B.3.2   Examples

```
ct @ct_args.txt
ct /r:Stepper.dll /iut:ClientServerImpl.Stepper.Create
     /testSuite:ContractTest.txt
ct /r:ClientServer.dll ClientServer.Factory.Create /r:Stepper.dll
     /iut:ClientServerImpl.Stepper.Create /fsm:Scenario.txt /runs:1
```

B.3.3   Options

`/?, /help`
Displays usage information and exits.

`/iut:<string>`
Implementation under test, a fully qualified name of a factory method that returns an object that implements IStepper.

`[/strategy:<string>]`
A fully qualified name of creator method that takes arguments (ModelProgram modelProgram, string[] coverage) and returns an object that implements IStrategy. If left unspecified, the default model stepper is used that ignores coverage point names (if any). (If a testSuite is provided, this option is ignored.)

`/reference:<string>+`
Referenced assemblies. (Short form: /r)

`[/coverage:<string>]*`
Coverage point names used by model stepper. (If a testSuite is provided, this option is ignored.)

`[/steps:<int>]*`
The desired number of steps that a single test run should have. After the number is reached, only cleanup tester actions are used and the test run continues until an

accepting state is reached or the number of steps is MaxSteps (whichever occurs first). 0 implies no bound and a test case is executed until either a conformance failure occurs or no more actions are enabled. (If a testSuite is provided, this value is set to 0.) Default value: '0'.

[/maxSteps:<int>]*

The maximum number of steps that a single test run can have. This value must be either 0, which means that there is no bound, or greater than or equal to steps. Default value: '0'.

[/runs:<int>]*

The desired number of test runs. Testing stops when this number has been reached. Negative value or 0 implies no bound. (If a testSuite is provided, this value is set to the number of test cases in the test suite.) Default value: '0'.

[/observableAction:<string>]*

Action symbols of actions controlled by the implementation. Other actions are controlled by the tester. (Short form: /o)

[/cleanupAction:<string>]*

Action symbols of actions that are used to end a test run during a cleanup phase. Other actions are omitted during a cleanup phase. (Short form: /c)

[/internalAction:<string>]*

Action symbols of tester actions that are not shared with the implementation and are not used for conformance evaluation. Other tester actions are passed to the implementation stepper. (Short form: /i)

[/waitAction:<string>]*

A name of an action that is used to wait for observable actions in a state where no controllable actions are enabled. A wait action is controllable and internal and must take one integer argument that determines the time to wait in milliseconds during which an observable action is expected.

[/timeoutAction:<string>]*

A name of an action that happens when a wait action has been executed and no obsevable action occurred within the time limit provided in the wait action. A timeout action is observable and takes no arguments.

[/timeout:<int>]*

The amount of time in milliseconds within which a tester action must return when passed to the implementation stepper. Default value: '10000'.

[/continueOnFailure[+|-]]*

Continue testing when a conformance failure occurs. Default value: '+'.

[/logfile:<string>]*

File name where test results are logged. The console is used if no log file is provided.

[/randomSeed:<int>]*

A number used to calculate the starting value for the pseudo-random number sequence that is used by the global choice controller to select tester actions. If a negative number is specified, the absolute value is used. If left unspecified or if 0 is provided, a random number is generated as the seed. Default value: '0'. (Short form: /seed)

[/overwriteLog[+|-]]*

If true, the log file is overwritten; otherwise the test results are appended to the log file. Default value: '+'.

[/testSuite:<string>]*

File name of a file containing a sequence of action sequences to be used as the test suite.

[/fsm:<string>]*

File name of a file containing the term representation fsm.ToTerm() of an fsm (object of type FSM). Multiple FSMs are composed into a product.

[/startTestAction:<string>]*

Name of start action of a test case. This value is used only if a testSuite is provided. The default 'Test' action symbol is considered as an internal test action symbol. If another action symbol is provided, it is not considered as being internal by default. Default value: 'Test'.

<model>*

Fully qualified names of factory methods returning an object that is a subclass of ModelProgram. Multiple models are composed into a product.

@<file>

Read response file for more options.

C Glossary

Undefined terms

The following technical terms are used but not defined in this glossary. We assume their usual meanings from computer science or C#.

agent, algorithm, allocate, argument, Boolean, call, callback function, code, code branch, compile, compiler, data structure, data type, declaration, decrement, developer, directory, element, execute, execution, expression, field, file, file type, framework, global variable, input, instance variable, interleave, key, local variable, main method, method, memory, memory leak, multithreaded, negate, object, object ID, output, overloading, program, programming language, parameter, return, return value, software, statement, static method, static variable, synchronize, system, text file, type, value, variable

Definitions

a priori testing. *Offline testing*.

abstract value. A value whose only operation is equality. Abstract values can be used to eliminate *isomorphic states*. NModel considers *term labels* for object IDs to be abstract values.

abstraction. Considering certain details and ignoring the rest. Choosing a *level of abstraction*. We distinguish *data abstraction*, *behavioral abstraction*, and *environmental abstraction*.

abstraction function. *State property*.

accepting state. A *state* where a *run* is allowed to stop. Usually, accepting states are chosen where some goal has been reached or some work has been completed.

accepting state condition. A *predicate* that defines *accepting states*.

action. The smallest unit of *behavior* at the chosen *level of abstraction*. A discrete, discontinuous, *atomic* execution step. Executing an action causes a *state transition*. In a *reactive system*, we distinguish *controllable actions* from *observable actions*. In a *model program*, the actions are *invocations* of *action methods*. In the NModel framework, actions are represented by *terms*.

action method. A method in a *model program* that is associated with an *action*. Contrast to *helper method*.

action symbol. The name of an *action*. The action symbol is often the same as the name of the corresponding *action method*, but not always.

action vocabulary. The collection of *action symbols* used by a *model program*.

active state. A *state* in which all *enabled actions* are *controllable*.

adaptive. A *strategy* that remembers the history of previous *action* selections. An adaptive strategy is said to *learn*. Contrast to *memoryless*.

analysis. See *model-based analysis*, *preliminary analysis*, *safety analysis*, *liveness analysis*, *static analysis*.

animation. *Simulation*.

API. *Application Programming Interface*.

application. Software that a user can start to perform some activity. In .NET, an application is an *assembly* with a main method, and usually has the file type exe. An application can use *libraries*.

application programming interface (API). The facilities provided by a *library*. In C#, its public types and methods.

approximation. An *FSM* that contains some, but not all, of the *states* and *transitions* of another, larger FSM. *Exploration* that is not *exhaustive*, but uses *sampling* or *pruning*, generates an approximation of the *true FSM*.

arc. *Link*.

arity. The number of parameters of an *action*.

assembly. In .NET, the output from compiling a *source program*. Assemblies are the *components* of the .NET framework. An assembly can be an *application* or a *library*.

assertion. A *predicate* that is supposed to be true when execution reaches it. In the xUnit testing framework, assertions are used as *oracles* to determine whether tests pass or fail. Assertions can be used for *run-time checks*.

assignment. To replace the previous value of a variable with a new one. Also called *update*. Assigning a *state variable* causes a *transition*.

assurance method. A technique for exposing *defects* in software or gathering other information about software for the purpose of improving its quality. *Testing*, *inspections*, and *static analysis* are assurance methods.

asynchronous stepper. A *stepper* for testing a *reactive system*. An asynchronous stepper maintains an *observation queue*.

atomic. An activity that runs to completion, without being interrupted or pre-empted by other activities. An *action* must be atomic.

atomic action. A single *action* associated with both the call and return of an *action method* that has no return value, or `out` or `byref` parameters. Contrast to *split action*.

attribute. In C#, a label applied to a declaration, which is stored in the *assembly* and can be accessed when the program is run. The NModel library defines attributes for labeling *actions* and other parts of a *model program*.

bag. An unordered collection of possibly repeating elements. Also called a *multiset*. In the NModel library, bag is a *compound value*.

behavior. The complete collection of all *runs* that a program or system can execute.

behavioral abstraction. *Abstraction* applied to statements and methods. A higher *level* of behavioral abstraction uses fewer statements or methods, where each statement or method in the *model program* represents more behavior in the *implementation*.

behavioral coverage. *Coverage* that measures aspects of *behavior*, such as *state* coverage or *transition* coverage. Contrast to *structural coverage*.

binary relation. A *set* of *pairs*.

bug. A word which is sometimes used for *defect* and sometimes used for *failure* – which are two different things!

Chinese postman tour. *Postman tour*.

cleanup action. An action that makes *progress* toward an *accepting state* in order to finish a *test run* during *on-the-fly testing*. Closing a file is an example of a cleanup action.

closed system. A system where all actions are *controllable*. Contrast to *reactive system*.

component. A unit of software that can be deployed independently. *Assemblies* are the components of the .NET framework.

composition. An operation that combines separate *model programs* into a new model program called the *product*. Under composition, model programs synchronize steps for *shared actions* and interleave actions not found in their common *action vocabulary*.

compound value. An NModel data type which is a *value type* that can handle tree-structured and variable-length data. The NModel data types *set*, *map*, *sequence*, *value array*, and *bag* derive from compound value.

concurrent system. A system where more than one program runs at a time. Multithreaded programs and *distributed systems* are examples of concurrent systems.

conform. To be in *conformance*.

conformance. Agreement between an *implementation* and a *model program*.

conjunction. An expression that contains the *and* operator, && in C#. Contrast to *disjunction*.

contract model program. A *model program* intended to act as a *specification*. Contrast to *scenario model program*.

control state. The part of the *state* that determines which *actions* are *enabled*. The *state variables* that appear in *enabling conditions*. Contrast to *data state*.

control structure. Code that controls which statements are executed and in which order. In *model programs*, control structure is replaced by *enabling conditions*.

controllable action. An *action* that can be invoked under the control of a *test harness*. Also called *tester action*. Contrast to *observable action*.

cover. To visit a *coverage point* by exercising some program part or property.

coverage. A measure of how much testing has been done.

coverage point. A part or property of a program used to measure *coverage*, by counting how many times it is executed, visited, or otherwise exercised. A state, an action, or a branch in the code could be a coverage point. A *strategy* can use coverage points. In the NModel framework, coverage points are represented by *terms*.

current state. The *state* before a *transition*.

cycle. A loop in a *graph*. A cycle in an *FSM* indicates repetitive behavior and might indicate a *livelock*.

data abstraction. *Abstraction* applied to variables. A higher *level* of data abstraction uses fewer variables, fewer values for those variables, and simpler data types.

data state. The part of the *state* that does not determine control flow. Contrast to *control state*.

dead state. A *state* from which an *accepting state* cannot be reached. A system that reaches a dead state experiences a *liveness failure*. Dead states indicate *deadlocks* or *livelocks*.

deadlock. A *liveness failure* where a program stops executing because it reaches a *state* where no *actions* are *enabled*.

decrementing action weight. In a certain kind of *strategy*, a number associated with an *action* that determines its probability of selection. The weight is initially assigned to some value and decremented each time the action is executed.

De Morgan's Law. Describes how to negate expressions involving *and* and *or*: `!(p && q) == !p || !q`.

defect. Incorrect code or missing code that can cause a *failure*. Also called a *fault* or a *bug*.

delegate. In C#, a type whose instances are methods. In an *asynchronous stepper*, the *observer* is assigned to a delegate.

dependent feature. A *feature* with no *state variables* of its own. Dependent features are often used for *scenario control*.

derived state. Methods or properties that query the *state* but do not change it.

design. A description of how a system or program is built up from parts and how the parts communicate. Contrast to *specification*.

deterministic. A *reactive system* where if an *observable action* happens in a certain *state*, then the same observable action will happen again when the same state is visited. This fact can be used by an *adaptive strategy*.

difference. A *set* that contains the elements of a set that are not found in a second set. Or, the operation on two sets that returns their difference.

directed graph. A *graph* where each *link* has a direction. An *FSM* can be represented by a directed graph where the nodes represent *states* and the links represent *transitions*, and each link is directed from the *current state* to the *next state*.

disabled. Not *enabled*.

disjunction. An expression that contains the *or* operator, `||` in C#. Contrast to *conjunction*.

distributed system. A system with more than one computer. A distributed system is also a *concurrent system*.

domain. A set from which the values for a parameter of an *action* are drawn during *exploration*. In order to be *explorable*, each parameter for every action in a *model program* must have a finite domain.

dynamic function. A key/value relationship that evolves during the *run* of a system. A dynamic function can be represented by a *map*.

edge. *Link*.

enabled. An *action* is enabled when it can occur, when it is allowed to be invoked, when its *enabling condition* is true.

enabling condition. A *predicate* associated with an *action*. The action is *enabled* when its *enabling condition* is true. Enabling conditions control the sequence of actions when a *model program* executes. Enabling conditions are also called *pre-conditions* or *guards*.

end state. *Next state*.

environmental abstraction. *Abstraction* applied to control structure. A higher *level* of environmental abstraction replaces control structure with *nondeterminism*.

event-driven system. *Reactive system*.

exhaustive. An analysis that considers every possibility. For example, exhaustive *exploration* generates the *true FSM*. Exhaustive analysis of an *"infinite"* program is not feasible.

explorable. A *model program* whose every parameter has a finite *domain*.

exploration. An analysis technique that generates an *FSM* from a *model program*.

factory method. A method that returns an object. In the NModel framework, factory methods are applied to a *library model program*, an *FSM model program*, or an *FSM text file* to create an instance of the ModelProgram class than can be used for *exploration* or testing.

fail. Of an *assertion*, to evaluate to false. Of a program, to experience a *failure*. Of a *test case*, to cause a program to experience a *failure*.

failure. An occurrence where a program does not satisfy its *specification* or violates *conformance*. Some failures are caused by *defects*.

fault. *Defect*.

feature. A group of related *state variables* and *actions* that might be included or excluded from a *model program*.

feature-oriented modeling. Where a *model program* is built up by combining separate *features*.

field map. A table that relates an object identifier to an associated data value. The NModel framework uses field maps to support *object-oriented modeling*.

finish action. The second *action* in a *split action*, associated with the return of the *action method*.

finite state machine (FSM). A finite collection of *state transitions*, along with an identification of the *initial state* and any *accepting states*. An FSM can express a *scenario*. *Exploration* generates an FSM from a *model program*.

finitely branching. A *model program* where only a finite number of *transitions* are *enabled* in each state. A finitely branching model program is *explorable*. Contrast to *infinitely branching*.

finitize. To write a finite model program that models an *"infinite"* system, or to limit *exploration* of an "infinite" model program to produce a *finite state machine*. *Pruning* and *sampling* are ways to finitize exploration.

formal. Expressed in a notation that can be analyzed automatically, such as a programming language. Contrast to *informal*.

frontier. During *exploration*, the *states* which have been reached but whose *enabled transitions* have not yet been executed.

functional. *State-independent*.

FSM. *Finite state machine*

FSM model program. A *model program* coded in C# as a sequence *terms* that represent the *transitions* of an *FSM*.

FSM text file. A *model program* coded in a text file as a *term* that represents an *FSM*.

fully qualified name. In C#, the *namespace* name prefixed to the *simple name*. The fully qualified name should be unique.

GAC. *Global Assembly Cache*.

generic failure. A *failure* that does not require an *oracle* to detect, such as a crash (unhandled exception), a memory leak, or a *deadlock*.

Global Assembly Cache (GAC). In .NET, a special directory where *assemblies* for installed software are stored. Assemblies may also be located elsewhere.

graph. A data structure consisting of *nodes* connected by *links*. An *FSM* can be represented by a *directed graph*.

group label. *State property*.

grouping. *State grouping*.

guard. *Enabling condition*.

guarded update program. A program that consists of *guarded update rules*. Our *model programs* are guarded update programs.

guarded update rule. An *action* along with its *enabling condition*.

helper method. A method in a *model program* that is not an *action method*.

hidden state. *State* in the *implementation* that is not represented in the *model program*.

immutable. A data type whose values cannot be changed. Operations on immutable values must construct a new value of the type. In C#, the string type is immutable. The data types defined in the NModel library are immutable.

implementation. The program, system, or component that is described by a *specification* or a *model program*.

implementation under test (IUT). The *implementation* that is the subject of *testing*, that is executed during *test runs*.

indexer. In C#, a construct that accesses a data structure using indices, as if it were an array. The NModel library provides access to the arguments of an *action term* through an indexer.

"infinite." Perhaps not mathematically infinite, but too large to store each element, or to consider each element one by one. Exhaustive analysis of an *"infinite"* program is not feasible; the analysis must be *finitized*.

infinitely branching. A *model program* where an *"infinite"* number of transitions are *enabled* in some states, because *actions* have "infinite" *domains*. An infinitely branching model program is not *explorable*, but can be made explorable by appropriate *parameter generation*.

informal. Expressed in a notation that cannot be analyzed automatically, such as natural language or hand-drawn diagrams. Contrast to *formal*.

initial state. The *state* where a *run* begins. It is necessary to identify the initial state of an *FSM*.

inspection. An *assurance method* where people examine documents or code, checking for errors. *Informal* documents can be inspected.

interesting. A *state* that is *partially explored* or that has a path leading to a partially explored state. A *strategy* might give priority to *actions* that lead to interesting states.

internal action. An action in a *model program* that has no corresponding action in the *implementation* and is not executed by the *stepper*. Internal actions are typically used to select among *test cases* in a *test suite*.

intersection. A *set* that contains the elements shared by two sets. Or, the operation on two sets that returns their intersection. In *composition*, the allowed *traces* of the *product* belong to the intersection of the traces of the *loop extensions* of the individual *model programs*.

invariant. A *predicate* that is supposed to be true in every *state* that is *reachable*. Invariants express *safety requirements*.

invocation. A method call, including the method name and all of its arguments. Or, the execution of that method call. The invocation of an *action method* is an *action*.

isomorphic states. *States* where there exists a substitution of *abstract values* that makes them equal. Isomorphic means "same shape." For example, states are isomorphic if they store data structures which have the same shape and store the same values, except for object IDs. Excluding isomorphic states can greatly reduce the number of states that must be considered during *exploration*.

IUT. *Implementation Under Test*.

lazy. An algorithm that does not compute an element until it is needed. The *exploration* algorithm discussed in this book is lazy.

learn. What an *adaptive strategy* is said to do.

level of abstraction. The amount of detail from the *implementation* that is represented in the *model program*. A lower level of abstraction represents more detail; a higher level represents less.

level of integration. A qualitative measure of the number of program *units* assembled for testing or other project activities, ranging from the unit level (just one, or a few, units) up to the system level (all units).

library. A *component* that provides an *API* that can be used by *applications* or other libraries. In .NET, a library is an *assembly* without a main method and usually has the file type `dll`.

library model program. A *library* created by compiling a *model program* coded in C# with *state variables*, *action methods*, and *enabling conditions*.

link. A connection between two *nodes* in a *graph*. Also called *edge* or *arc*. In an *FSM*, the links represent *transitions*.

livelock. A *liveness failure* where execution continues endlessly, never reaching an *accepting state*.

liveness. The property that something good will happen: execution will reach an *accepting state* and will avoid *dead states*, *deadlock*, and *livelock*. Or, a given *scenario* will be executed. Contrast to *safety*.

liveness analysis. Checking *liveness*, by searching for *dead states* or attempting to execute a given *scenario*.

lockstep execution. In *model-based testing*, simultaneous execution of the actions of the *model program* and the *implementation*. Lockstep execution is supported by a *test harness* called a *stepper*.

loop extension. In *composition*, the *model program* formed by adding *actions* that are *self-loops* for each of the actions in the other model programs that are not *shared actions*.

map. A collection that associates unique keys with values. In the NModel library, map is a *compound value*.

match. Determining which *actions* in separate *model programs* will be combined in *composition*. Matching considers both *action symbols* and argument values.

memoryless. A *strategy* that does not remember the history of previous *action* selections. Contrast to *adaptive*.

model checking. An analysis technique similar to *exploration* that usually checks a property expressed as a formula in temporal logic.

model program. A program that describes the *behavior* of another program, system, or component called the *implementation*. A model program can act as a *specification* or a *design*. We distinguish *contract model programs* from *scenario model programs*.

model-based analysis. Using a *model program* to debug and improve *specifications* and *designs*. *Simuluation, exploration*, and *composition* are model-based analysis techniques. They can be used for *safety analysis* or *liveness analysis*.

model-based testing. Using a *model program* to generate *test cases* or act as an *oracle*. Model-based testing includes both *offline testing* and *on-the-fly testing*.

multiplexing. A technique that produces a single sequence of events generated by multiple agents in a *concurrent system*. Multiplexing must consider *partial order*.

multiplicity. The number of times an element appears in a collection, particularly a *bag*.

multiset. *Bag*.

namespace. In C#, a name applied to a group of type declarations. The namespace identifies the group and is prefixed to the *simple names* within the group to form *fully qualified names*.

next state. The *state* after a *transition*. Also called the *target state* or *end state*.

node. One of the elements in a *graph* that are connected by *links*. In an *FSM*, the nodes represent *states*.

nondeterminism. Unpredictability. Nondeterminism occurs where there is more than one alternative, and it is not possible to predict which alternative will be taken.

object-oriented modeling. Using instance variables as *state variables*.

observer. In a *model program*, a *probe*. In an *asynchronous stepper*, a callback function that enters *observable actions* into an *observation queue*.

observable action. An *action* that cannot be invoked by a *test harness*; it can only be awaited and observed. A system that has observable actions is a *reactive system*. Contrast to *controllable action*.

observation queue. A queue of *observable actions* that are observed during a test run that is managed by an *asynchronuous stepper*.

offline testing. Testing where *test suites* are generated before running the tests. Contrast to *on-the-fly* testing.

on-the-fly testing. Testing where each *test case* is generated while the *test run* executes. Contrast to *offline testing*.

online testing. *On-the-fly testing*.

oracle. The authority which provides the correct result for a *test case*, used to judge whether the test *passed* or *failed*. A *model program* can act as an oracle.

pair. A data record with two elements in order. A *set* of pairs represents a *binary relation*. The pair data type in the NModel library is a *value type*.

parameter generation. Specifying *domains* and selecting parameter values from those domains during *exploration*. Parameter generation is an aspect of *scenario control*.

partial order. A relation where some, but not all, pairs of elements occur in order. Partial orders arise in *concurrent systems* where it is not always possible to know whether an event in one program precedes or follows an event in another. Partial order must be considered in *multiplexing*.

partially explored. A *state* where an unexplored *action* is *enabled*.

pass. Of a *test case*, to not *fail*.

passive state. A *state* in which all *enabled actions* are *observable*.

passive testing. A special case of *on-the-fly testing* where all the *actions* are *observable*. For example, passive testing could be used to check a log file for *conformance*.

path coverage. A measure of how many execution paths have been executed. The number of possible paths is often *"infinite,"* so full path coverage is rarely feasible. Contrast to *transition coverage*.

placeholder. An *action* argument which *matches* any value when matching actions during *composition*.

postman tour. An algorithm used in *offline testing*, which generates a *test suite* from an *FSM* by *traversal*. The postman tour produces a test suite that has *minimal transition coverage*. Also called the *Chinese postman tour*.

precondition. *Enabling condition*.

predicate. A Boolean expression or method that has no *side effects*.

preliminary analysis. Preparation for writing a *model program*, including selecting the *features* to include, choosing the *level of abstraction*, identifying the *state* and *actions*, and writing some sample *traces*.

probe. An *action* that checks the *state*, usually for purposes of testing. A probe does not change the state; the resulting *transition* is a *self-loop*.

product. The *model program* that results from the *composition* of two or more model programs.

progress. Closer approach to a goal, such as an *accepting state*. A program that does not make progress experiences a *liveness failure*.

protocol. An agreement about how two or more agents work together. A protocol is defined by rules for forming messages and rules that constrain the ordering of the messages. When modeling a protocol, the messages are *actions*.

pruning. To limit *exploration* by systematically excluding some *transitions*. Examples of pruning techniques include *state filters*, *strengthening enabling conditions*, *state groupings*, and *stopping rules*. Pruning is a way to *finitize*. Contrast to *sampling*.

pure. A statement or expression that has no *side effects*. An *enabling condition* or any other *predicate* must be pure.

random. A simple *strategy* that randomly selects an enabled action to execute next.

reachable. Of a *state*, that it is visited by some possible *run*. A reachable state might be visited during *exploration*. Of an object, that it occurs within a global *state variable*, or occurs within an instance field of a reachable object. The keys of a *field map* contain all reachable instances of its class.

reactive system. A system that responds to its environment. In a reactive system, some of the actions are *observable*. Contrast to *closed system*.

reference equality. Where two variables are equal when occupy the same location in memory. In C#, the default equality for objects. Contrast to *structural equality*.

restricted model. A *scenario model program* created by restricting a *contract model program*, especially by limiting *domains*.

review. *Inspection*.

reward. A quantity that a *strategy* seeks to maximize, by choosing the best *action* in each *state*.

run. A sequence of *actions*. A run begins in the *initial state* and should stop in an *accepting state*; otherwise, it is considered a *liveness failure*.

run-time check. To execute an *assertion* to check that the program or its environment is behaving as intended.

safety. The property that nothing bad will happen: execution will not reach any *unsafe states* that violate *safety requirements*. Or, no unsafe *scenarios* will be executed. Contrast to *liveness*.

safety analysis. Checking *safety*, by searching for *unsafe states* or attempting to execute a *scenario*.

safety requirement. *Invariant*.

sampling. To limit *exploration* by selecting desirable paths to explore, rather than excluding undesirable transitions as with *pruning*. Sampling is a way to *finitize*.

sandbox. A *test harness* in which normally *observable* actions are made *controllable*, so a normally *reactive* system can be tested as a *closed system*.

scenario. A collection of related *runs* (perhaps just one). A scenario can be expressed by a *scenario model program*.

scenario control. Limiting analysis and testing to particular *runs* of interest.

self-loop. A *transition* where there is no change of *state*; the *current state* and *next state* are the same. So called because of its appearance in a *state transition diagram*.

sequence. An ordered collection of (possibly repeating) elements. In the NModel library, sequence is a *compound value*.

set. An unordered collection of distinct elements. In the NModel library, set is a *compound value*.

scenario FSM. A *scenario model program* expressed as an *FSM*.

scenario model program. A *model program* that defines a *scenario*, usually intended for *scenario control*. Contrast to *contract model program*.

shared action. An *action* whose *action symbol* appears in the *action vocabulary* of two or more programs. Under *composition*, model programs synchronize steps for shared actions.

side effect. Any effect of evaluating an expression or executing a statement, other than computing a value. *Updating* variables, allocating storage, or performing input or output are examples of side effects.

signature. The name and parameters of a method, or the *action symbol* and parameters of an *action*.

simple name. In C#, a name not including the namespace. A simple name need not be unique. Contrast to *fully qualified name*.

simulation. A *model-based analysis* technique, where *runs* of a *model program* are observed. Each run of a model program is a simulation of some *behavior* of the *implementation*. Simulation can include *run-time checks*. Sometimes called *animation*. Compare to *exploration*.

slice. A collection of *features*.

sliding window. A *protocol* that uses a pool of resources (the "window") whose contents change ("slide") as time progresses.

source program. In C#, the collection of source code files (perhaps just one) that are compiled to produce an *assembly*.

specification. A description of what a program, *component*, or system is supposed to do. A specification should be a complete description of *behavior* that describes everything the system must do, might do, and must *not* do. A *model program* can act as a specification. Contrast to *design*.

split action. A pair of *actions*, the *start action* and the *finish action*, associated with the call and return of a single *action method* that has a return value and/or `out` or `byref` parameters. Contrast to *atomic action*.

start action. The first *action* in a *split action*, associated with the call of the *action method*.

state. The information stored in a system at one point in time. In a *model program*, the state is the collection of all *state variables* and their values.

state filter. A *predicate* that must be satisfied in the *next state* of a *transition* for that transition to be included in *exploration*. State filters are a *pruning* technique.

state grouping. A collection of *states* that have the same value for a *state property*. In *exploration*, a *pruning* technique can exclude a state that does not provide a new value for one of the properties. In testing, an *adaptive strategy* can select *actions* that lead to state groupings that have not yet been visited.

state-independent. A method that does not read or update any *state*. It only reads its parameters and returns a value.

state property. A value computed from a *state*. All states where the property has the same value belong to the same *state grouping*. Also called an *abstraction function* or a *group label*.

state transition. *Transition*.

state transition diagram. A picture of the *directed graph* that represents an *FSM*, where bubbles represent *states*, arrows represent *transitions*, and labels on the arrows represent *actions*.

state transition table. A table that represents an *FSM*, with one row for each transition (or group of transitions with "don't care" or "don't change" values).

state variable. A variable in a *model program* that stores *state*. In the NModel framework, static variables and instance variables, but not parameters or local variables, are state variables.

static analysis. Analysis that checks code without executing it. Contrast to *testing*.

static class. In C#, a class labeled with the *static* modifier. A static class can only have static variables and static methods.

step. The execution of an *action*.

stepper. A *test harness* used with the NModel framework, which supports *lockstep execution*.

stochastic. An algorithm that combines random and directed aspects. Some *strategies* and *sampling* algorithms are stochastic.

stopping rule. A rule which causes *exploration* to stop, possibly before it generates the *true FSM*. For example, a rule might stop exploration when a certain number of *transitions* have been explored. Stopping rules are the simplest *pruning* strategy.

strategy. A function that selects which *action* to execute next during each step of *on-the-fly testing*. A strategy can be designed to achieve good *coverage*. A strategy may be *random*, *memoryless*, or *adaptive*.

strengthen. To add constraints, often by *conjunction*. Strengthening *enabling conditions* is a *pruning* technique. Contrast to *weaken*.

structural coverage. *Coverage* that measures execution of parts of the *model program*, such as method coverage or code branch coverage. Constrast to *behavioral coverage*.

structural equality. Where two variables are equal when they contain the same values. Structural equality is needed for state comparison. The data types defined in the modeling library use structural equality. Contrast to *reference equality*.

system testing. Testing that executes an entire *application* or an even larger *level of integration*. Contrast to *unit testing*.

target state. *Next state*.

temporal property. A property that is defined by a *scenario*, instead of a set of *states*. Temporal properties can be checked by *composition*.

term. A data structure used in the NModel framework to represent *actions*, *transitions*, *FSMs*, *coverage points*, *term labels*, etc.

term label. A *term* representation of an object ID.

test. (Noun) *Test case*, especially in xUnit.

test case. A *run* used for *testing*.

test-driven development. Where developers write *test cases* before they write code.

test fixture. In the xUnit framework, a class that contains *test methods*, which acts as a *test harness*.

test harness. Code that enables a *test runner* to execute an *implementation*. A test harness for the NModel framework is called a *stepper*.

test method. In the xUnit framework, a method that executes a *test case*.

test run. *Test case*.

test runner. An *application* that executes *test cases* and reports the results.

test suite. A collection of related *test cases*.

tester action. *Controllable action*.

testing. An *assurance method* that checks software by executing it. This book discusses *model-based testing*.

time-out action. An *observable action* that occurs after a *wait action* if the *observation queue* is empty. A time-out action is usually considered a *conformance failure*.

trace. A description of a *run*.

transition. The effect of executing an *action*. A transition is uniquely identified by the action, the *current state* before the transition, and the *next state* after the transition.

transition coverage. A measure of *behavioral coverage* that measures the number of *transitions* that have been executed. The *postman tour* achieves full transition coverage of a given FSM. Contrast to *path coverage*.

traversal. A *run* produced by tracing a path through the *transitions* of an *FSM*.

triple. A data record with three elements in order. The triple data type in the NModel library is a *value type*.

true FSM. The *FSM* that describes all of the *runs* of a *model program*. The FSM that is generated from a model program by *exhaustive exploration*. It is not feasible to generate the true FSM of a *"infinite"* model program; we can only generate an *approximation* instead. Contrast to *scenario FSM*.

union. A *set* that contains all the elements of two other sets. Or, the operation on two sets that returns their union.

unit. The smallest amount of software which is reasonable to test. In C#, the units are usually classes (or other types).

unit testing. Testing that executes some (perhaps just one) of the *units* from which a program is constructed. Contrast to *system testing*.

update. An *assignment*, or several.

update rule. *Action method.*

unsafe state. A *state* that violates an *invariant*.

unwind. To generate a less compact but possibly more useful representation from a more compact one. For example, to *explore* a *model program* to generate an *FSM*, or to *traverse* an *FSM* to generate a *test suite*.

validate. To show that a *specification* or *model program* expresses the intended *behaviors*.

value array. A data type in the NModel library which is similar to a C# array, but is *immutable* and uses *structural equality*. Value array is a *compound value*.

value type. A data type that uses *structural equality* and is *immutable*. The data types in the NModel library are value types because value types are needed to compare *states*.

vertex. (plural vertices) *Node.*

wait action. An *internal action* invoked when testing a *reactive system*, when there are no tester actions enabled and the *observation queue* is empty. A wait action may be followed by a *time-out action*.

weaken. To relax constraints, often by *disjunction*. Constrast to *strengthen*.

wrapper. A method that calls another method, but provides a different (usually shorter or simpler) list of parameters. Or, an *API* that consists of wrapper methods.

Bibliography

J.-R. Abrial. *The B Book: Assigning Programs to Meanings*. Cambridge University Press, 1996.

ASM. Abstract State Machines, 2006. URL: `http://www.eecs.umich.edu/gasm/`.

R. Alur, C. Courcoubetis, and M. Yannakakis. Distinguishing tests for nondeterministic and probabilistic machines. In *STOC '95: Proceedings of the Twenty-Seventh Annual ACM Symposium on Theory of Computing*, pages 363–372, ACM Press, New York, 1995.

R. Alur, T. A. Henzinger, O. Kupferman, and M. Vardi. Alternating refinement relations. In *Proceedings of the Ninth International Conference on Concurrency Theory (CONCUR'98)*, volume 1466 of *Lecture Notes in Computer Science*, pages 163–178. Springer, 1998.

M. Barnett, W. Grieskamp, L. Nachmanson, W. Schulte, N. Tillmann, and M. Veanes. Towards a tool environment for model-based testing with AsmL. In A. Petrenko and A. Ulrich, editors, *Formal Approaches to Software Testing, FATES 2003*, volume 2931 of *Lecture Notes in Computer Science*, pages 264–280. Springer, 2003.

M. Barnett, R. Leino, and W. Schulte. The Spec# programming system: An overview. In M. Huisman, editor, *Construction and Analysis of Safe, Secure, and Interoperable Smart Devices: International Workshop, CASSIS 2004*, volume 3362 of *Lecture Notes in Computer Science*, pages 49–69. Springer, 2005.

B. Beizer. *Software System Testing and Quality Assurance*. Van Nostrand Reinhold, New York, 1984.

B. Beizer. *Software Testing Techniques*, 2nd edition. Van Nostrand Reinhold, New York, 1990.

B. Beizer. *Black-Box Testing: Techniques for Functional Testing of Software and Systems*. John Wiley & Sons, 1995.

R. V. Binder. *Testing Object-Oriented Systems: Models, Patterns, and Tools*. Addison-Wesley, 1999.

A. Blass and Y. Gurevich. Background, reserve, and Gandy machines. In *Proceedings of the 14th Annual Conference of the EACSL on Computer Science Logic*, pages 1–17. Springer-Verlag, London, 2000.

A. Blass and Y. Gurevich. Ordinary interactive small-step algorithms, I. *ACM Transactions on Computation Logic*, 7(2):363–419, April 2006.

A. Blass, Y. Gurevich, L. Nachmanson, and M. Veanes. Play to test. In W. Grieskamp and C. Weise, editors, *FATES*, volume 3997 of *Lecture Notes in Computer Science*, pages 32–46. Springer, 2005.

E. Börger and R. Stärk. *Abstract State Machines: A Method for High-Level System Design and Analysis*. Springer, 2003.

C. Boyapati, S. Khurshid, and D. Marinov. Korat: Automated testing based on Java predicates. *SIGSOFT Software Engineering Notes*, 27(4):123–133, 2002.

E. Brinksma and J. Tretmans. Testing transition systems: An annotated bibliography. In *Summer School MOVEP'2k – Modelling and Verification of Parallel Processes*, volume 2067 of *Lecture Notes in Computer Science*, pages 187–193. Springer, 2001.

M. Broy, B. Jonsson, J.-P. Katoen, M. Leucker, and A. Pretschner, editors. *Model-Based Testing of Reactive Systems*, volume 3472 of *Lecture Notes in Computer Science*. Springer, 2005.

C. Campbell, W. Grieskamp, L. Nachmanson, W. Schulte, N. Tillmann, and M. Veanes. Testing concurrent object-oriented systems with Spec Explorer (extended abstract). In *FM 2005: Formal Methods*, volume 3582 of *Lecture Notes in Computer Science*, pages 542–547. Springer, 2005a.

C. Campbell and M. Veanes. State exploration with multiple state groupings. In D. Beauquier, E. Börger, and A. Slissenko, editors, *12th International Workshop on Abstract State Machines, ASM'05*, March 8–11, 2005, Laboratory of Algorithms, Complexity and Logic, University Paris 12 – Val dc Marne, Créteil, France, pages 119–130, 2005.

C. Campbell, M. Veanes, J. Huo, and A. Petrenko. Multiplexing of partially ordered events. In F. Khendek and R. Dssouli, editors, *17th IFIP International Conference on Testing of Communicating Systems, TestCom 2005*, volume 3502 of *Lecture Notes in Computer Science*, pages 97–110. Springer, 2005b.

K. M. Chandy and J. Misra. *Parallel Program Design: A Foundation*. Addison-Wesley, 1988.

E. M. Clarke, E. A. Emerson, and A. P. Sistla. Automatic verification of finite-state concurrent systems using temporal logic specifications. *ACM Transactions on Programming Languages and Systems*, 8(2):244–263, April 1986.

E. M. Clarke, O. Grumberg, and D. Long. Verification tools for finite-state concurrent systems. In J. W. De Bakker, W.-P De Roever, and G Rozenberg, editors, *A Decade of Concurrency, Reflections and Perspectives*, volume 803 of *Lecture Notes in Computer Science*. Springer, 1994.

E. M. Clarke, O. Grumberg, and D. A. Peled. *Model Checking*. MIT Press, 1999.

D. E. Comer. *Internetworking with TCP/IP, Principles, Protocols, and Architectures*, 4th edition. Prentice-Hall, 2000.

J. Davies and J. Woodcock. *Using Z: Specification, Refinement, and Proof*. Prentice-Hall, 1996.

L. de Alfaro. Game models for open systems. In N. Dershowitz, editor, *Verification: Theory and Practice. Essays Dedicated to Zohar Manna on the Occasion of His 64th Birthday*, volume 2772 of *Lecture Notes in Computer Science*, pages 269–289. Springer, 2004.

L. de Alfaro and T. A. Henzinger. Interface automata. In *Proceedings of the 8th European Software Engineering Conference / 9th ACM SIGSOFT International Symposium on Foundations of Software Engineering*, volume 26(5) of *ACM SIGSOFT Software Engineering Notes*, pages 109–120. ACM Press, 2001.

R. Douence, P. Fradet, and M. Südholt. *Aspect-Oriented Software Development*. Addison-Wesley, September 2004.

T. Elrad, M. Aksit, G. Kiczales, K. Lieberherr, and H. Ossher. Discussing aspects of AOP. *Communications of the ACM*, 44(10):33–38, 2001.

J. Filar and K. Vrieze. *Competitive Markov Decision Processes*. Springer-Verlag, New York, 1996.

J. Fitzgerald and P. G. Larsen. *Modelling Systems: Practical Tools and Techniques for Software Development*. Cambridge University Press, 1998.

FSE. Foundations of Software Engineering, 2006. URL: `http://research.microsoft.com/fse/`.

W. Grieskamp, Y. Gurevich, W. Schulte, and M. Veanes. Generating finite state machines from abstract state machines. In P. G. Frankl, editor, *Proceedings of the ACM SIGSOFT 2002 International Symposium on Software Testing and Analysis (ISSTA-02)*, volume 27 of *Software Engineering Notes*, pages 112–122. ACM, 2002.

W. Grieskamp, N. Kicillof, and N. Tillmann. Action machines: A framework for encoding and composing partial behaviors. *International Journal on Software and Knowledge Engineering*, 16(5):705–726, 2006.

W. Grieskamp, N. Tillmann, and M. Veanes. Instrumenting scenarios in a model-driven development environment. *Information and Software Technology*, 46(15):1027–1036, 2004.

Y. Gurevich. Evolving algebras 1993: Lipari Guide. In E. Börger, editor, *Specification and Validation Methods*, pages 9–36. Oxford University Press, 1995.

Y. Gurevich, B. Rossman, and W. Schulte. Semantic essence of AsmL. *Theoretical Computer Science*, 343(3):370–412, 2005.

Y. Gurevich and N. Tillmann. Partial updates. *Theoretical Computer Science*, 336:311–342, May 2005.

P. Hamill. *Unit Test Frameworks*. O'Reilly, 2004.

D. Harel and R. Marelly. *Come, Let's Play: Scenario-Based Programming Using LSCs and the Play-Engine*. Springer, 2003.

A. Hartman and K. Nagin. The AGEDIS tools for model based testing. In G. S. Avrunin and G. Rothermel, editors, *Proceedings of the ACM/SIGSOFT International Symposium on Software Testing and Analysis, ISSTA 2004*, pages 129–132. ACM, 2004.

A. Hejlsberg, S. Wiltamuth, and P. Golde. *The C# Programming Language*, 2nd edition, Addison-Wesley, 2006.

C. Hertel. *Implementing CIFS: The Common Internet File System*. Prentice-Hall, 2003.

G. J. Holzmann. *The Spin Model Checker: Primer and Reference Manual*. Addison-Wesley, 2004.

J. E. Hopcroft and J. D. Ullman. *Introduction to Automata Theory, Languages, and Computation*. Addison-Wesley, 1979.

IEEE (Institute of Electrical and Electronics Engineers). *Standard Glossary of Software Engineering Terminology*, 1983.

R. Iosif. Symmetry reductions for model checking of concurrent dynamic software. *STTT*, 6(4):302–319, 2004.

D. Jackson. *Software Abstractions: Logic, Language, and Analysis*. MIT Press, 2006.

D. Jackson and C. A. Damon. Elements of style: Analyzing a software design feature with a counterexample detector. *IEEE Transactions on Software Engineering*, 22(7):484–495, July 1996.

J. Jacky. *The Way of Z: Practical Programming with Formal Methods*. Cambridge University Press, 1997.

C. Jard and T. Jéron. TGV: Theory, principles and algorithms. A tool for the automatic synthesis of conformance test cases for non-deterministic reactive systems. *International Journal on Software Tools for Technology Transfer*, 7(4):297–315, 2005.

C. Kaner, H. Q. Nguyen, and J. L. Falk. *Testing Computer Software*. John Wiley & Sons, Inc., 1993.

R. Keller. Formal verification of parallel programs. *Communications of the ACM*, 371–384, July 1976.

L. Lamport. Time, clocks, and the ordering of events in a distributed system. *Communications of the ACM*, 21(7):558–565, 1978.

L. Lamport. *Specifying Systems: The TLA+ Language and Tools for Hardware and Software Engineers*. Addison-Wesley, 2002.

K. G. Larsen, M. Mikucionis, B. Nielsen, and A. Skou. Testing real-time embedded software using UPPAAL-TRON: An industrial case study. In *EMSOFT '05: Proceedings of the 5th ACM International Conference on Embedded Software*, pages 299–306. ACM Press, New York, 2005.

D. Lee and M. Yannakakis. Principles and methods of testing finite state machines – a survey. *Proceedings of the IEEE*, 84(8):1090–1123, August 1996.

S. Lipschutz. *Set Theory and Related Topics, Schaum's Outline Series*. McGraw-Hill, 1998.

N. Lynch and M. Tuttle. Hierarchical correctness proofs for distributed algorithms. In *Proceedings of the Sixth Annual ACM Symposium on Principles of Distributed Computing*, pages 137–151. ACM Press, New York, 1987.

B. D. McKay. Practical graph isomorphism. *Congressus Numerantium*, 30:45–87, 1981.

A. Miller, A. Donaldson, and M. Calder. Symmetry in temporal logic model checking. *ACM Computing Surveys*, 38(3):8, 2006.

J. S. Miller and S. Ragsdale. *The Common Language Infrastructure Annotated Standard*. Addison-Wesley, 2004.

M. Musuvathi and D. L. Dill. An incremental heap canonicalization algorithm. In P. Godefroid, editor, *SPIN*, volume 3639 of *Lecture Notes in Computer Science*, pages 28–42. Springer, 2005.

G. J. Myers. *The Art of Software Testing*. John Wiley & Sons, New York, 1979.

G. J. Myers, T. Badgett, T. M. Thomas, and C. Sandler. *The Art of Software Testing*, 2nd edition. John Wiley & Sons, New York, 2004.

L. Nachmanson, M. Veanes, W. Schulte, N. Tillmann, and W. Grieskamp. Optimal strategies for testing nondeterministic systems. In *ISSTA'04*, pages 55–64, 2004.

D. Peled. *Software Reliability Methods*. Springer, 2001.

R. M. Poston. *Automating Specification-Based Software Testing*. IEEE Computer Society Press, 1996.

M. L. Puterman. *Markov Decision Processes: Discrete Stochastic Dynamic Programming*. Wiley-Interscience, New York, 1994.

J. B. Rainsberger. *JUnit Recipes*. Manning Publications Co., 2005.

S. Reiff-Marganiec and M.D. Ryan, editors. *Feature Interactions in Telecommunications and Software Systems VIII*. IOS Press, June 2005.

M. Robby, B. Dwyer, and J. Hatcliff. Domain-specific model checking using the Bogor framework. In *ASE '06: Proceedings of the 21st IEEE International Conference on Automated Software Engineering (ASE'06)*, pages 369–370. IEEE Computer Society, Washington, DC, 2006.

Spec Explorer, 2006. URL: http://research.microsoft.com/specexplorer, released January 2005, updated release September 2006.

M. Spivey. *The Z Notation: A Reference Manual*, 2nd edition, Prentice-Hall, 1992.

W. R. Stevens. *Unix Network Programming*. Addison-Wesley, 1990.

D. Stutz, T. Neward, and G. Shilling. *Shared Source CLI Essentials*. O'Reilly, March 2003.

H. Thimbleby. The directed Chinese postman problem. *Software Practice and Experience*, 33(11):1081–1096, 2003.

J. Tretmans. Testing concurrent systems: A formal approach. In J. C. M. Baeten and S. Mauw, editors, *CONCUR '99*, volume 1664 of *Lecture Notes in Computer Science*, pages 46–65. Springer, 1999.

J. Tretmans and A. Belinfante. Automatic testing with formal methods. In *Euro STAR'99: 7th European International Conference on Software Testing, Analysis and Review*, Barcelona, Spain, November 8–12, 1999. EuroStar Conferences, Galway, Ireland.

J. Tretmans and E. Brinksma. TorX: Automated model based testing. In *1st European Conference on Model Driven Software Engineering*, Nuremberg, Germany, pages 31–43, December 2003.

J. R. Ullmann. An algorithm for subgraph isomorphism. *Journal of the ACM*, 23(1):31–42, 1976.

M. Utting and B. Legeard. *Practical Model-Based Testing: A Tools Approach.* Morgan Kaufmann, 2006.

M. van der Bijl, A. Rensink, and J. Tretmans. Compositional testing with IOCO. In A. Petrenko and A. Ulrich, editors, *Formal Approaches to Software Testing: Third International Workshop, FATES 2003*, volume 2931 of *Lecture Notes in Computer Science*, pages 86–100. Springer, 2004.

M. Veanes, C. Campbell, W. Grieskamp, L. Nachmanson, W. Schulte, and N. Tillmann. Model-based testing of object-oriented reactive systems with Spec Explorer. In: R. Hierons, J. P. Bowen, and M. Harman, editors, *Formal Methods and Testing*, Springer, in press.

M. Veanes, C. Campbell, and W. Schulte. Composition of model programs. In J. Derrick and J. Vain, editors, *27th International Conference on Formal Methods for Networked and Distributed Systems, FORTE'07*, Tallinn, Estonia, June 2007, volume 4574 of *Lecture Notes in Computer Science*. Springer 2007a.

M. Veanes, J. Ernits, and C. Campbell. State isomorphism in model programs with abstract data structures. In J. Derrick and J. Vain, editors, *27th International Conference on Formal Methods for Networked and Distributed Systems, FORTE'07*, Tallinn, Estonia, June 2007, volume 4574 of *Lecture Notes in Computer Science*. Springer, 2007b.

M. Veanes, C. Campbell, W. Schulte, and N. Tillmann. Online testing with model programs. In *ESEC/FSE-13: Proceedings of the 10th European Software Engineering Conference Held Jointly with 13th ACM SIGSOFT International Symposium on Foundations of Software Engineering*, pages 273–282. ACM Press, New York, 2005.

M. Veanes, P. Roy, and C. Campbell. Online testing with reinforcement learning. In K. Havelund, M. Núñez, G. Rosu, and B. Wolff, editors, *FATES/RV*, volume 4262 of *Lecture Notes in Computer Science*, pages 240–253. Springer, 2006.

J. Woodcock and M. Loomes. *Software Engineering Mathematics*. Addison-Wesley, 1989.

T. Xie, D. Marinov, W. Schulte, and D. Notkin. Symstra: A framework for generating object-oriented unit tests using symbolic execution. In N. Halbwachs and L. D. Zuck, editors, *TACAS*, volume 3440 of *Lecture Notes in Computer Science*, pages 365–381. Springer, April 2005.

M. Yannakakis. Testing, optimizaton, and games. In *LICS'04: Proceedings of the 19th Annual IEEE Symposium on Logic in Computer Science (LICS'04)*, pages 78–88. IEEE Computer Society, Washington, DC, 2004.

Index